Published for
OXFORD INTERNATIONAL AQA EXAMINATIONS

International GCSE
COMPUTER SCIENCE

Alison Page

OXFORD
UNIVERSITY PRESS

Great Clarendon Street, Oxford, OX2 6DP, United Kingdom

Oxford University Press is a department of the University of Oxford. It furthers the University's objective of excellence in research, scholarship, and education by publishing worldwide. Oxford is a registered trade mark of Oxford University Press in the UK and in certain other countries

British Library Cataloguing in Publication Data
Data available

978-0-19-841730-9

5 7 9 10 8 6

Paper used in the production of this book is a natural, recyclable product made from wood grown in sustainable forests. The manufacturing process conforms to the environmental regulations of the country of origin.

Printed in Great Britain by CPI Group (UK) Ltd., Croydon CR0 4YY

Acknowledgements
The author would like to thank Howard Lincoln for his contribution to chapter 11.

The questions and example answers that appear in this book were written by the author.

The publishers would like to thank the following for permissions to use their photographs:

Cover image: Paper Boat Creative/Getty Images; p130: Rusm/ iStockphoto; p137: From Computer Science Unplugged (csunplugged. org); p145 Icedesigner/Shutterstock; p160t: Russell Burden/Getty; p160m: Rich Stock/Shutterstock; p160b: Fajne obrazki/Shutterstock; p184: Vjom/Shutterstock; p185: Grzegorz Knec/Alamy Stock Photo; p204: jultud/Shutterstock; p205: urapongNaowasate/Shutterstock; p206: Roman Sigaev/Shutterstock; p208: Christophe Testi / Shutterstock; p209: Natalia Siverina/Shutterstock; p227t: Weerayut Kongsombut/123RF; p227b: ESB Professional/Shutterstock; p232: Ethernet Alliance; p233: WiFi Alliance; p246: The Washington Post/ Getty Images; p247: metrue/Shutterstock.

All other images by Alison Page. HTML examples by Howard Lincoln.

Artwork by Aptara and OUP.

Introduction

If you are studying Computer Science for the Oxford AQA International GCSE, then this book is designed for you. Its purpose is to help you achieve your best in the course and examination, equipping you with the knowledge you need to study the subject at a higher level.

The book matches the syllabus exactly and consists of eleven chapters: chapters 1-3 cover exam paper 1 of the syllabus (**Programming**), while chapters 4-11 cover exam paper 2 (**Concepts and Principles of Computer Science**).

To help you make the most of this student book, the following features are used to organise the content:

Syllabus reference

The explicit syllabus reference allows you to frame your learning and build connections between different topics.

Introduction

The short introduction will make it clear what you will learn in each lesson.

Example

Examples are given to show you what your screen should look like or to give step-by-step guidance on what to do.

Test yourself & Learning activity

The "Test yourself" and "Learning activity" questions will help you check your understanding after each lesson and give you further opportunities to practise what you have learnt.

Extension activity

The Extension Activities go beyond the requirements of the syllabus and will not be tested in the examination. They are intended to give you a broader understanding of computer science and hopefully you'll find them good practice.

Programming

In this student book, Python is used as an example programming language. There are many other programming languages and your teacher might have chosen a different one. However, the features you will learn about are found in almost all languages.

Contents

## Chapter 1

Syllabus reference

3.2.2 Programming concepts

Students should be able to write programs.

1.1 Begin programming

Introduction to Python

Introduction

This book will help you to learn about Computer Science. The first thing you will learn is how to write computer programs. As you learn to write programs, you will learn more about how a computer works.

You will learn to write programs in the Python programming language.

Begin programming

In this chapter you will learn how to write computer programs. The Python programming language is used as an example. There are many other programming languages. The features you will learn about are found in almost all languages. You will write Python programs that use variables, loops, and other key features. Programs written in other languages also have these features.

To extend your understanding of programming you could work independently to learn about an additional language and see how it compares to Python. This is not essential.

What is Python?

Python is a programming language. You can write programs in the Python language. Then you can run the programs. You will control the actions of the computer.

You do not have to pay to use Python. You can download Python onto your own computer at home. That means you can practise programming outside of classroom time. To download Python go to the main Python website:

https://www.python.org/

Choose "Downloads" from the menu.

Versions

There are several versions of Python. Each version has a different number. Some start with 2, for example 2.7.10. Some start with 3, for example 3.5.3. In this book we use version 3. You can download and use any version as long as it begins with 3.

Integrated development environment (IDE)

Like many programming languages, Python comes with an integrated development environment (IDE). The Python IDE is called IDLE. An IDE is similar to a word processor. An IDE lets you type up your program and save it like a document. However, a typical IDE has extra features you don't find in a word processor. For example, IDLE:

- uses colour to show different features of the program code

- lets you run the code
- gives you guidance about errors in your code.

Python Shell

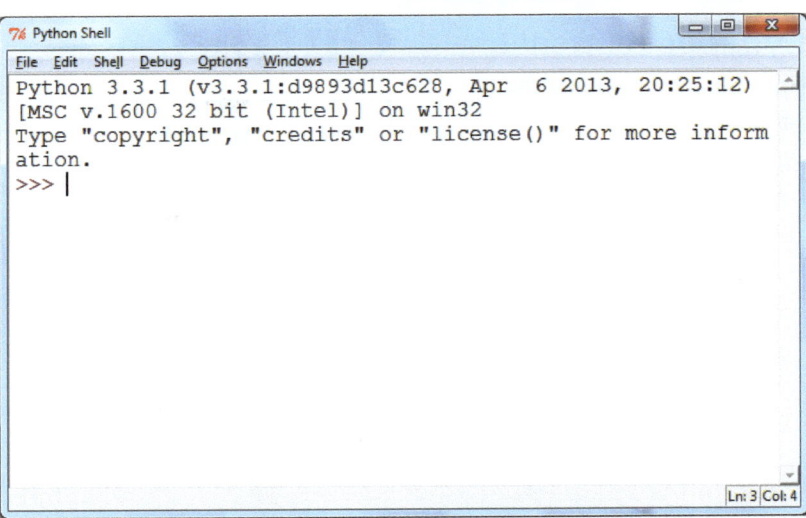

▲ The Python Shell

When you start IDLE you will see a window with the title "Python Shell" at the top. You can type Python commands in the Python Shell. Python will carry out the command that you type.

For example, type these commands. You must use lower-case letters only (no capital letters). Press the Enter key after each command.

```
print("12 + 5")
print(12 + 15)
```

The result of each command appears below it in the Shell window. What does the print command do? What is the difference between these two commands? You will learn more about these issues soon.

Program Editor

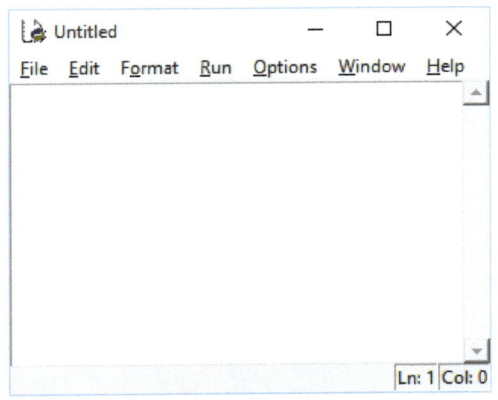

▲ The Program Editor

At the top of the Python Shell is a menu bar. Open the File menu and choose "New Window". A second window will open. It has the heading "Untitled" as shown in the picture.

The new window you opened is called the Program Editor. This is where you will write program code. Then you can **run** the programs you write. When you run a program, the results will appear in the Python Shell window.

The Program Editor has a menu bar across the top. The File menu will let you save the programs you make, and open saved programs. The Edit menu will let you cut, copy and paste text. If you can use a word processor you will be able to use this software with no problems.

Learning activity

Here are some Python commands. Enter these commands in the Python Shell. Some of the commands have deliberate errors in them.

```
Print(4)
print(Hello world)
print(99 + 12 - 104)
print("12 + 14 =",12 + 14)
Print("Hello world")
```

1. Which of these commands have errors?

2. If you type a command with an error what happens?

Extension activity

Try to correct the errors in the commands above. Run the corrected code to see the results of the commands.

Test yourself

1. What does IDE stand for? What is the purpose of IDE software?

2. What features does an IDE have that you would not find in an ordinary word processor?

3. In this section you used a Python IDE called IDLE. IDLE has two different windows. What are their names?

4. In future sections you will use IDLE to write and run programs. Where will you see the results of the programs?

Syllabus reference

3.2.7 Input/output and file handling

Be able to output data and information from a program to the computer display.

Output

> **Introduction**
>
> The "output" of a program means the results that appear when you run the program. In this section you will learn how to produce output from a program using the print command.

Data values

The job of a computer is to process data values. Data can include text and number values. When you are writing a computer program, a piece of data is called a **data value**. A computer program can:

- **input** data values to the computer
- **store** data values in the computer's electronic memory
- **process** the data values
- **output** data values as results.

Expressions

An **expression** is a piece of computer code that represents a value. Here are some numerical expressions. They represent number values:

```
33.333
(2+7)*4
```

This is a string expression:

```
"What a wonderful world"
```

A series of characters inside quote marks is called a string. You can use single or double quote marks. A string is also called a "string literal".

Python output

The results of a program are called the program **output**.

The main output of a simple Python program is the on-screen display. To make Python display output on the screen you use the print command followed by brackets. Any Python expression can go inside the brackets.

```
print("What a wonderful world")
print(123.456)
```

The expression inside the brackets represents a value. When you run the program, the value will appear on the screen. You will see it in the Python Shell window

To print a blank line you enter this code:

```
print("\n")
```

Predefined function

The word "print" is a predefined function. A predefined function is a command which comes as part of standard Python code.

Python comments

Programmers often add comments to their code. The computer will ignore all comments. Comments are used by programmers to add notes for a human reader.

In Python comments are marked by the hash symbol:

    #

Any text that follows this sign is ignored by the computer. IDLE makes all comments red so they stand out.

Example

This example of a Python program uses the print command and comments.

```
# Program name: myfirst
# Code written by: Alison Page
# This program demonstrates use of the print command

print("========================")
print("       W E L C O M E       ")
print(" This is my first program ")
Print("========================")
```

When you type a program in IDLE some pieces of code are shown in different colours:

- A predefined function is shown in purple.
- A string is shown in green.
- Comments are shown in red.

If you make a mistake you may spot the colours are wrong. What is the error in the example above? How do colours help you spot it?

Save your work

You can save your file to edit it or run it another day. To save the program code choose Save from the file menu and enter a name for the program. Pick a name that reminds you what the program does.

Run the code

"Running the code" means Python will carry out the commands in your program and display the output in the Python Shell. To run the program code, open the Run menu. Choose Run Module.

Syntax errors

"Syntax" means the rules of a language. If you make a mistake in the program code, this is a syntax error. The code will not run. An error message will appear in the Python Shell window.

The error message will tell you what the error is. It will say what line of the code has the error. Go back to the code. Correct the error. Save and run the program again. It is OK to make mistakes in code. All programmers do this.

Test yourself

1. What is a string?
2. What does the computer do with comments added to a program?
3. Explain the syntax of a print command. What goes in the brackets?
4. Describe what happens when you run a Python program.

Learning activity

1. Invent a name for a new computer game.
2. Make a Python program that displays a welcome screen for the game. Use print commands and comments.
3. Save and run the program.

Extension activity

You can create complex designs from simple print statements. This is called ASCII art. Carry out Internet research to find examples of ASCII art. Try making your own examples of ASCII art using Python print statements.

Syllabus reference

3.2.2 Programming concepts

Use, understand and know how the following statement types can be combined in programs: variable declaration, assignment.

Use meaningful identifier names and know why it is important to use them.

Additional information

Identifier names include names for variables.

Variables

> ## Introduction
> You have learned that an expression represents a data value. In this section you will learn to store these values in the computer's electronic memory.

Variable

When the computer is running it stores data values in its memory. A computer's memory is made up of millions of different storage areas called locations. You can set aside a memory location to store a value. You give the memory location a name. A named memory location is a **variable**.

The electrical signals of computer memory can change. That means you can change the value stored in the variable.

When you close the program, or turn off your computer, the electrical signals will stop. That means the computer will lose the value stored in the variable when the program stops.

Naming variables

You must choose a name for every variable you use in your program. Names that you give to variables are called 'identifiers'. In later lessons you will give 'identifiers' to other program elements. Identifiers must be unique. Do not give two variables the same name. Here are some other rules about identifiers:

- The name must not include spaces.
- You can use only letters, numbers and the underscore character (_).
- The name must start with a letter of the alphabet.

It is important to choose identifiers carefully. Well-chosen identifiers will help other programmers to read and understand your code. Well-chosen identifiers make it easier for you to write code without making mistakes.

- Choose a name that reminds you of what value the variable stores. This will make your program easier to write and easier for other people to understand.
- Many Python programmers use only lower-case letters for variable names.

In this book many variable names start with a capital (upper-case) letter to make them stand out in the text.

Assign a value

Storing a value in a variable is called **assigning** a value to the variable. The equals sign is used to assign a value. To assign a value to a variable, you enter code using this pattern:

- the name of the variable
- an equals sign
- a value.

This code assigns the value 23 to the variable `Age`:

```
Age = 23
```

This code assigns the value `"Bond"` to the variable `CodeName`:

```
CodeName = "Bond"
```

Declaring variables

In some programming languages you must create a variable with a special command before you can use it. When you create the variable you give it an identifier and a data type (find out more about data types on page 16). The variable is empty – it doesn't have a value. Creating a variable is called 'declaring' or 'initialising' the variable. In Python, you do not need to declare variables using a special command. Just start using the variable when you need it in your program. A variable is declared when you assign a value to it for the first time.

Output a variable

You have learned that a print command will output a value. You can put the name of a variable into the print command. The computer will output the value stored in the variable:

```
print(Age)

print(CodeName)
```

When you output a variable you do not put quote marks round the variable name. You don't want the computer to print out the name of the variable as a word. You want it to print the value that is stored in the variable.

You can combine a string and a variable in the same output command. Put a comma between them:

```
print("Your code name is ", CodeName)
```

Test yourself

1. What is the name for code that represents a data value?

2. Give the command to assign the value 19.99 to the variable `TicketCost`.

3. Give the command to output the value stored in the variable `TicketCost`.

4. Here are four variable names. For each one say whether it is a good or bad variable name and say why.

   a   `Character Name`

   b   `firstName`

   c   `5Star`

   d   `myvariable`

   e   `Star*Rating`

Learning activity

Open the computer game program you started writing in the last lesson.

1. Create a variable called `Score`.

2. Assign the value 0 to this variable.

3. Add a command to print out the variable.

Input

Introduction

You have learned that every computer program has input and output. You can make program output using the print command. In this section you will learn how to get program input from the user. You will save the input value as a variable.

The user

The person who works with your program is called the user. The user will run the program. He or she will input the data values, usually by typing at the keyboard. The user will see the output, usually on the computer screen.

Input a value

"Input" means the data values that are entered when the program is running. Typically, the input is typed by the user. An input command looks like this:

```
input()
```

The word must be shown in lower-case letters. You must include brackets. You normally add some text inside the brackets. The text inside the brackets is called the prompt. The prompt is a message that tells the user what to input. When you run the program, the computer will display the prompt, and wait for the user to type something. For example:

```
input("Enter the password")
```

Save the value

You usually want the computer to store the value that is input by the user, so you will assign the input value to a variable. Remember the code pattern:

```
variable = value
```

The value can be an input value. This command will take the user input and store it as a variable called `Password`:

```
Password = input("Enter the password")
```

The variable is called `Password`. Whatever value the user types will be stored in the variable.

Sequence

You have created short programs with several lines of code. The commands in a computer program are carried out in order. This is called the program sequence. The command at the top of the program is carried out first. Then the next line, then the next and so on.

It is very important that you get the sequence right. The lines must be in the right order. For example, you must assign a value to a variable before you output the variable.

Program errors

If your program has a syntax error, it will not run. You will see an error message. Syntax errors may be caused by:

- commands that **break the rules of the language** – for example starting the print command with a capital letter, or leaving out the brackets

- commands **in the wrong sequence** – for example, printing a variable before you have assigned a value to the variable.

```
76 Python Shell
File  Edit  Shell  Debug  Options  Windows  Help
Python 3.3.1 (v3.3.1:d9893d13c628, Apr  6 2013, 20:25:1
tel)] on win32
Type "copyright", "credits" or "license()" for more inf
>>> ================================ RESTART ==========
>>>

==========================
       W E L C O M E
 This is my first program
Traceback (most recent call last):
  File "C:/Python33/myfirst.py", line 9, in <module>
    Print("==========================")
NameError: name 'Print' is not defined
>>>
```

Introduction

You have learned to write simple computer programs including input and output. You have used the Python programming language. In this section you will learn that programmers plan and record their programs as algorithms. You will learn to draw a flowchart that represents an algorithm.

What is an algorithm?

An algorithm describes a set of steps to solve a problem. For example, a recipe is a simple algorithm. Algorithms are used in mathematics to describe how to solve problems.

An algorithm can also describe the logical structure of a program. An algorithm sets out all the actions that the program will carry out. It shows:

- which data values are **input**
- how data values are stored as **variables**
- the new data values that are produced as **output**.

An algorithm describes a program but it is not a working program. You can run a program but you cannot run an algorithm. An algorithm is not written in a particular programming language. Turning an algorithm into a program is called coding.

Why do programmers write algorithms?

Why do programmers spend time writing algorithms? Why don't they just start writing program code? There are several reasons. Setting out the solution in the form of an algorithm helps programmers to:

- plan their solution and check that it makes sense before they begin writing code
- share their solution with other programmers, including people who use a different programming language
- keep a record of their solution.

There are lots of different programming languages. A programmer can read an algorithm and turn it into code in any language. A good algorithm can be used by many different programmers.

Flowchart boxes

A flowchart is a diagram. It uses boxes connected by arrows to show an algorithm. The boxes stand for actions. Different shapes of box stand for different actions. The boxes are connected by arrows. The arrows show the flow or sequence of the program.

Every flowchart has a start box and most have a stop box. They look like this.

START   STOP

Output is shown by a box like this.

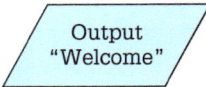

Words inside the box give you more detail about what the output is. It could be a text string, the name of a variable, or any other expression.

Input is shown by a box like this.

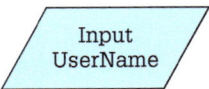

Inside the box put the word "Input" and the name of the variable that will store the input.

To assign a value to a variable show a box like this.

Score = 0

Inside the box put the name of the variable, and the value assigned to the variable.

Using these boxes you can make an algorithm with all the programming commands that you have learned so far. Just pick the box that matches the command you want to use in your algorithm.

Make a flowchart

To make a flowchart you have to connect the boxes with arrows. The arrows show the sequence of commands. Here is an example of a complete flowchart algorithm.

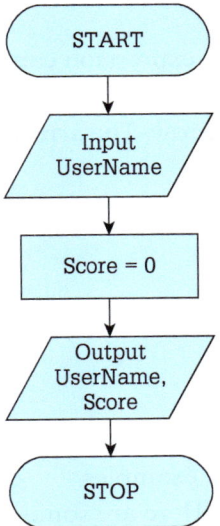

A flowchart shows the sequence of commands. The sequence starts at the top and goes down the flowchart diagram. The commands are carried out in order.

Test yourself

1. What is an algorithm? Why do programmers create algorithms before they start to write program code?

2. In a flowchart, input and output are shown by the same shape of box. How can you tell whether a box stands for input or output?

3. Draw the shapes of three different flowchart boxes. Write alongside each box what program feature it represents.

4. How is sequence shown in a flowchart algorithm?

Learning activity

1. Using any graphics package, create the flowchart shown on this page.

2. Write a Python program to match this flowchart.

Extension activity

You wrote a program that creates the Welcome screen for a computer game. Design a flowchart to match the program you wrote.

Syllabus reference

3.1.1 Representing algorithms

Understand and explain the term "algorithm".

Use a systematic approach to problem solving and algorithm creation, representing algorithms using pseudocode.

Explain simple algorithms in terms of their inputs, processing and outputs.

Additional information

Students must be able to identify where inputs, processing and outputs are taking place within an algorithm.

3.2.2 Programming concepts

Students should be able to interpret algorithms that include these statement types: variable declaration, assignment.

Pseudocode

Introduction

You have learned to draw a flowchart. A flowchart represents an algorithm as a diagram. Pseudocode is a way of writing out an algorithm in words. In this section you will learn how to make a simple pseudocode algorithm.

What is pseudocode?

Pseudocode is a way of setting out an algorithm in words. Pseudocode is similar to program code – but it is not exactly the same. Pseudocode helps you plan your program. Pseudocode is not a real program. You cannot run pseudocode on a computer.

In this book you will see algorithms set out in pseudocode. The pseudocode used in this book looks very similar to Python.

Pseudocode style

Different programmers use different styles of pseudocode. When you write your own pseudocode try to copy the style shown in this book:

- Command words such as PRINT and INPUT are shown in capital (upper-case) letters.
- Names of variables have capital letters.
- String literals are shown inside quote marks.

Remember that you will not run pseudocode on your computer, so the exact syntax is not as important as it is in program code. The important thing is that other people can understand it.

Assign a value to a variable

Remember that data values are represented by expressions. An expression can be a string literal, a number value or a variable. In pseudocode you can assign a value to a variable. To assign a value to a variable, draw an arrow. The arrow points from the value to the variable. Here are some examples:

```
FirstName    ← "Jason"

Age          ← 17

Cost         ← 49.99
```

The arrow does the same job as the equals sign in Python.

Input in pseudocode

You can also assign input to a variable. Use an arrow (as in the examples above) but instead of an expression, put the word USERINPUT. Here are some examples:

```
FirstName    ← USERINPUT

Age          ← USERINPUT

Cost         ← USERINPUT
```

Output in pseudocode

If you want to show output in pseudocode use the word OUTPUT. Include an expression after the word OUTPUT. The command will output the value of the expression. Here are some examples:

```
OUTPUT      "Welcome"

OUTPUT      44

OUTPUT      FirstName
```

Comments

You can include comments in your pseudocode. The comments will help to explain the algorithm. Comments are not used for input or output. Just as in Python, comments are shown by the symbol #. Here are some examples:

```
# Program written by Alex Khan

# The user will input his or her age
```

A complete algorithm

Here is an example of a pseudocode algorithm. It represents the start of a video game.

```
# Start of a video game

OUTPUT      "Welcome to the Maze of Doom"

PlayerName  ← USERINPUT

Hitpoints   ← 50

OUTPUT      PlayerName, Hitpoints
```

Test yourself

1. In this line of pseudocode, what is the variable? What is the expression and what type of expression is it?

```
Month ← "January"
```

2. Write a line of pseudocode to assign user input to a variable called EmailAddress.

3. Write a line of pseudocode to output the message Game Over.

4. Write a line of pseudocode to assign the value 99 to a variable called Height.

Learning activity

There is a complete pseudocode algorithm on this page. It has five lines of text.

1. Explain the meaning of each line of the algorithm.

2. Write a Python program that matches the algorithm .

Extension activity

You wrote a program that creates the Welcome screen for a computer game. Design a pseudocode algorithm to match the program you wrote.

Syllabus reference

3.2.3 Arithmetic operations in a programming language

Be familiar with and be able to use:

- addition
- subtraction
- multiplication
- real division.

1.2 Calculation

Numerical expressions

> **Introduction**
>
> People often use computer programs to work out the results of complex calculations. In this section you will learn to write programs that find the answers to calculations. Using this skill, you can write many useful Python programs.

What are numerical expressions?

An expression is code that represents a value. Numerical expressions represent number values. Numerical expressions can include minus numbers and numbers with decimal places. Here are some simple numerical expressions:

```
66

7.5

-99
```

A calculation is another type of numerical expression. The computer will work out the result of the calculation. The result of the calculation is the value of the expression. Here are some examples. Can you work out the value of each of these numerical expressions?

```
66+4

7.5*4

-99*9
```

Using the print command, you can output the value of any numerical expression.

```
print(23-13)
```

Assign a numerical expression

You have learned that you can assign a value to a variable using the equals sign.

```
variable = expression
```

You can assign the result of a calculation to a variable.

```
variable = numerical expression
```

For example, the following line of code will work out 240 + 270 and assign the result to a variable called Cost:

```
Cost = 240 + 270
```

The variable Cost now stores the result of the calculation. If you output the variable you will see the result of the calculation:

```
print("The cost is ", Cost)
```

Arithmetic operators

Calculations in Python use symbols to stand for the main mathematical processes. These symbols are called arithmetic operators. Here are the main arithmetic operators.

Operator	Meaning
+	add
−	subtract
*	multiply
/	divide

Order of operation

You may see an expression with more than one operator. The computer will do the calculation inside brackets first.

```
(4+6)/2
```

The computer works out the part in brackets first. That adds up to 10. Then the computer divides 10 by 2. The result is 5.

Using variables in calculations

The calculations you have seen so far use numerical values. You can also use the name of a variable in a calculation. The computer will use the value of the variable.

```
Pay = 150.00
Tax = Pay*0.25
print(Tax)
```

The output is 37.50.

You can also change the value of a variable using a calculation.

```
Age = Age+1
```

This command will increase the value stored in the variable Age. It will go up by 1.

Test yourself

1. List the four main arithmetic operators and their meanings.

2. What are the values of these four numerical expressions?

```
9/2
6-15
8*-7
7*2.5
```

3. Write the Python code to output the value of −4 times −5.

4. Write the Python code to assign the value of 81 divided by 7 to a variable called Result.

Learning activity

Write a Python program with these commands:

- Every year is identified by a number (such as 2018 or 2021). Assign this year's number to a variable called ThisYear.

- You have a birthday this year (it might have already happened). Assign your age at this birthday to a variable called MyAge.

- Use a numerical expression operating on these two variables to work out the year you were born. Output this value.

- Add one or more comment lines to the program.

Syllabus reference

3.2.1 Data types

Understand the concept of a data type.

Understand and be able to use the following appropriately:

- integer
- real
- Boolean
- character
- string.

Data types

Introduction

Expressions have values. The values can be stored in variables. The computer uses different methods to store different types of data. These are called data types. You must understand data types in order to do calculations.

Data types

Expressions represent data values. These values can be stored in variables. The computer uses different methods to store different types of data. When you create a variable, the computer has to decide what type of storage to use, depending on what type of data it is. Here are some important data types:

- **Integer:** an integer variable will only store a whole number, with no decimal point.
- **Real number:** a real number variable will store a number with a decimal point. In Python this data type is called float.
- **String:** a string variable stores one or more text characters. Strings have quote marks at the start and end.
- **Boolean:** a Boolean variable stores a True or False value. We will look at this type of variable in a later section.
- **Character:** stores a single text character. This variable type in not used in Python.

Any number with a decimal place in it is the real number data type. In Python we call this the float data type. This applies even if the number after the decimal place is zero.

Value	Data type
6	integer
6.0	real number (float)
"6"	string

What data type should you use?

In some programming languages you tell the computer what data type to use. You would do that when you declare a variable. In Python you do not need to tell the computer what data type to use. The computer picks a data type when you assign a value to the variable:

- If you assign a whole-number value, it will make an integer variable.
- If you assign a number value with a decimal point, it will make a float variable.
- If you assign a string value, it will make a string variable.

Data type of input values

You can use a variable to store a value that is input by the user. The computer does not know what type of data the user might type in.

What data type will the computer use?

Answer: if a variable holds a value input by the user, the computer makes the variable the string data type.

Data type of calculated values

You can also assign calculated values to variables. The computer will use a different data type depending on the calculation. Here are the rules it uses:

- If you add, subtract or multiply integer values, the computer will use an integer data type to store the results.
- If any value in your calculation is the float data type, the computer will use the float data type for the result.
- If your calculation includes division, the computer will use the float data type for the result.

String data type and calculations

String expressions do not have a numerical value. Even if a string has digits it is not a number value. Here is an example string variable:

```
"07884123099"
```

This has numbers in it, but it is not a numerical value. It might be a phone number or a code number. Here are some points about string variables:

- String variables cannot be used in mathematical calculations.
- The result of a numerical calculation is never the string data type.

Test yourself

1. Here are some numerical expressions. What data type results from each expression?

```
36

36.0

36 * 10

36 + 1.0

36 / 6
```

2. Here are some commands that assign values to variables. What is the data type in each case?

```
Age = "Over 21"

Age = 22

Age = 22.0

Age = input("Enter your age")
```

3. A computer programmer is writing a Python program. The user will input the amount he or she earns. What data type is this value?

4. Write the Python code to assign the value 33 to the variable Age. Make sure it is stored as float data type.

Learning activity

Question 1 in "Test yourself" includes a range of numerical expressions. Write a program that prints out the value of each of these expressions. What is different about the way the computer prints integer and real data types?

Syllabus reference

3.2.8 String handling operations in a programming language

Understand and be able to use

String conversion operations:

- string to integer
- string to real
- integer to string
- real to string.

Convert data type

Introduction

Input values are always stored as string data type. This creates a problem for Python programmers; string variables cannot be used in calculations. In this section you will learn how to solve that problem.

A problem for Python programmers

- Input values are stored as the string data type.
- The string data type cannot be used in calculations.

Does that mean we cannot use input values in calculations? That would be a big problem for programmers. The problem is avoided because we can change the data type.

Example

This program shows the problem:.

```python
# use input in a calculation

itemcost = input("enter the cost of the item: ")
deliverycharge = 5.50

total = itemcost + deliverycharge

print("You must pay ",total)
```

If you run the program, you will see this error message:

```
enter the cost of the item: 35
Traceback (most recent call last):
  File "C:/Users/Alison/AppData/Local/Programs/Python/Python35-32/datatype.py",
line 7, in <module>
    total = itemcost + deliverycharge
TypeError: Can't convert 'float' object to str implicitly
```

The error message tells us there is a data type error. The error is in line 7. Line 7 is the calculation:

```
total = itemcost + deliverycharge
```

The computer has to add together the two variables: `itemcost` and `deliverycharge`. However, `itemcost` is string data type. String variables cannot be used in calculations, so the program doesn't work.

Convert string to a numerical data type

There is a way to avoid the data type error described above. If you want to use an input variable in a calculation you can change it from string to a different data type. You can turn it into integer or float.

This command will turn `itemcost` into the integer data type:

```
itemcost = int(itemcost)
```

This command will turn `itemcost` into the float data type:

```
itemcost = float(itemcost)
```

Either of these data types may be used in a calculation. If the value has a decimal place you should use the float data type. If the value is a whole number you can use the integer data type.

Corrected example

Here is the program with the problem corrected:

```
# use input in a calculation
itemcost = input("enter the cost of the item: ")
itemcost = float(itemcost)
deliverycharge = 5.50
total = itemcost + deliverycharge
print("You must pay ",total)
```

You can run this program and there will be no error message.

Convert integer and float to string

You can convert integer and float data types to the string data type. Here is an example:

```
Age = str(Age)
```

This command converts the variable `Age` to the string data type. Integer or real data can be converted to a string using this command.

Some numbers should not be used in calculations. An example would be a phone number. It is good practice to store these values as strings.

Learning activity

Write a program for use in a supermarket. The user enters the value of three different items. The program adds up the total cost and outputs this value.

Test yourself

Here is an example program:

```
HourlyRate = 12.00
Hours = input("Enter how many hours you worked")
Pay = Hours * HourlyRate
print(Pay)
```

1. What predefined functions are used in this program?

2. What are the names and data types of the three variables used in this program?

3. When you run this program you will see an error message. Explain why.

4. Write a corrected version of this program.

Extension activity

Extend the supermarket program from the Learning activity to calculate sales tax at 17.5% and add it to the value of the total.

Print the bill showing:

- cost of all items
- total cost without sales tax
- sales tax
- total cost with sales tax.

Syllabus reference

3.2.3 Arithmetic operations in a programming language

Be familiar with and be able to use integer division, including remainders: a two-stage process using modular arithmetic.

Introduction

You have learned the four main arithmetic operators: plus, minus, divide and multiply. In this section you will learn two new arithmetic operators. They are used in a type of maths called integer division.

Data type and division

You have already learned about the division operator. The division operator is used to create a calculated value from two numbers. The two numbers have these names:

- The number before the division operator is called the **dividend**.
- The number after the division operator is called the **divisor**.

Here are some examples of expressions that use the division operator.

```
30/4

38/4

7.6/4
```

What are the dividend and divisor in each case? What is the value of each of these expressions?

Python will store the results of these calculations as float data type. Python will always use the float data type for the result of division. That is because division does not always produce a whole number.

What is integer division?

There is another way to do division, which is by using remainders. You may have learned to use remainders at school. For example, divide 38 by 4. There are two ways to show the result:

- normal division: 9.5
- integer division: 9 remainder 2.

When we use integer division the result has two numbers. In this example they are 9 and 2. This is how we refer to them:

- The first number is called the **quotient**.
- The second number is called the remainder or **modulus**.

When we carry out integer division we must do two calculations. One calculation will give us the quotient, and the other calculation will give us the modulus.

Quotient

"Quotient" means the result of integer division without the remainder. If the divisor and the dividend are both integer data type, then the quotient will be integer data type.

The arithmetic operator that produces the quotient looks like this:

```
//
```

Here is an arithmetic expression that uses this operator:

```
23//7
```

What is the value of this expression? What is its data type?

Modulus

"Modulus" means the remainder from an integer division. If the divisor and dividend are both integers, then the modulus will be an integer. The modulus operator looks like this:

```
%
```

Here is a numerical expression that uses the modulus operator:

```
23%7
```

What is the value of this expression? What is its data type?

Note: In Python the percentage symbol (%) is used as the modulus operator. This can be confusing, because in maths we use this symbol to indicate percentages. Remember the symbol has a special meaning in Python code.

Example

This Python program shows the result of integer division:

```
# demonstrate integer division

dividend = 79
divisor  = 10

quotient = dividend // divisor
modulus  = dividend %  divisor

print(dividend, " divided by ", divisor)

print(quotient, " remainder ", modulus)
```

Learning activity

There is an example program shown on this page. Adapt this program to use input values in the calculation.

Test yourself

1. Give the meaning of these four terms:

   a dividend

   b divisor

   c quotient

   d modulus.

2. Here is a short extract from a Python program. What are the values stored in the two variables at the end of this code?

```
Minutes = 220

Hours = Minutes // 60

Minutes = Minutes % 60
```

3. Write a Python program that will convert 40 days into a whole number of weeks and remaining days.

Extension activity

Write a Python program to do this task:

- The user inputs a number of days.

- The program outputs how many whole weeks this is.

- The program outputs how many days are left over .

Constants

Introduction

You have learned how to write programs using variables. A variable is an area of memory. A variable can store a changing value.

Your programs can also have constants. A constant is like a variable. A constant stores a value, but it stores a value that will **not** change while the program is running.

Variables and constants

A variable is a memory location that has a name. You can assign a value to the variable, which means you store a value in that memory location.

```
variable = value
```

A constant is like a variable. It is a named memory location. You assign a value to the constant just as you assign a value to a variable. For example, this command assigns the value 7 to a constant that stores the number of days in a week.

```
DAYS_IN_WEEK = 7
```

This value will not change in your program. It is a constant.

In some programming languages there are special commands to declare constants. In Python there isn't a special command. Constants are made in the same way as variables. Be careful not to change the value once it is set. In this example, the number of days in a week will always be 7. You should not change this value in your program.

Examples of constants

Here are some examples of values that will not change while you are running a program:

- the number of kilometres in a mile
- the rate of acceleration due to gravity
- the number of hours in a week.

Find out the value of these constants. You might need to do some internet research.

Why use constants?

We could just type in the number value instead of using a constant. For example we could use the number 7 throughout the program instead of the constant 'DAYS_IN_WEEK'. But using a constant has two advantages:

- It makes your program easier to understand.
- It makes your program easier to change.

In some languages constants are defined differently from variables. In these languages the value of a constant can never be changed, not even by accident, after it has been declared. This helps to protect the programmer from making errors.

Example – converting speed

A programmer wrote a program to convert units of speed. The program would convert speed from miles per hour to kilometres per second. To do this you must:

- divide by the number of seconds in an hour
- multiply by the number of kilometres in a mile.

Here is the first program he made:

```
### conversion  from mph (miles per hour)
###              to   kps (kilometres per second)

mph = input("enter speed in miles per hour: ")
mph = float(mph)

kps = mph/3600*1.6

print("kilometres per second: ",kps)
```

Here is the same program, using constants to store the conversion factors:

```
### conversion  from mph (miles per hour)
###              to   kps (kilometres per second)

seconds = 3600     # seconds in an hour
kilometres = 1.6   # kilometres in a mile

mph = input("enter speed in miles per hour: ")
mph = float(mph)

kps = mph/seconds * kilometres

print("kilometres per second: ",kps)
```

Why use constants?

The example program shows the advantages of using constants in your programs. Using constants makes the program easier to understand. The main calculation in the first program is shown as:

```
kps = mph/3600*1.6
```

In the second program (using constants) the calculation looks like this:

```
kps = mph/seconds * kilometres
```

The second version is easier to understand. The two values have been replaced by words: divide by seconds, multiply by kilometres.

Using constants makes the program **easier to change**. The programmer found a more precise conversion factor from miles to kilometres: 1.60934 instead of 1.6. He only had to change one line, right at the top of the program:

```
kilometres = 1.60934
```

A constant might be used in many places in a program. You only need to change one line of code to change your whole program.

Test yourself

1. You would never use a constant to store user input. Why not?

2. A programmer wrote a program to add up the bill in a restaurant. The size of the bill is not a constant. Why not?

3. The acceleration due to gravity is usually abbreviated to "g". It is a value in metres per second squared. On Earth this value is 9.8. Write a line of Python code that stores this value as a constant called g.

4. A programmer wrote a program to calculate tax. The tax rate was 40% or 0.4. Give two reasons why the programmer should store this as a constant.

Learning activity

Write a program that converts miles per hour into metres per second. Note that 100 miles per hour is almost exactly 44.7 meters per second. Does your program give this result?

Extension activity

Write a program that converts a value in one currency (for example US dollars) to another currency (for example euros). Research the exchange rate by looking online. Store the exchange rate as a constant. Use the constant in your program.

Syllabus reference

3.1.1. Representing algorithms

Explain simple algorithms in terms of their inputs, processing and outputs.

Additional information

Students must be able to identify where inputs, processing and outputs are taking place within an algorithm.

Processing values

Introduction

You have learned that an algorithm can be used to describe a program. In this section you will see how algorithms describe the calculations in a program.

Processing

An algorithm describes the logical structure of a program. An algorithm sets out all the actions that the program will carry out.

Every program includes these features:

- Data values are **input**.
- Data values are changed by **processing**.
- The new data values are **output**.

"Processing" means changing data values. Calculation is one way of changing data values.

Processing in flowcharts

A flowchart box like this is used to assign a value to a variable. Inside the box put the name of the variable, and the value assigned to the variable.

> Score = 0

You can also use the box to assign a calculation to a variable.

> Score = Score + 1

This command increases the value of the variable Score by 1. Use the same arithmetic operators as you would in Python.

Processing in pseudocode

You have learned that the arrow symbol is used in pseudocode. It is used to assign a value to a variable. You can also assign a calculated value to a variable. Here are two examples:

```
Tax ← Pay * Taxrate
Score ← Score + 1
```

The main arithmetic operators are the same as in Python.

Integer division

In pseudocode you might see text used in integer division instead of operators:

- The word DIV is used instead of // to get the quotient.
- The word MOD is used instead of % to get the modulus.

Here is the example of 23 divided by 6 using integer division:

```
Quotient ← 23 DIV 6

Modulus ← 23 MOD 6
```

What would be the values of `Quotient` and `Modulus` after these two calculations?

Input, output and processing

With these different commands you can make an algorithm that has input, processing and output. This is how they are shown in a flowchart:

- Input is shown by a slanted box with the word `INPUT` in it.
- Output is shown by a slanted box with the word `OUTPUT` in it.
- Processing is shown by a straight-sided box. The box assigns a value to a variable. It could be a calculated value.

This is what is shown in a pseudocode algorithm:

- Input is shown by the word `USERINPUT`.
- Output is shown by the word `OUTPUT`.
- Processing is shown by an arrow. An arrow assigns a value to a variable. It could be a calculated value.

Test yourself

Here is a pseudocode algorithm. Read it and then answer the questions.

```
Pi ← 3.14159

Radius ← USERINPUT

Circumference ← 2 * Pi * Radius

OUTPUT Circumference
```

1. This program includes a constant. What is the name of the constant? Why is this value a constant not a variable?

2. The program has four lines. Which line represents input?

3. Which line represents processing? Describe the processing.

4. Which line represents output? What value is output by this algorithm?

Learning activity

Create a pseudocode algorithm with these features:

- input the cost of a purchase
- calculate sales tax at 15%
- output the total cost
- input the amount of cash paid over
- calculate the change (cash minus total cost)
- output the value of the change.

Extension activity

Write a pseudocode algorithm that converts a value in one currency (for example US dollars) to another currency (for example euros). You may already have written a Python program that does this – now turn it into an algorithm.

1.3 # String handling

Strings

> ### Introduction
> You have learned to do calculations using number values. In this section you will learn to process string values. You will learn to alter strings and take parts of strings.

A string expression is a series of characters. It is enclosed in quote marks. You have learned that string values cannot be used in numerical calculations. However, now you will learn some useful things you can do with strings in your programs.

String length

You can find the length of a string and store that value in a variable. Every character inside the string counts as part of the length. This is the command:

```
len()
```

Put a string inside the brackets.

```
len("This is an example string")
```

This command makes a number value. In the example shown here, what is that number? Remember that spaces count as part of the length of a string.

You can print the number value.

```
print(len("This is an example string"))
```

Or you can store the value in a new variable. In this example the variable is called `stringlength`.

```
stringlength = len("This is an example string")
```

Length of a string variable

You have learned that string variables store strings. Here is an example:

```
UserName = "JatinderSingh"
```

If we use the `len()` function with this variable it will tell us the length of the stored string.

```
stringlength = len(UserName)
```

String length holds the value 13, which is the length of `"JatinderSingh"`.

Concatenation

You can join two or more strings together to make one big string. This is called **concatenation**.

Join the strings together with a + sign. The + sign is used to add number values together. The + sign will concatenate string values. Here is an example:

```
FirstName = "Brigit"

SecondName = "O'Neill"

FullName = FirstName + " " + SecondName
```

What value is held in the variable `FullName` after these commands? Why has the programmer added a short string in between the two names?

Extension – repetition

You can also use the multiplication sign `*`. This sign will repeat a string. Here is an example:.

```
print("=" * 20)
```

This command will print a line of 20 equals signs on the screen.

```
====================
```

This command can be used to underline a string for emphasis. We can use the `len()` function command to find out how many times to repeat. Here is an example:

```
UserName = input("enter your username")

NameLength = len(UserName)

print(UserName)

print("=" * NameLength)
```

Try running this program a few times. Notice that the underlining changes size to fit each user name you input.

Test yourself

1. Write a Python command to ask the user for a password and store it as a variable. Choose a suitable name for the variable.

2. Write a Python command to find the length of the password and store it as a variable.

3. Write a Python command to print out this message.

```
Your password has 10 characters
```

The number in the message will vary depending on the length of the password you enter.

4. When you enter a password, the computer often displays it using a string of asterisks. It looks like this:.

```
Enter Password: ******
```

Write a Python program that asks you to enter your password and then prints it as a string of asterisks. The number of asterisks should be the same as the length of your password.

Learning activity

1. Write a program that asks users for several facts about themselves, such as name, age and date of birth.

2. Concatenate these variables to make a single string variable and print this out.

Extension activity

The width of the screen is about 70 characters. To print a string in the centre of the screen you must put spaces in front of the string. The number of spaces is 35 minus half the length of the string.

Use this information to write a program where the user inputs a string. The program prints out that string in the centre of the line.

Substrings

> ## Introduction
>
> In the last section you learned to concatenate strings. You also learned how to find the length of a string. In this section you will learn how to work with substrings. A substring is part of a string.

String position

A string is a series of characters. It is enclosed in quote marks. The quote marks are not part of the string.

Python numbers every character position in the string. The numbering starts at 0. The first character is 0, the next is 1 and so on. This may seem confusing at first. This type of numbering, which starts with 0, is common in many programming languages.

You can use this method to pick out a single character in a string. Put the position number in square brackets after the string name.

Example

This code assigns a value to a string variable.

```
UserName = "robot44"
```

This code prints out the first character in the string.

```
print(UserName[0])
```

The result of this command is:

```
r
```

What is the result of this command?

```
print(UserName[5])
```

Substring

You have learned how to pick out a single character from a string. You can also pick out a substring. A substring is a series of characters from inside a string.

In Python you find a character by putting the position of the character inside square brackets. You find a substring by putting two numbers inside the square brackets. You record:

- the position of the first character of the substring.
- the position of the first character after the end of the substring.

These two numbers are separated by a colon (two dots):

```
:
```

Substring example

This command assigns a value to a string variable.

```
UserName = "Max Power"
```

Here is the string inside a table to show the position number of each character. You will not see a string set out in this way – you have to do the counting in your head.

M	a	x		P	o	w	e	r
0	1	2	3	4	5	6	7	8

Let's say we want to print the substring "Max":

- The position of the first character of the substring is 0.
- The position of the first character after the end of the substring is 3.

So the command is:

```
print(UserName[0:3])
```

Using substrings in your code

This code assigns a value to a string variable:.

```
GameTitle = "Maze Of Doom"
```

This code prints out the first four characters in the string:

```
print(GameTitle[0:4])
```

The result of this command is:

```
Maze
```

What is the result of this command?

```
print(GameTitle[5:7])
```

What is the command to print out the word "Doom"?

Shortcut

There is a shortcut you can use. If the string starts at position 0, you can leave out the number 0 before the colon.

So instead of:

```
print(GameTitle[0:4])
```

You can use this shortened command:

```
print(GameTitle[:4])
```

If the string ends at the final position, you can leave out this number after the colon, so instead of:

```
print(GameTitle[8:12])
```

You can use this shortened command:

```
print(GameTitle[8:])
```

What is printed out by this command?

Learning activity

A social network site lets users share messages of 140 characters or less. Longer messages are truncated. That means only the first 140 characters are shared.

Write a program that lets you type in a message and then prints out the first 140 characters of your message.

Test yourself

This command assigns a value to a string variable:.

```
BankCode =
"TAX40078"
```

Write the character or substring that would be printed by each of the following commands.

a `print(BankCode[2])`

b `print(BankCode[1:3])`

c `print(BankCode[:5])`

d `print(BankCode[3:])`

e `print(BankCode[:])`

Extension activity

You have learned to store the length of a string as a number. You have learned to do integer division with numbers. You have learned to define a substring by giving the first and last positions of the string.

Putting these ideas together, write a program that divides a string into two substrings of equal size. If the string is an odd number of characters, then one of the substrings will be larger by one character. Print out the two substrings.

Syllabus reference

3.1.1 Representing algorithms

Use a systematic approach to problem solving and algorithm creation, representing algorithms using flowcharts.

3.2.4 Relational operations in a programming language

Be familiar with and be able to use:

- equal to
- not equal to
- less than
- greater than
- less than or equal to
- greater than or equal to.

Additional information

Students should be able to interpret these operators when used within algorithms. We will use the following symbols: $=, \neq, <, >, \leq, \geq$.

1.4 Selection

Logical decision

Introduction

You have learned to write a program that makes output. In this section you will learn how the computer can produce different output depending on the results of a logical test. This is called selection or a conditional structure.

Select between two options

The programs you have written so far have been based on a simple sequence of commands. There is one path through the algorithm.

A more complex type of program has a branching structure. There are two paths and the computer selects one of the paths. In order to select the right path, the computer carries out a logical test.

Logical test

A logical test is a test that gives an answer of either True or False. If the test result is True, the computer takes one path. If the test result is False, the computer takes the other path.

A logical test compares two values. Remember that the result of a logical test is always True or False. To compare two values, you use a type of operator called a "relational operator". You may see the following relational operators used in algorithms such as flowcharts and pseudocode.

Operator	Meaning
$=$	equal to
$\neq$	not equal to
$<$	less than
$\leq$	less than or equal to
$>$	more than
$\geq$	more than or equal to

Here are some logical tests made using relational operators.

Logical test	Meaning
Age $>$ 17	Age is more than 17
Price $=$ 9.99	Price is equal to 9.99
Name $\neq$ "Leon"	Name is not Leon

When the computer sees a logical test like these it does the comparison. For example, it compares the variable Age with the value 17. Is Age bigger than 17? The answer will be Yes (True) or No (False). That is a logical test.

Decision box

In a flowchart a logical test is shown inside a box called a decision box. A decision box is diamond shaped. One arrow goes into the decision box. Two arrows come out of the box. The arrows are labelled YES and NO.

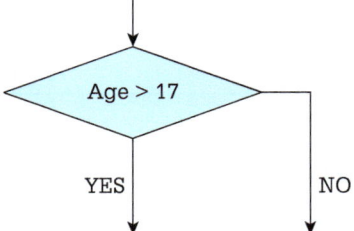

This is how it works:

- If the answer to the logical test is YES you follow the YES arrow.
- If the answer to the logical test is NO you follow the NO arrow.

It is usual in flowcharts for the YES arrow to go straight down. The NO arrow goes out to one side.

Example

In this example the algorithm decides whether you are old enough to go to college.

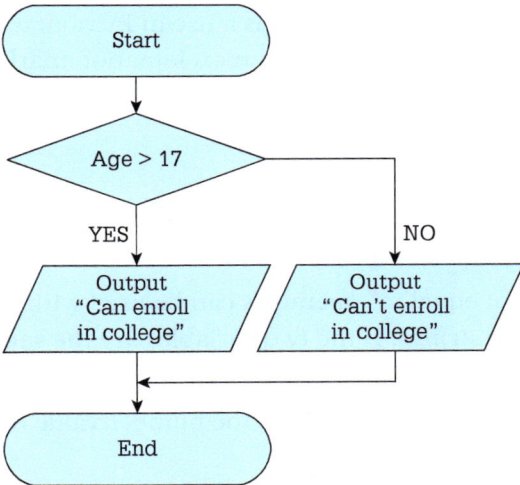

If the age is over 17, the computer outputs a message saying "Can enroll in college". If the result of the test is No (False) the computer outputs a message saying "Can't enroll in college".

Learning activity

1. Copy the flowchart shown on this page.
2. Create a flowchart for a program where the user inputs a password. If the password is "Outstanding99" the computer will output the message "You entered the correct password". If the result of the test is False the computer will output the message "Wrong password. Goodbye".

Test yourself

1. In an algorithm with two paths, how does the computer choose which path to take?
2. List the relational operators, giving the meaning of each one.
3. How are relational operators used to make logical tests?
4. Draw the flowchart symbol used to represent a decision. Label the YES and NO arrows.

Selection

> ### Introduction
>
> In the previous section you learned about the concept of selection, using a logical test. In this section you will see how logical tests are used in Python programming.

Applying your understanding

In this section you will create part of a program to sell tickets for a ride on the Nightmare Roller Coaster. Nightmare is an extreme ride. People must be age 15 or over to buy a ticket for this roller coaster. You will write the code to check the age of someone who wants to buy a ticket.

Logical tests in Python

The relational operators used in Python programming are slightly different to those used in algorithms. Make sure you use these relational operators when writing a Python program.

As the table shows, "equal to" is indicated using a double equals sign. That is because a single equals sign already has a use in Python: to assign a value to a variable. "Not equal to" is shown as an exclamation mark plus an equals sign. You can see that the Python operators are easy to type with a normal keyboard.

Operator	Meaning
==	equal to
!=	not equal to
<	less than
<=	less than or equal to
>	more than
>=	more than or equal to

Data type and comparison

You have to understand data types to use these relational operators:

- "Equal to" and "not equal to" operators can be used with variables of any data type including strings. If the two variables are the same value and the same data type, the result will be true.

- "Less than" and "more than" compare the number value of number data types (float and integer).

- "Less than" and "more than" operators compare the alphabetical order of string variables. A string that is later in alphabetic order counts as "more than" a string that is earlier in the alphabet.

Collect the comparison data

A logical test carries out a comparison. Before you can apply the logical test you must collect the data for comparison. Before we can decide whether someone is old enough to ride on the roller coaster we must find out the person's age.

In this program the data is input by the user and stored in a variable called Age. We need to do a numerical comparison. The variable Age is converted to integer data type.

```
7% show_if.py - C:/Python33/show_if.py                    [ - ][ □ ][ x ]
File  Edit  Format  Run  Options  Windows  Help
# program: show_if
# code by: Alison
# purpose: show how the 'if' structure works

print("Buy a ticket for the Nightmare Roller Coaster")
print("You must be 15 or over")

Age = input("Please enter your age: ")
Age = int(Age)
                                              Ln: 14 Col: 0
```

if…

The code that uses a logical test to select between two commands is called a conditional statement or an `if` statement. In Python an `if` statement has this structure:

- the word "if" (lower case)
- the logical test
- a colon (two dots, like this ":").

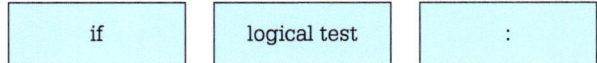

| if | logical test | : |

In this section you will create part of a program to sell tickets for a ride on the Nightmare Roller Coaster. If you are younger than 15 years old you cannot buy a ticket. The logical test is `Age<15` (age is less than 15). Following the `if` statement, you enter the command or commands that you want the computer to carry out if the result of the logical test is True.

This example program will output the message "sorry come back when you are older". It will only show this message if the result of the logical test is True.

```
print("Buy a ticket for the Nightmare Roller Coaster")
print("You must be 15 or over")

Age = input("Please enter your age: ")
Age = int(Age)

if Age < 15:
    print("sorry come back when you are older")
```

Use of indentation

Indentation gives an empty space at the start of a line of code. The line is set in from the left margin. Indentation is very important in Python. If you get the indentation wrong, your program will not work properly.

The `if` statement you typed ends with a colon. The colon tells Python that the next line you type must be indented. The indentation shows that the line belongs inside the `if` statement. There might be one indented line, or there might be many indented lines. The indented lines all belong inside the `if` statement.

How to indent a line

IDLE adds indentation automatically. You can use the Tab key on your keyboard to add indentation. Press Tab before you start typing a line of code. This adds an indentation at the start of the line. To remove indentation, you can delete the Tab, using the Backspace or Delete key on your keyboard.

Test yourself

1. What is the final symbol on the first line of an `if` statement?

2. What does indentation show in an `if` statement?

3. Where does a logical test appear in an `if` statement?

4. In the example on this page, why was the `Age` variable converted to integer data type?

Learning activity

1. Copy the program shown on this page and make sure it works properly.

2. Create a program that checks a user's password for a computer game. Choose the correct password. If the user enters the correct password display the message "Welcome to the game".

if... else...

Introduction

In the previous section you learned to write Python code using an `if` statement. The commands inside the `if` statement are carried out if result of the logical test is True. In this section you will extend the `if` statement to include commands carried out if result of the logical test is False.

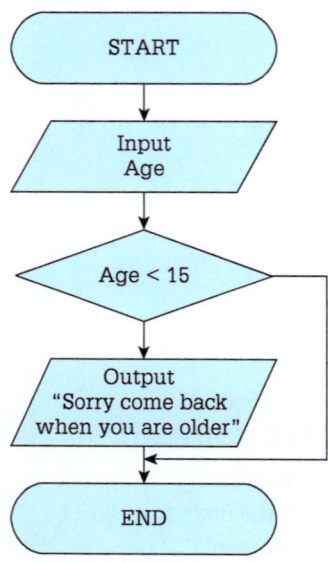

Algorithm

In the previous section you wrote a program that asked for the user's age. The logical test was `Age<15`. If the age was less than 15 the message "Sorry come back when you are older" appeared. On the left of this page is a flowchart that matches that structure.

Now we will extend the program. We will add a second message. This message will be output if the test result is False. Here is a flowchart that shows the structure of the extended program.

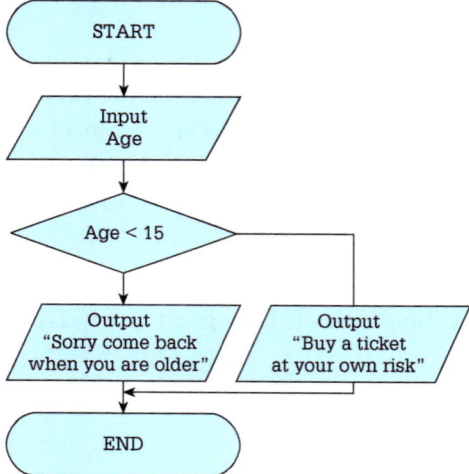

if... else...

In Python you can make the computer choose between two different actions. You use an `if` statement, then you use the word `else`:

- The indented code that follows the `if` statement is carried out if the test result is True.

- The indented code that follows `else` is carried out if the test result is False.

Using this code we can extend the Nightmare Roller Coaster example.

```python
print("Buy a ticket for the Nightmare Roller Coaster")
print("You must be 15 or over")

Age = input("Please enter your age: ")
Age = int(Age)

if Age < 15:
    print("sorry come back when you are older")

else:
    print("you can buy a ticket at your own risk")
```

Use of indentation

Indentation shows which code belongs inside the `if` statement:

- The `if` statement and the `else` statement are not indented.
- The lines that follow the `if` statement and the `else` statement are indented.

The indented lines that follow the `if` statement will be carried out if the test result is True. The indented lines that follow the `else` statement will be carried out if the test result is False.

Example

This program carries out a calculation for the user:

- The user enters two numbers. They are stored as the variables `Num1` and `Num2`.
- Then the user chooses what calculation to do. This input is stored as the variable `Choice`.
- The computer chooses an action using `if... else`.

Here is the extended program. Can you work out what this code does?

```
# program plusminus

print("Plus/Minus. A calculation that does addition and subtraction.")

Num1 = input("enter a number: ")
Num2 = input("enter another number: ")

Num1 = int(Num1)
Num2 = int(Num2)

choice = input("Type + to add the numbers together (else subtract)")

if choice == "+":
    answer = Num1 + Num2
else:
    answer = Num1 - Num2

print("The answer is :", answer)
```

Read through the program code and think about what it does. Now try typing in the program and using it to see what happens. Did the program do what you expected?

Learning activity

1. Enter and run all the examples of code shown on these two pages.
2. On page 33 you created a program that checks a user's password. Extend the program to show an appropriate message if the user types the wrong password.

Test yourself

1. Why are the variables `Num1` and `Num2` converted to integer data type in this program?
2. What does the computer do if the user types +?
3. What does the computer do if the user presses the Enter key with no typing?
4. This program uses whole numbers such as 99. What happens if you type a decimal number such as 99.9? Try it and see.
5. How would you change the program so it allows decimal numbers?

Extension activity

1. Adapt the calculation program so it accepts decimal values.
2. Make a calculation program that selects multiply or divide.
3. Adapt the calculation program so it outputs the question as well as the answer.

Nested `if`

Introduction

You have learned to write a program that includes an `if` statement. The `if` statement uses a logical test. Sometimes programmers need to use more than one logical test.

One way to do this is to put an `if` statement inside another `if` statement. This double structure is called a "nested `if`". In this section you will learn to create a nested `if`.

A test inside a test

Sometimes a programmer needs to make a program where one test follows another. Here is an example. Have you ever logged on to a network, for example at school? There are two tests:

- **Test user ID:** usually the computer has a list of the IDs of all the people who are allowed to use the network.

- **Test password:** if you enter a valid user ID, the computer asks for your password. The computer has a list that links each user to his or her current password.

If you pass both tests, then you can use the network.

The second test only happens if the first test result is True. If the first test result is False – if you do not have a network ID – then the computer will not carry out the second test. It does not ask you for your password.

There are two `if` statements. One is "nested" inside the other.

Example

Now you will write a Python program to check user ID and password. You will learn to work with lists of data in a later lesson. For now, we will check the login of a single user.

Here are the facts about that user:

- **User ID:** JehanD8
- **Password:** Metropolis

First we must input and test the user ID.

```
UserID = input("enter your network ID")
if UserID == "JehanD8":
```

The next few lines will be indented because they are inside the `if` structure. These lines will only be carried out if the `UserID` is `"JehanD8"`. If the result of this test is True, the program will input and test the password.

```
UserID = input("enter your network ID")
if UserID == "JehanD8":
    Password = input("enter your password")
    if Password == "Metropolis":
```

Finally, we add the lines that go inside the second `if` structure. These lines have a double indentation.

```
UserID = input("enter your network ID")

if UserID == "JehanD8":

        Password = input("enter your password")

        if Password == "Metropolis":

                print("Login successful")
```

In real life there would be more commands after this. The computer would not just say "Login successful", it would actually connect the user to the network.

Use of indentation

A nested `if` structure uses a double indentation. To get to the final line of the program the user must pass two tests – so the final line is indented twice.

Here is another example program that uses a nested `if` structure. It is used by a teacher to grade students. The students do two exams. They must get 50 marks or more in each exam to pass the course.

```
Exam1 = input("enter student mark for Exam 1")

Exam1 = int(Exam1)

if Exam1 >= 50:

        Exam2 = input("enter student mark for Exam2")

        Exam2 = int(Exam2)

        if Exam2 >= 50:

                print("Student has passed the course")
```

What are the two logical tests used in this program? What is the relational operator used in these tests? Why are the variables converted to integer data type before the logical test?

Use `else` in an indented structure

We can use if... else in a nested `if` structure. Each `else` statement is linked to one of the `if` statements. The `else` statement has the same level of indentation as the `if` statement that it belongs with.

Extension

Try making this program using Python.

```
UserID = input("enter your network ID")

if UserID == "JehanD8":

        Password = input("enter your password")

        if Password == "Metropolis":

                print("Login successful")

        else:

                print("Incorrect password")

else:

        print("User ID not found")
```

Be careful to match the pattern of indentation shown here. Run the program and see what happens if you enter the wrong user ID. What if you enter the right user ID but the wrong password?

Syllabus reference

3.2.5 Boolean operations in a programming language

Be familiar with and be able to use:

- NOT
- AND
- OR.

Be able to use these operators and combinations of these operators within conditions for selection structures.

Boolean operators

Introduction

In the last section you learned to write a program that uses two logical tests. You used a nested structure. That means one `if` statement is put inside another.

In this section you will learn another way of using two logical tests. In this example tests are linked to make one big test. They are linked by a kind of operator called a Boolean operator.

Why are these operators called Boolean?

Boolean operators are named after George Boole. He was an English mathematician. He was the first person to describe and explain what we now call Boolean operators. This was in the 19th century, long before computers were invented. His calculations were all on paper. Now we use his ideas when we write computer programs.

Operators

You have learned to use different operators:

- Arithmetic operators such as + and * are used to carry out calculations.
- Relational operators such as == and > are used to make logical tests.

In this section you will learn about another type of operator. They are called **Boolean** operators. A Boolean operator is used to join two logical tests together to make one big logical test.

There are three important Boolean operators:

- AND
- OR
- NOT

The meaning of these words in a program is just like the meaning of these words in real life.

AND

The Boolean operator AND is used to join two tests together. It makes one big test. The test result is True if both of the joined test results are True.

In the previous section you saw a nested `if` structure. First the computer tested `UserID`. Then the computer tested `Password`. We can join these two tests into one big test.

```
UserID = input("enter your network ID")

Password = input("enter your password")

if UserID == "JehanD8" and Password == "Metropolis":

    print("Login successful")
```

This test result is True if the `UserID` test result is True **and** the `Password` test result is True.

OR

Sometimes you want to join tests together in a different way. For example, in this program the user must type Y to play a computer game.

```
Play = input("Do you want to play this game? (Y/N)")

if Play == "Y":

    print("Welcome to the game")
```

What if the user types a lower-case "y"? This would not pass the test. The computer does not realise that "Y" and "y" are the same letter. We can fix that using a Boolean operator.

```
Play = input("Do you want to play this game? (Y/N)")
if Play == "Y" or Play == "y":
        print("Welcome to the game")
```

The Boolean operator OR makes a test by joining two tests together. The result of the big test is True if any of the small test results are True. This example is true if the user types "Y" OR "y".

NOT

Sometimes you want to reverse a test. The Boolean operator NOT makes this easy. If you put "not" in front of a test, this makes a test that is the opposite of the smaller test. Here is an example:

```
UserID = input("enter your network ID")
if not UserID == "JehanD8":
        print("You are not the registered user")
```

In the example above the result of the test is True if the user is **not** `"JehanD8"`.

The Boolean operator NOT is similar to the word "not" in everyday speech.

Test yourself

1. This section is about Boolean operators. What are the other two types of operator?

2. What is the job of a Boolean operator?

3. Explain why the and operator in Python is like the word "and" in English.

4. A class was open to students aged 16–18. A Python programmer wrote this code. Explain what is wrong with this code. Rewrite the code without the mistake.

```
print("You must be aged 16 to 18 ")
age = input("enter your age")
age = int(age)
if age<16 and age>18:
        print ("you are the wrong age")
```

Learning activity

Write a program that asks the user to enter a number between 1 and 9. If the number is not in this range, the program prints an error message.

Extension activity

Write a computer game where players have to make three choices. If they pick the right choice three times they win the game. You can decide what the three choices are. You can decide which conditional structure to use.

Syllabus reference

3.1.1 Representing algorithms

Use a systematic approach to problem solving and algorithm creation, representing algorithms using pseudocode.

3.2.4 Relational operations in a programming language

Students should be able to interpret relational operators when used within algorithms. We will use the following symbols: =, ≠, <, >, ≤, ≥

Selection in pseudocode

Introduction

You have learned to use `if`, `else` and nested `if` in Python. Pseudocode has similar structures. In this section you will learn to understand and use pseudocode selection structures.

Selection

In pseudocode, selection uses a logical test. Pseudocode is very similar to Python. Now you have learned to use `if`, `else` and nested `if` in Python you will find it easy to use similar structures in pseudocode.

You may see the following relational operators used in algorithms such as flowcharts and pseudocode.

Pseudocode and flowcharts	Python	Meaning
=	==	equal to
≠	!=	not equal to
<	<	less than
≤	<=	less than or equal to
>	>	more than
≥	>=	more than or equal to

Some of these operators are the same in pseudocode and in Python, and some are different. However, the way they make logical tests is exactly the same in pseudocode and in Python.

IF... THEN... ELSE... ENDIF

In Python command words are shown in lower-case letters. In pseudocode the command words are shown in upper-case letters. The structure of a pseudocode `IF` statement looks like this:

```
IF test THEN

        commands

ELSE

        commands

ENDIF
```

There are many similarities between pseudocode and Python. Remember that the logical test in pseudocode will typically compare two values using a relational operator, just as in Python.

There are some differences between pseudocode and Python. This is what you see in pseudocode:

- The command words are in upper-case letters.

- Instead of using a colon, the end of the first line is shown by the word `THEN`.

- The end of the whole `IF` statement is marked by the word `ENDIF`.

Indentation and line breaks are not as important in pseudocode as they are in Python. You can put all the code on a single line of pseudocode instead of spreading it out over several lines.

Example

Here is a pseudocode version of the roller coaster program you made on page 34:

```
Age ← USERINPUT

IF Age<15 THEN

        OUTPUT "sorry come back when you are older"

ELSE

        OUTPUT "Buy a ticket at your own risk"

ENDIF
```

If you understand Python, then you will understand programs set out in pseudocode.

Nested `IF`

You learned to use a nested `if` structure. Here is an example of a nested `if` structure in pseudocode:

```
UserID ← USERINPUT

IF UserID = "JehanD8" THEN

        Password ← USERINPUT

        IF Password = "Metropolis" THEN

                OUTPUT "Login successful"

        ENDIF

ENDIF
```

There is an `ENDIF` for each `IF` statement. To find out which `ENDIF` goes with each `IF` statement, see how they line up. Each `ENDIF` belongs to the `IF` statement it is lined up with.

Test yourself

1. Compare the pseudocode and Python versions of the roller coaster program. List the similarities and differences between the two versions.

2. Look at the pseudocode algorithm showing Nested `IF`. Write this algorithm in full. Each `IF` statement has a matching `ENDIF`. Draw a line between the `IF` and `ENDIF` statements to show which ones belong together.

3. The Nightmare Roller Coaster now has two rules. You have to be over 15 years old to ride on it. Also, you have to sign an agreement form. Change the roller coaster algorithm on this page so that it includes a nested `IF` structure with both these tests.

Extension activity

In the previous section you created a simple computer game with three choices. Turn this game into a pseudocode algorithm. Use a nested `IF` structure.

Learning activity

Make a Python version of the pseudocode 'nested `IF`' algorithm on this page.

Syllabus reference

3.1.1 Representing algorithms

Use a systematic approach to problem solving and algorithm creation, representing algorithms using flowcharts.

3.2.2 Programming concepts

Use definite and indefinite iteration.

1.5 Repetition

Loops

Introduction

Programs use loops. Loops are sections of a program that repeat over and over again. In this section you will look at loops in flowcharts.

What is a loop?

You have learned about program sequence, which is when commands are carried out in order. You have learned about program selection, which is when the computer uses a logical test to choose between different options. In this section you will learn about program repetition. A loop is a section of code that is repeated. The program loops back on itself. Using loops makes programs much more powerful. Just a few lines of code can make a program that will run for a long time.

Exit condition

It is important that there is a way to stop the loop. Every loop must have an exit condition. The exit condition is a logical test. The exit condition tells the computer when to stop repeating the loop.

There are two types of iterations or loops: definite iteration (counter-controlled loops) and indefinite iteration (condition-controlled loops). The two types of iterations have different exit conditions. In every program the exit condition must come true. Otherwise, the loop will never stop.

Definite iteration

In a definite iteration the computer counts how many times the loop repeats. When it reaches a set number, the loop stops. You use definite iteration when you know how many times you want the loop to repeat. A counter-controlled loop uses a variable called the counter. The counter goes up by 1 every time the loop repeats. When it reaches a maximum value the loop stops. You will learn more about definite iteration on page 44.

Indefinite iteration

In an indefinite iteration you set a logical test. The result of the test tells the computer whether to repeat the loop. The loop might repeat once, or a million times. You use the condition-controlled loop when you do not know how many times you need to repeat the loop. You will learn more about indefinite iteration on page 46.

Flowchart loop

In a flowchart the exit condition is shown using a decision box. The decision box has a logical test inside it. A decision box has two arrows coming out of it. The loop that comes out of the side of the decision box goes back up the page. It re-joins the main arrow that shows the flow of the program.

Example

This flowchart shows an algorithm. The program asks a mathematics question and checks the user's answer. Note these important features:

- The exit condition uses a variable called `Answer`.

- A box inside the loop lets the user change the value of the variable `Answer`.

Look at the flowchart structure. When will the program stop looping?

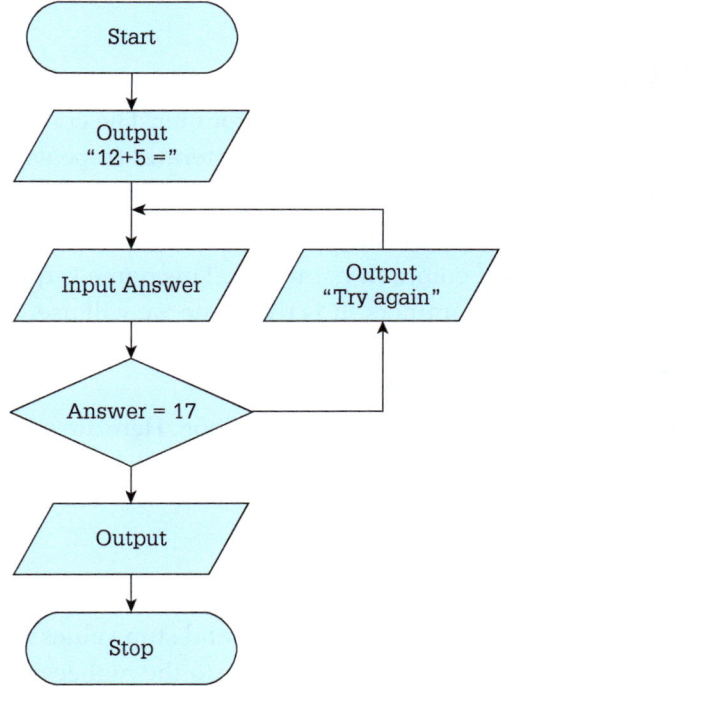

Key words

Two key words are very useful when talking about loops:

- "Increment" means increase a value by 1.

- "Iteration" means repetition of a loop.

Test yourself

1. What is an exit condition?

2. What does "increment" mean?

3. There are two types of loop. Explain how they differ by contrasting the exit conditions for each type.

4. A teacher wrote a program to process the results of exactly 100 student tests. What type of program loop does she need?

5. A student wrote an indefinite iteration. The exit condition checked a variable called `finish`. She forgot to include a command inside the loop to change the value of finish. What happened when she ran the program?

Extension activity

Write a quiz program that keeps asking each question until the user gets the answer right. You can decide the questions and the right answers.

Learning activity

1. Draw the flowchart shown on this page.

2. Draw a flowchart for a program that asks for a password. It loops until the user gives the correct password. You can choose what the correct password is.

Counter loops

Introduction

You have learned there are two types of iterations: definite and indefinite iteration. In this section you will learn how to make a definite iteration. In Python this is called a `for` loop.

Definite iteration

A definite iteration repeats a set number of times. You set the number of iterations in advance. This is also called a counter-controlled loop. That is because the loop repeats a definite number of times. You know exactly how many times it will repeat.

Counter variable

A definite iteration uses a variable as the counter. The counter variable will increment (go up by 1) every time the loop iterates (repeats). When the counter reaches the maximum value the loop will stop.

You can choose any name for the counter variable. Some programmers call it `counter`, but the most common name is `i`. This name is quick to write, and understood by all programmers. It is the name we will use.

Start the `for` loop

In Python a definite iteration is called a `for` loop. Here are some examples. Each example is the first line of a `for` loop. In each case the counter is called `i`.

```
for i in range (1, 100):
for i in range (0, 5):
for i in range (4, 8):
```

The two numbers in brackets are the start and stop values for the counter. The program will count from the lower number to the higher number. It will stop just before it reaches the higher value. For instance, in the first example the program will count from 1 to 99, then stop. If you do not specify a start value, Python will start at 0. You do not need to write any code to increment the counter variable. Python will do that on its own.

Indented lines are repeated

You have learned that indentation is important in Python. Indentation is added automatically by IDLE after you type a colon. Or you can add indentation yourself using the Tab key. Indentation shows which lines belong inside the loop. There might be one indented line, or more. The indented lines will be repeated. How many times will these lines be repeated? The computer will count the iterations until it reaches the right number. Then the loop will stop.

Loop structure

The Python structure looks like this:

```
for i in range (start, stop):
    commands
```

The indented commands will be repeated

Example

Here is an example Python program with a `for` loop:

```
# program forloop
# demonstrates the 'for' loop in Python

for i in range(1, 5):
    print("count number ", i)

print("now the loop has stopped")
```

Inside the loop there is a command to print the counter variable. The computer will print the counter variable every time the loop repeats. The value will be bigger each time. When the counter variable reaches the stop value, the loop stops.

```
count number   1
count number   2
count number   3
count number   4
now the loop has stopped
```

Input the stop value

In the following program the user can choose the number of iterations. The user inputs a number. The user's input is stored as a variable called `howmany`. The program repeats until it reaches that value.

```
# program forloop
# demonstrates the 'for' loop in Python

howmany = input("how many loops do you want?")
howmany = int(howmany)

for i in range(1, howmany+1):
    print("count number ", i)

print("now the loop has stopped")
```

These are features of this program:

- The user inputs a value. It is stored in the variable `howmany`.
- Input variables are always string data type, so the next line converts the variable to an integer.
- The variable `howmany` is used as the stop value of the `for` loop.

The stop value for the loop is set at `howmany + 1`. This is because the loop stops 1 before this value.

Step count

Typically, the Python for loop command will count up in increments of 1. However, a different step size can be used. You simply add the step size you want to use as a third number inside the brackets. The command:

```
for i in range (0, 100, 10):
```

will count up from 0 to 100 in increments of 10. You can even use a negative number and Python will count backwards.

Test yourself

1. If the start and stop values of a Python loop are set at 1 and 11, how many times will the loop iterate?

2. How does Python know which commands to repeat inside the `for` loop?

3. In the second example program on this page the user sets the number of iterations for the loop. In your own words explain the reason for this command:

```
howmany =
int(howmany)
```

Learning activity

An example of a Python program where the user sets the number of iterations of the loop is given above. The user does this by setting the upper value of the counter range. Create a new version of this program so the user sets the upper and lower value of the counter range.

Extension activity

Create a program so the user enters a number value and the program shows the value of that number multiplied by 1, by 2, by 3 and so on up to 12.

Syllabus reference

3.2.2 Programming concepts

Use indefinite iteration with the condition at the start of the iterative structure.

Condition loops

Introduction

You have learned there are two types of iterations: definite and indefinite iterations. In this section you will learn how to make an indefinite iteration. In Python this is called a `while` loop.

Indefinite iteration

An indefinite iteration is controlled by a test not by a counter. This is also called a condition-controlled loop. That is because the loop repeats an indefinite number of times. You do not know exactly how many times it will repeat.

Loop while a test result is True

Many different types of indefinite iteration are used in programming. Python uses just one – the `while` loop. These are key facts about the `while` loop:

- A `while` loop starts with a logical test.
- If the test result is True, the loop repeats.
- If the test result is False, the loop stops.

Other types of loop are used in different programming languages but not in Python. You can learn about other types of loop on pages 48–53.

Loop structure

The first line of a `while` loop is very easy to write. It consists of:

- the word "while"
- a logical test
- a colon (":").

The line or lines that follow this are indented. The indentation shows you which lines belong inside the loop. The indented lines will be repeated.

Every time the loop repeats the computer carries out the logical test again. If the test result is True the loop repeats again. If the test result is False the loop stops.

Test variable

The loop will stop if the test result is False. You must make it possible for the loop to stop. To use the `while` loop, remember these rules:

- The logical test at the top of the loop must have a variable in it.
- You must make sure the variable has a value before the loop starts.
- You must make sure the variable can change value inside the loop.

This program starts with introductory comments. Then there are five lines of code. These lines are not indented. They only happen once, at the start of the game. They do not loop. Then the player is asked to input a letter that stands for north, south, east or west. The player's input is stored in a variable called `Direction`.

Example

In this example you will make a computer game made using a single `while` loop. The game is called The Maze of Doom. Here is how it starts.

```
# program mazeofdoom
# this program is a game where the user has to escape from a maze
# it demonstrates the 'while' loop in Python

print("GAME: The Maze of Doom")
print("You are surrounded by thick hedges. You cannot see over them.")
print("You can go North, South, East or West. Which do you choose.?")
print("\n")
Direction = input("Type one letter: N, S, E, W: ")
```

Now we will extend the program, using a `while` loop.

```
# program mazeofdoom
# this program is a game where the user has to escape from a maze
# it demonstrates the 'while' loop in Python

print("GAME: The Maze of Doom")
print("You are surrounded by thick hedges. You cannot see over them.")
print("You can go North, South, East or West. Which do you choose.?")
print("\n")
Direction = input("Type one letter: N, S, E, W: ")

while Direction != "W":
    print("The hedges continue on either side of you.")
    print("You are getting tired and hungry")
    print("Which direction do you want to go?")
    Direction = input("Type one letter: N, S, E, W: ")
    print("\n")

print("You see the way out ahead of you.")
print("WIN: you have escaped the Maze of Doom")
```

Start the loop

The loop starts with a logical test. It looks like this:

```
while Direction != "W":
```

- The variable is called `Direction`.
- The relational operator `!=` means "does not equal".

The loop will repeat while the variable `Direction` does not hold the value `"W"`.

Inside the loop

There are five indented lines. These five lines are inside the loop. This is how they work:

- Three lines tell the user that he or she is still in the maze.
- Then there is a line that takes the user's input:

```
Direction = input("Type one letter: N, S, E, W: ")
```

This is the line that lets the user change the value of the variable `Direction`. This is how the user can stop the loop.

After the loop

The lines at the end of the program are not indented. They are not inside the loop. They will be carried out only once, after the loop has stopped.

Test yourself

Answer these questions are about the game called The Maze of Doom.

1. How many lines are inside the loop?

2. What would happen in this game if the user entered "W" right away?

3. What would happen if the user entered a lower-case "w"?

4. You want to change the game so that typing "W" makes the loop continue and anything else makes the loop stop. Which line would you change, and how would you change it?

Learning activity

1. Enter the program shown on this page. Run the program and try playing the game.

2. Use the `while` loop to create a password system. The program will loop unless the user enters the correct password.

Extension activity

Create a different game. The player must escape from a lion. The only way to escape is to get a feather and tickle the lion. Give the player several choices. When the player picks "tickle with a feather" the lion will run away.

Nested loops

Introduction

You have learned how to use loops in Python. In this section you will learn how to put a loop inside another loop. This is called a nested loop.

Loop reminder

A `for` loop uses a counter variable. The value of the counter variable starts at 0. The value increases by 1 each time. When the variable reaches a set value, the loop will stop.

This loop will print the message "1 times table", "2 times table"... up to "12 times table".

```
for i in range (1,13):
        print(i, "times table")
```

Loop inside a loop

Now we will put a loop inside the loop. The second loop uses a different counter variable. In this example we have called the second counter variable `j` (see bold type below).

```
for i in range(1,13):
        print(i, "times table")
        for j in range(1,13):
                print(i * j)
```

The second loop is inside the first loop. When the first loop repeats once, the second loop is carried out 12 times. The second loop will print the full times table for each value. This short program will produce almost 200 lines of output.

Improved loop

When you run the program the lines of output may shoot past so fast you can hardly see them. We will improve the loop to make the output more useful.

We will use an input command to pause the program before each times table. The new line is shown in bold.

```
for i in range(1,13):
        print(i, "times table")
        input("press Enter to continue")
        for j in range(1,13):
                print(i * j)
```

We will add a message to each print statement to explain what each value is. The change is shown in bold.

```
for i in range(1,13):
        print(i, "times table")
        input("press Enter to continue")
```

```
    for j in range(1, 13):
        print(i,"x",j,"=",i*j)
```

This short nested loop program will produce almost 200 lines of useful and well-formatted output.

Nested `while` loop

This program lets the user enter a series of numbers. It adds up the total value of the numbers. The loop will stop if the user enters the value 0.

The programmer wanted to stop people from entering minus numbers. To do this, she added an extra `while` loop. It was nested inside the other loop. The nested `while` loop is shown in bold.

```
total = 0
number = "-"
while number !=0:
    number = input("enter a number (0 to quit) ")
    number = int(number)
    while number < 0:
        number = input("cannot be minus number ")
        number = int(number)
    total = total + number
print("total:",total)
```

The nested loop will repeat if the user enters a number smaller than 0.

You can put a `while` loop inside a `for` loop. You can put a `for` loop inside a `while` loop. Any nested structure is allowed, and can be used to solve your programming problem.

Test yourself

1. Here is a sample of code. How many times will this code print out the word "Hello"?

```
for i in range(4):
    print("Hello")
```

2. Here is another sample of code. How many times will this code print out the word "Hello"?

```
for i in range(4):
    for j in range(2):
        print("Hello")
```

3. Here is a sample of code. What numbers will be printed out by this code?

```
number = 1
for i in range(4):
    for j in range(2):
        print(number)
        number = number + 1
```

Syllabus reference

3.1.1 Representing algorithms

Use a systematic approach to problem solving and algorithm creation, representing algorithms using pseudocode.

3.2.2 Programming concepts

Use definite and indefinite iteration

Loops in pseudocode

Introduction

You have learned to write loops in Python. You have learned to use `for` and `while` loops. Pseudocode also includes loops of this type. In this section you will learn to write FOR loops and WHILE loops using pseudocode.

FOR loops

A `for` loop is a definite iteration. The counter variable will count up to a maximum value. Here is an example of a pseudocode `for` loop. The counter variable will start at 1 and finish at 5.

```
FOR i ← 1 TO 5

        OUTPUT i

ENDFOR
```

This loop will print out the numbers from 1 to 5. Pseudocode looks different from Python in several ways:

- Words are in upper-case (capital) letters.
- An arrow symbol is used instead of the words "in range".
- There is no colon at the end of the line.
- The whole loop structure ends with the command ENDFOR.

This pseudocode loop is shown with indentation. You may see loops where there is no indentation. The top and bottom of the loop is shown by the terms FOR and ENDFOR.

The counter range

There is another important difference between Python and pseudocode:

- In Python the counter will stop before the maximum value.
- In pseudocode the counter will stop at the maximum value.

The example pseudocode algorithm shown at the top of the page would output these numbers.

1

2

3

4

5

What would be the output of a similar Python program?

WHILE loops

A `while` loop is an indefinite iteration. The loop begins with a logical test. If the result of the test is True, the loop will repeat. Here is an example of a `while` loop in pseudocode.

```
Password ← USERINPUT
WHILE Password ≠ "Pluto"
        OUTPUT "Wrong password"
        Password ← USERINPUT
ENDWHILE
```

This loop will repeat until the user enters the correct password. A pseudocode WHILE loop is very similar to a Python while loop. There are some differences. These are the features of pseudocode:

- Words are in upper-case letters.
- There is no colon in the first line.
- The structure ends with the command ENDWHILE.

The pseudocode WHILE loop above is shown with indentation. You may see loops where there is no indentation. The top and bottom of the loop is shown by the terms WHILE and ENDWHILE.

Features of a WHILE loop

A WHILE loop begins with a logical test. The logical test is at the top of the loop. A logical test typically tests the value of a variable. In the example on this page the variable is called Password.

A WHILE loop has these features:

- The test variable must have a value before the loop begins, so it can be tested.
- If the result of the logical test is False, the loop will not run even once.

You can see these features in the example pseudocode program. The password is input before the loop begins. If the user gets the password right first time, the loop does not run. The user will never see the message "Wrong password".

Test yourself

1. A Python loop begins with this command:

```
for i in range(1,11):
```

Write the equivalent command in pseudocode.

2. A Python loop begins with this command:

```
while choice != "Y":
```

Write the equivalent command in pseudocode.

3. In Python you can tell which lines belong inside a loop because of indentation. Pseudocode does not always use indentation. How can you tell which lines belong inside a loop?

4. Sometimes the commands inside a "while" loop are not carried out even once. Explain why.

Extension activity

Refer to your extension program to unlock a bank vault. Your program used a nested loop structure. Convert this program into pseudocode.

Learning activity

You have created a number of Python programs using loops. Create pseudocode versions of any two programs: one that uses a FOR loop, and one that uses a WHILE loop.

Syllabus reference

3.1.1 Representing algorithms

Use a systematic approach to problem solving and algorithm creation, representing algorithms using pseudocode.

3.2.2 Programming concepts

Use indefinite iteration with the condition at the end of the iterative structure.

3.2.5 Boolean operations in a programming language

Be familiar with and be able to use:

- NOT
- AND
- OR.

Additional information

Students should be able to use these operators and combinations of these operators within conditions for selection structures.

End-conditional

Introduction

You have learned to write and recognise loops in pseudocode. You have learned the FOR and WHILE loops. These are very similar to Python loops. Pseudocode has another type of loop called a REPEAT loop. This type of loop is not found in Python.

The REPEAT loop

Pseudocode includes another type of loop structure. This is called a REPEAT loop. It is an indefinite iteration. That means it has a logical test.

The pseudocode structure looks like this:

```
REPEAT
        commands
UNTIL test
```

A REPEAT loop has different rules from a WHILE loop:

- The test comes at the end of the loop.
- When the test result is True the loop will stop.

Example

Here is the game called The Maze of Doom, made using a REPEAT loop:

```
REPEAT
        OUTPUT "You are stuck in a maze"
        Direction ← USERINPUT
UNTIL Direction = "W"
OUTPUT "You have escaped!"
```

Differences from the WHILE loop

A REPEAT loop is controlled by a logical test. The test is at the bottom of the loop. This changes the way you use the loop in a program:

- You do not have to set the test variable before the loop starts. The value can be set by the commands inside the loop.
- The commands inside the loop are always carried out at least once, no matter whether the result of the test is True or False. In programming terms "the code repeats at least once".

Using Boolean operators

You have learned that Boolean operators can be used to join logical tests together (see page 38). This table shows the three operators.

Operator in Python	Operator in pseudocode	Meaning
and	AND	The test is true if both test results are True
or	OR	The test is true if one or both test results is True
not	NOT	This operator reverses the test result of True

In Python these operators are shown in lower case. In pseudocode they are shown in upper case.

REPEAT loops and WHILE loops are controlled by logical tests. You can combine two logical tests with **AND** or **OR** to make a single logical test. In this example the test at the end of the REPEAT loop uses **OR** to combine two tests. The user can type "W" or "w" to escape the maze.

Example

Here is the game called The Maze of Doom, made using a REPEAT loop:

```
REPEAT
        OUTPUT "You are stuck in a maze"
        Direction ← USERINPUT
UNTIL Direction = "W" OR Direction = "w"
OUTPUT "You have escaped!"
```

Test yourself

1. You want to make a loop, with the test at the top of the loop. What type of loop will you use?

2. You want to make a loop that stops when the test result is True. What type of loop will you use?

3. You want to make a loop that repeats until the username and password are correct. What Boolean operator will you use?

4 Explain the main differences between the WHILE and REPEAT loops in pseudocode.

Learning activity

Write an algorithm for a password login, using the REPEAT loop.

Extension activity

Refer to your pseudocode algorithm to unlock a bank vault. A passcode must be entered correctly three times. The algorithm used a WHILE loop nested in a FOR loop. Change this program so it uses a single REPEAT loop.

Syllabus reference

3.2.6 Data structures

Understand the concept of data structures.

Use arrays (or equivalent) in the design of solutions to simple problems.

2.1 Data structure

Lists

> **Introduction**
>
> You have learned to use a variable to store a single data value. In this section you will learn about a new kind of variable called a list. This type of variable lets you store a list of different values.

Data structures

A data structure is a way of storing a collection of several data values in an organised way. A list is an example of a data structure.

Make a list

A teacher made a Python list to store the names of her students. She called the list `Studentlist`.

Here is the command to make the list:

```
Studentlist = ["caspar", "soo-lin", "ali", "roberto"]
```

The list is shown in square brackets. In this example it is a list of four names.

The different items in a list are called elements. The elements in a list are separated by commas. There are four elements in this list. The elements are of string data type.

You can also make a list of numbers. A scientist made a list to store the result of an experiment each day for a week. Here is the command:

```
Resultslist = [2.3, 2.2, 4.5, 6.6, 1.9, 8.7, 6.0]
```

Numerical values do not have quotation marks. How many elements are there in this list? Which data type is used in this list?

Features of a list

A list is a variable that stores multiple elements. Each element in the list has its own name. The name of an element is the name of the list plus an index number. The numbering starts at 0.

```
Studentlist[0]
```

has the value:

```
"caspar"
```

Each element is identified by an index number.

```
Studentlist[3]
```

has the value:

```
"roberto"
```

The index number tells you the position of the element in the list. The index number is in square brackets.

Working with elements

Once you have made a list you can work with the elements. Each element in a list can be treated as a variable in its own right. You can print a single element:

```
print(Studentlist[0])
```

You can assign the value to another variable:

```
ClassLeader = Studentlist[0]
```

You can use a list variable in logical tests:

```
if Studentlist[0] == "caspar":
```

Working with the full list

You can also work with the full list. For example, with a single command you can print the entire list:

```
print(Studentlist)
```

This will print the whole list, showing all the elements, including the square brackets, the commas, and the quote marks. The output will look like this:

```
['caspar', 'soolin', 'ali', 'roberto']
```

Change value of a list element

You can change the value of a list element using the = sign. It is like changing the value of a variable.

```
Studentlist[1] = "soo-lin"
```

If you print the list, you will see the change.

```
['caspar', 'soo-lin', 'ali', 'roberto']
```

Example

This program uses the commands you have learned:

```
Resultslist = [2.3, 2.2, 4.5, 6.6, 1.9, 8.7, 6.0]
print("The first result was", Resultslist[0])
Resultslist[1] = 2.9
print("Here is the full list of results")
print(Resultslist)
```

Learning activity

1. Enter the example `Resultslist` program shown on this page. Run the program and see what outputs there are.

2. A soccer team has 11 players. Create a program that stores the names of 11 players in a list called `Team`. You can use real soccer players, and make your dream team, or just make up names.

3. Add lines to the soccer program so it prints out the names of the first three players.

Test yourself

1. What symbols mark the start and end of a list?

2. How are the elements of a list separated?

3. What is the index number of the first element in a list?

4. Give the command to create a list called `Rainbow` with seven elements. Choose the values you would store in this list.

5. Give the command to print the second element in the list called `Rainbow`.

6. Give the command to print the whole list called `Rainbow`.

Extension activity

Extend the soccer program by adding an indefinite loop. Each time the program loops the user will enter a number from 0 to 10. The program will print out the element of the soccer list that matches that number. If the user enters a number bigger than 10 the loop will stop.

Syllabus reference

3.2.2 Programming concepts

Use definite iteration.

3.2.6 Data structures

Understand the concept of data structures.

Use arrays (or equivalent) in the design of solutions to simple problems.

Output a list

Introduction

You have learned to make a list. You know how to print a single element from the list, or print the whole list. In this section you will learn how to use a `for` loop to print all the elements in a list one by one.

Example

In this section we will use an example list `Rainbow`. Here is the command to create the list:

```
Rainbow = ["red", "orange", "yellow", "green",\
"blue", "indigo", "violet"]
```

This command shows a new Python feature. If a command is too long to fit on one line of your program, a symbol like this:

```
\
```

lets you continue onto a second line.

Print an element

The command:

```
print(Rainbow)
```

will print the whole list including square brackets, commas and quote marks. Or you can print a single element:

```
print(Rainbow[3])
```

This will print the word "green" with no square brackets or quote marks.

Print all elements

There are seven elements in the list. To print all the elements one by one would take seven lines of code. A list with 100 items would need a program with 100 lines of code. To make the program shorter, we can use a counter-controlled loop. The loop will count through the elements of the list, printing each one in turn.

Counter variable

A counter-controlled loop needs a counter variable. We will use the variable i as the counter variable. Every time the loop iterates, the counter variable will increment by 1. We will use the variable i as the list index number. Every time the loop iterates, the list index number will count up by 1.

Start and stop values

Every counter-controlled loop has a start and stop value. The start value is 0, because the first element of a list is number 0. The stop value is the number of elements in the list. This list has seven elements, so we will use 7 as the stop value.

Example

This program will count through all the elements in the list. It will print the counter variable. It will print the element with that index number. It will start at 0 and end at 6. Remember that a counter-loop stops one before the stop value.

```
# program Rainbow
# shows how to print the elements of a list
# using a counter-controlled loop


Rainbow = ['red', 'orange', 'yellow', 'green', 'blue', 'indigo', 'violet']

for i in range(0,7):
    print(i, Rainbow[i])
```

The output looks like this. This program prints elements 0 to 6: all the elements in the list.

```
0 red
1 orange
2 yellow
3 green
4 blue
5 indigo
6 violet
```

How many iterations?

In the previous example the stop value was 7 because the list had exactly seven elements. We can adapt the program so it works for a list of any length. Instead of entering a number, such as 7, we ask the computer to tell us the length of the list.

This command `len(Rainbow)` will find the length of the list called `Rainbow`. It counts how many elements there are in the list.

This command will store the value in a variable called `Listlength`:

```
ListLength = len(Rainbow)
```

Now we can use the variable `ListLength` as the stop value of the counter-controlled loop. Here is the first line of the loop:

```
for i in range (0, ListLength):
```

This means the counter will increment from 0, up to the length of the list. Then it will stop.

Extension activity

A soccer manager has a team of 11 players. The manager will select one player to take a penalty kick.

1. Write a program with these features:
   - The program contains 11 players as a list.
   - The manager enters a number and the computer prints out the name from the list that matches that number.
   - Remember that the elements are numbered from 0 to 10. If the manager enters a number that is bigger than 10, the program loops until a valid number is entered.

2. Extend the program so that the program also loops if the manager enters a number smaller than 0.

Learning activity

1. Copy the Rainbow program shown above, and run it to see what the result is.

2. Change the Rainbow program to use the `ListLength` variable as shown on this page.

3. In the extension activity you created a list for a soccer team. Use the skills you have learned on this page to print the name of every player in the soccer team.

Syllabus reference

3.2.2 Programming concepts

Use definite iteration.

3.2.6 Data structures

Understand the concept of data structures.

Use arrays (or equivalent) in the design of solutions to simple problems.

Add elements to a list

Introduction

In the previous section you learned how to use a counter-controlled loop to output all the elements of a list. In this section you will learn how to use a counter-controlled loop to input elements to a list.

Append

Adding an element to a list is called appending. The new element is added at the end of the list. Here is an example. This command will add the element "Ultra Violet" to the list called Rainbow:

```
Rainbow.append("Ultra Violet")
```

You enter the name of the list, then a dot, then the word "append". You end the command with the element you want to add, in brackets.

Append to an empty list

The simplest way to put elements in a list is to start with an empty list. Then append as many elements as you want.

You can create an empty list (a list with no elements in it). Here is an example that makes an empty list called Rainbow:

```
Rainbow = [ ]
```

You can give the list any name.

Counter loop

Next you use a counter-controlled loop to append elements to the empty list. The start value of the loop is 0. The stop value of the loop depends on how many elements you want to add. In this example we will add seven elements:

```
for i in range (0,7):
```

You can use any number for the stop value. The list will have that number of elements.

There must be two commands inside the loop. The first command will get a new value from the user. The second command will append that value to the list. We use a variable to store the input from the user. In this example the variable is called NewValue:

```
NewValue = input("enter the next element of the list:")
Rainbow.append(NewValue)
```

Example

Here is the completed program, using the commands from this page.

You can add extra lines at the end of the program to print out all the elements of the list.

```
# program Rainbow
# append to a list

Rainbow = [ ]

For i in range(0, 7):
    NewValue = input("enter the next element of the list: ")
    Rainbow.append(NewValue)
```

Extension – choose how many elements

If you are a confident programmer, try this activity. You can let users choose how many elements to add to the list before they begin:

- Input a value and store it as an integer variable.
- Use this value as the stop value of the `for` loop.

Here is a program showing these commands:

```python
# program Rainbow
# append to a list

Rainbow = [ ]

HowMany = input("How many elements in the list? ")
HowMany = int(HowMany)

for i in range(0, HowMany):
    NewValue = input("enter the next element of the list: ")
    Rainbow.append(NewValue)
```

Add extra lines at the end of the program to print all the elements of the list.

```python
print("\n")
print("The elements of this list...")

for i in range(0, HowMany):
    print(i, Rainbow[i])
```

Extension – append using a `while` loop

Here is an activity for the most confident programmers. Write a program that uses a `while` loop to add elements to an array. After adding an element, the user is asked whether he or she wants to add another. If the user inputs "Y" the loop iterates.

Test yourself

These questions are about creating a list called `Months`. It has 12 elements, the names of the months.

1. Write the command to make an empty list called `Months`.

2. Write the first line of a counter-controlled loop that will let the user add 12 elements to the list.

3. Write two lines that will (a) take user input and (b) append that value to the list.

Learning activity

1. Make the program shown on this page that inputs values to the list called `Rainbow`.

2. Make a program that lets you input the names of 12 months to make a list.

3. Add lines at the end of your `Months` program so that the list of months is printed using a counter-controlled loop.

Extension activity

1. Use the `Months` program to input the names of the months in a different language, for example French.

2. Complete one or both of the extension activities described on this page.

Syllabus reference

3.1.1 Representing algorithms

Use a systematic approach to problem solving and algorithm creation, representing those algorithms using pseudocode.

3.2.6 Data structures

Use arrays (or equivalent) in the design of solutions to simple problems.

Arrays in pseudocode

Introduction

You have learned to use lists in Python. Other languages have similar data structures called arrays. In this section you will learn to recognise pseudocode commands that process arrays.

Arrays

You have learned that Python includes a data structure called a list. A list stores a series of values. Each value is identified by an index number. In other programming languages a very similar structure is available called an **array**.

When you see pseudocode programs you may see arrays used. Arrays in pseudocode look just like lists in Python. They are processed using similar commands. If you can write a Python program that uses a list, you can write a pseudocode algorithm that uses an array.

Make an array and assign values

Assigning values to an array is exactly the same in pseudocode as in Python. The arrow symbol is used instead of the equals sign. This commands creates an empty array called results:

```
results ← []
```

This command makes an array called results with four elements. The elements are floating point numbers. Elements of any data type can be stored in an array.

```
results ← [7.0, 12.3, 4.4, 9.1]
```

Just as in Python, the first element is results[0], the final element is results[3]. What is the value of results[1]?

Append to an array

Pseudocode does not have the append command that we use in Python to add a value to a list. However, it is easy to add elements to an empty array. Here is an example:

```
countries ← []
countries[0] ← "Brazil"
countries[1] ← "Uruguay"
countries[2] ← "Argentina"
```

What would be the contents of the array after these commands?

Input values to an array

You can use a for or while loop to input elements to an array. Here is an example using a for loop. In pseudocode, a for loop counts from a start to a stop value. The first element of an array has the index number 0. 0 is the start value. The final element of an array has an index number one less than the length of the array. This is the stop value.

```
results ← []
FOR i ← 0 TO 9
        results[i] ← USERINPUT
ENDFOR
```

This loop will add 10 values to the array, numbered from 0 to 9.

Output an array

Just as in Python, you can output a single element of an array by giving the index number.

```
OUTPUT results[9]
```

You can also use a `for` loop to output all elements of an array. Remember the final element of the array has an index number one less than the length of the array. We can store this value as a variable called 'stop'.

```
stop = LEN(results) - 1
FOR i ← 0 TO stop
        OUTPUT results[i]
ENDFOR
```

Extension – using a `while` loop

We can use a `while` loop to assign values to an array. This is a longer program. It has the advantage that users can add as many or as few elements to the array as they want.

```
results ← []
more ←"Y"
i = 0
WHILE more = "Y"
        results[i] ← USERINPUT
        i ← i + 1
        more ← USERINPUT
ENDWHILE
```

Test yourself

1. What type of data values can be stored in an array?

2. What is the index number of the first element in an array?

3. An array has ten elements. What is the index number of the final element in the array?

4. Write the command to append the value 44 to an array called `Marks` that already has 10 elements.

Learning activity

1. Write a pseudocode algorithm to add 12 user input values to an empty array called `Months`.

2. Extend the pseudocode algorithm to output the 12 elements of the array `Months`.

Extension activity

Write a two-line pseudocode algorithm that will allow you to append an element at the end of any array, regardless of its length.

Syllabus reference

3.2.6 Data structures

Use arrays (or equivalent) in the design of solutions to simple problems.

Additional information

One-dimensional (1-D) and two-dimensional (2-D) arrays are required.

In Python, a list is a suitable alternative to an array for this specification.

2-D arrays and lists

> ## Introduction
> You have learned to create and use lists and arrays. In this section you will learn about more complex versions of these structures. They are called two-dimensional (2-D) arrays.

In these examples you will use Python list commands. Very similar commands will work with pseudocode arrays.

2-D data structures

Sometimes data is provided in a grid or matrix structure. When we present this type of data we often show it as a table. Here is an example. We have numbered the rows and columns starting with 0 to match the way Python numbers a list's elements.

The numbers in the grid are imaginary data, just to give us values to work with in this exercise.

	Column 0	Column 1	Column 2
Row 0	23	17	100
Row 1	38	19	200
Row 2	18	11	120

Each element in the table may be identified by its row and column position. For example, the grid position row 1, column 2 has the value 200.

This type of structure is called a 2-D array. One dimension is the height of the table, indicated by row number. The other dimension is the width of the table, indicated by column number.

2-D lists

In Python, this structure is shown by making a list of lists. Each element in the list is a smaller list. We will call it a sublist. Here is the Python command that stores the grid shown on this page:

```
grid = [[23,17,100],[38,19,200],[18,11,120]]
```

It may be easier to understand if we break the command up into several lines using the \ symbol:

```
grid = [[23,17,100],\
        [38,19,200],\
        [18,11,120]]
```

Each element of the list is a sublist. Each of the sublists stands for one row of the table. This command:

```
print(grid[1])
```

will print one of the sublists. In this case, it will print row 1 – the middle row of the table:

```
[38, 19, 200]
```

Printing a single element

To print a single value from a 2-D array we must give two index numbers. The first index number identifies the row. The second index number identifies the column. This command:

```
print(grid[1][0])
```

will produce this output:

```
38
```

You can see that 38 is row 1, column 0 of the grid. To put it another way:

- Find element 1 of the grid. This is a sublist.
- Find element 0 of the sublist.

Changing values in a 2-D list

Typically, you will work with a 2-D list that already has values assigned to it. As a reminder, values are assigned with a command like this:

```
grid = [[23,17,100],\
        [38,19,200],\
        [18,11,120]]
```

You can then change the value of any element of the list. Remember that each element is identified by two numbers, the row and then the column.

You have seen that this element:

```
grid[1][0]
```

holds the value 38. This command:

```
grid[1][0] = 99
```

will change the value from 38 to 99.

Extension – printing values from a 2-D list

The command:

```
print(grid)
```

will print out the list of lists as a long string. It is not very easy to read. You can print out each row of the table, using a `for` loop. In this example we have called the counter variable `row` because it counts each row of the grid. It makes the program easier to read.

```
rows = len(grid)
for row in range(rows):
    print(grid[row])
```

This will print out every row as a separate list.

To print out every element within the row, you would need to use a nested loop structure.

```
rows = len(grid)
for row in range(rows):
    cols = len(grid[row])
    for col in range(cols):
        print(grid[row][col])
```

Try this program for yourself.

Test yourself

You have been working with a Python list. It has the name `grid`. These questions refer to the `grid` list.

1. What is the length of the list?

2. What is the command to print out the first element of the list? It stores three values that match the first row of the table.

3. What is the command to print out the first value in the list? In this example it has the value 23.

4. The final element in the list has the value 120. Write a command to change this value to 0.

Learning activity

Write a Python program that creates the 2-D grid structure shown above. Add commands that let the user enter a row and column, and then amend the value stored in that cell of the grid.

Extension activity

This activity uses a chess board.

Write a program that stores the position of pieces on a chess board using a 2-D list of eight rows and eight columns. A place where there is no chess piece will store the string `"-"`. A place where there is a piece will store the name of the piece, for example "Black King".

Use print commands to show the position of every piece on the board.

<table><tr><td>

Syllabus reference

3.2.6 Data structures

Use records (or equivalent) in the design of solutions to simple problems.

Additional information

In Python, classes can be used to create records.

</td><td>

Records

> ## Introduction
>
> You have learned to use 1-D and 2-D lists or arrays. We can also store data in more complex structures called records. In this section you will learn to create and use records.

Database records

Computer systems often need to store data. We store data in a structured way. Data can be about all kinds of things, for example:

- people
- objects
- places
- events.

In a database these things are called entities.

All the data about one entity is stored as a single database record. In this section you will see how Python can be used to make a database record. In chapter 10 you will learn to make a database using different software.

Fields

One database record stores the facts about one entity. For example, a wildlife park stored data about every animal in the park.

Each record stored these facts:

- code number
- name
- species
- date of birth (DOB).

Each animal record has the same facts in the same order.

These different facts are called fields. Each field stores one fact.

Create a class

To store this data we will make a new data structure called a class. Here is the command to make the data structure:

```python
class Animal():

    def __init__(self, code, name, species, DOB):

        self.code = code
        self.name = name
        self.species = species
        self.DOB = DOB
```

The special procedure __init__ is called a constructor. It tells the computer how to make animal records. It tells the computer what fields there are in an animal record. Note that there is a double underline before and after the word init.

</td></tr></table>

Create a new record

A new lion cub was born in the park. The park keeper made a new record. The lion cub did not have a name yet. It just had the code number "L233".

```
L233 = Animal("L233", "-", "Lion", "10-08-2019")
```

This command creates a new variable. It is a new `Animal` variable. The name of the variable is `L233`. The four facts about the animal are given in brackets.

Print fields

`L233` is made of four fields. Here are the field names. Each field stores a different piece of data.

Field	Data
L233.code	"L233"
L233.name	"-"
L233.species	"Lion"
L233.DOB	"10-08-2019"

Each field is accessed by the name of the variable. Then there is a full stop. Then the name of the field appears.

We can print any of the fields in the record.

```
print(L233.species)
```

Change the data in a field

Each field in the record has a different value. It is possible to change the value of any field in the record. The park keeper decided to call the new cub Simba. This command changes the value of the name field. It gives the name field the value "Simba".

```
L233.name = "Simba"

print(L233.code, L233.name)
```

Summary

A data record is a variable made of fields. Each field stores one fact. Each field is called by the name of the variable, then a full stop, then the name of the field. We can change the value of any field in the record. We can print the value stored in any field.

This gives us a new structured way to store facts about entities.

Syllabus reference

3.2.6 Data structures

Use records (or equivalent) in the design of solutions to simple problems.

Additional information

In Python, classes can be used to create records.

Make a list of records

> ## Introduction
>
> You have learned about records. You have learned about lists. In this section you will learn how you can store records in a list.

Create new records

Begin a new program by entering the Animal class definition from the previous page.

Once this definition is in place you can write a program so that the user can enter new values and make new records of the Animal class. If these commands are put inside a loop, the user can make as many new records as they like.

Here are the commands:

```python
add_more = "Y"

while add_more == "Y":

    newcode = input("enter the animal code: ")
    newname = input("enter the animal name: ")
    newspec = input("enter the animal species: ")
    newDOB  = input("enter the date of birth: ")

    newrecord = Animal(newcode, newname, newspec, newDOB)

    add_more = input("add another record (Y/N)? ")
```

This code will run, and you can test it out.

However there is a big problem with this code. Every record is stored using the same variable name ("newrecord"). Every time you go round the loop, the old record is lost.

Store the records in a list

To solve this problem you can store all the records in a list. To do this you must add two new commands:

- Before the start of the `while` loop, add this command to create a new, empty list:

  ```python
  animal_list = []
  ```

- Inside the `while` loop add, a command to append the new record to the list: `animal_list.append(newrecord)`. This command comes after the line which creates the variable "newrecord".

If you add these commands in the right location the records will be stored as items in `animal_list`.

Print out the records

You can add some further lines to the program to print out the contents of the list. The following extra lines will print out the name of every animal. You already know all these commands.

```
list_size = len(animal_list)

for i in range (list_size):

    print(animal_list[i].name)
```

Extension – an alternative `for` loop

When we print out items in a list there is a shorter, neater way of writing the `for` loop. Instead of using the counter variable I, we can just tell Python to count every item in the list. We don't need to find the list size or set a range for the loop. Python will take care of this.

We could use this command to start the loop

```
for item in animal_list:
```

But in this example we call each item 'animal'. Here is the alternative for loop structure:

```
for animal in animal_list:

    print(animal.name)
```

This makes the code shorter and easier for the reader to understand.

Test yourself

1. In this line of the program what is the data type of newcode?

```
newcode = input("enter the animal code: ")
```

2. In this line of the program what is the data type of newrecord?

```
newrecord = Animal(newcode, newname, newspec,
newDOB)
```

3. Explain why we use a 'while' loop to add records to the list, but a 'for' loop to print them out.

Learning activity

Make the program shown on this page – remember to add the two commands which create a list and append records to the list.

Adapt the program so it prints out the name and species of every animal in the list.

Extension activity

Amend the program you wrote so the code number of each animal is calculated automatically. The first record in the list will have code number 0. Each animal in the list will have a code number that is one bigger than this.

Permanent storage

In this lesson you have learned how to store several records in a list. However, if you close the program all these records will be lost. In the next section you will learn how to save data from a Python program to a storage file.

2.2 File handling

Write to a file

> ### Introduction
>
> You have learned about variables and data structures such as lists and arrays. These data structures are stored in the computer's electronic memory. The values are lost when the program closes. In this section you will learn how to store values permanently by writing them to text files.

Memory and storage

Data in the computer's memory is stored as electrical signals. When the computer is turned off, or when you close a program, the data in the program is lost. This includes all the variables you have used in your program. To save values after the program is closed you can write them to a text file. That means the values are stored in a file in permanent storage. The file will continue to exist after the program is closed. You can open the file and look at the contents.

Write to a file

Here is a Python program that saves a message to a text file:

```python
### write to a text file

filename = "example.txt"

with open(filename, "w") as myfile:
    myfile.write("here is a sample of text")
```

The first command in the program sets the name of the text file. In this program it is called `example.txt`. You can use any name. It is a good idea to use the ending `.txt`. This tells the computer that you are making a text file.

The final command of the program writes a message to the text file. In this program the message is:

```
here is a sample of text
```

You can write any text that you want. You can include more than one line of text.

Look at the output

When you run the program you won't see any results on the screen. Instead the computer has made a text file. Go to the storage area where you save your Python work. When you look in the file list you will see a file called `example.txt`. You can open the file and look at its contents. You can use any software that opens text files, for example Microsoft Notepad.

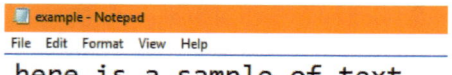

```
here is a sample of text
```

Write multiple lines

The first example program wrote only one line to the file. Here is an extended program that writes several lines to the file. Remember that this command adds an empty line:

```
"\n"
```

```
### write to a text file

filename = "example.txt"

with open(filename, "w") as myfile:
    myfile.write("saving line 1 \n")
    myfile.write("saving line 2 \n")
    myfile.write("saving line 3")
```

The previous contents of the file have been overwritten by the program.

⬆ If you open the file example now you will see it looks like this.

String data type

In these examples you have written a string to the text file. You can also write a string variable to the text file.

```
### write a variable to a text file

filename = "example.txt"
message  = "this is my text message"

with open(filename, "w") as myfile:
    myfile.write(message)
```

You cannot write integers and float data type directly to a text file. They would have to be converted into string data type first.

Overwrite

Sometimes you will write to a file that already exists. When you open the file for writing, the new lines of text you add will wipe out the old text in the file. The file will only contain the new text. This is called overwriting the file. The new contents will replace the old content of the file. None of the old content is left.

Append to a file

Sometimes you want to append to a file (add new content) instead of overwriting (wipe out old content). It is easy to make this change. Instead of this code:

```
with open(filename, "w") as myfile
```

use "a" for 'append':

```
with open(filename, "a") as myfile
```

Test yourself

These questions refer to this example Python code:

```
filename = "testresult.txt"

header = "Results of spelling test"

with open(filename, "w") as myfile:
    myfile.write(header)
    myfile.write("\n")
    myfile.write("Total marks = 10")
```

1. What is the name of the file created by this program?

2. What is the data type of the variable `header`?

3. What is the content of the text file after the program has been run?

Learning activity

Write a program that saves your name, address and phone number to a text file. Write several lines of text. Check the contents of the text file.

Extension activity

You have learned the commands to output all the elements of an array on the screen. Write a program that writes all the elements of an array to a text file.

Read from a file

Introduction

You have learned how to store text values in a permanent file. In this section you will learn to read the values from a stored file, so you can include them in your program.

Read a file

Writing to a text file means that the electronic contents of the computer's memory are copied into electronic storage.

Reading a text file means that text from the file is copied into the computer's memory. You can use the text in your program. For example, you can show the text on the screen.

In this section you will learn to read from a text file. If you have completed the previous section you can use the file you created.

Read the contents of a text file

Here is a Python program that reads from a text file:

```python
filename = "example.txt"

with open (filename) as myfile:
    text = myfile.read()

print(text)
```

The program reads `example.txt` and stores the contents of the file into a variable called `text`. The last line of program prints out the value stored in the variable `text`.

Select a file

You can use any file name you like. You must make sure of these things:

1. A file with that name exists.
2. The file is in the same storage area as your Python program.
3. It is a text file.

If any of these conditions are not true, your program will crash.

Write several variables to a file

You have learned that any string variable can be written or appended to a text file. You can save several different variables in the same write operation. This program will append two variables to a text file.

```
filename ="example.txt"

var1 = input("enter the first value: ")
var2 = input("enter the second value: ")

with open(filename, "a") as myfile:

    myfile.write(var1)
    myfile.write(var2)
```

But if you want to enter several values it may be best to store them as a list. Then each item in the list can be appended to the text file. Instead of the `write` command, we use the Python `writelines` command.

Here is an example. You may have written a program which inputs several values to a list. You can add the following extra lines to the program to save the list to a text file. In this example the list is called `mylist`:

```
with open(filename, "w") as myfile:

        for item in mylist:
            myfile.write(item + "\n")
```

This code writes each element of the list one at a time to the text file. It uses the shortcut `for` loop method (find out more on page 69). By adding "\n" to each item you make sure each one is stored on a different line of the text file.

Read several variables from a file

You have saved a list of variables to a text file. A different program can read the lines from the file. Here is the entire program. It will read the lines one by one into a list called `newlist`.

```
filename = "example.txt"
with open(filename) as myfile:
    newlist = myfile.readlines()
```

The following extra lines will print out the elements of newlist. The command `strip` takes out the "\n" values that you added in the last program, leaving just the text.

```
for item in newlist:
    item = item.strip()
    print(item)
```

Extension

You can read from a file that is not in the same storage location as your Python program. The file name you give must include the drive and folder where the file is stored. It is easier just to make sure the file is in the same folder as the Python program.

Test yourself

1. Write a Python program that will open a file called `password.txt` and read the contents into a variable called `mypass`.

2. What data type is the variable?

3. Why is a word-processed document not suitable for reading by this Python program?

4. Describe three ways in which you could create the file `password.txt`.

Learning activity

You have already made a program that writes your name and address to a text file. Write a program that reads this file and displays the contents on the screen.

Extension activity

Create a text file that stores a single word – the password for a website. Write a Python program that reads this word into a variable called `password`. Complete the program by adding a `while` loop that iterates until the user's input matches the `password` variable.

Files in pseudocode

Introduction

You have learned to write text to a text file. You have learned to read text from a text file. In this section you will learn the pseudocode commands to carry out these actions.

Write to a text file

The pseudocode commands for file handling are simpler than the Python commands. This is an example of a command to write to a text file. It writes one line of text to one line of a file.

```
WRITELINE(file, n, text)
```

Here are some notes to help you:

- **file**: instead of `file` write the name of the text file. You can give the text file any name you want. The name of a text file usually ends with `.txt`.

- **n** instead of the letter n write the line of the file. This is the line that will hold the text. You can store the text in line 1. Or you can write the text to line 100, or to any other line of the file. The file can have as many lines as you like.

- **text:** complete the command by giving the exact text you want to write to the file. Remember to write text values in quote marks.

Example

Here is an example:

```
WRITELINE(Password.txt, 3, "Engine99")
```

This command will write the text `Engine99` to the file `Password.txt`. It will write this text to line 3 of the file.

Overwrite

If the file already exists, the new content will overwrite the old contents. In pseudocode it will only overwrite one line. The other lines in the file will not change.

Example

A file called `password.txt` looked like this. The lines have been numbered for convenience.

```
1. Password
2. ********
3. Pluto
4. --------
```

A pseudocode algorithm includes this command:

```
WRITELINE(Password.txt, 3, "Engine99")
```

After this command the file looks like this:

```
1. Password
2. ********
3. Engine99
4. --------
```

The command overwrites one line of the file. The other lines stay the same.

Keep track of a file's contents

Remember that pseudocode does not make a real text file. You cannot run pseudocode programs on the computer. Pseudocode is used to plan the structure of a program before you begin writing the program code.

As you make a pseudocode algorithm, keep a record of the contents of the text file. For example, you could write this down on a piece of paper. Number all the lines on the page. Every time you see a `WRITELINE` command, write the contents into the numbered line. Remember to cross out any old contents on that line. The new text overwrites the old text. This will keep an accurate record of the contents of the file.

Read from a text file

Pseudocode also includes a command to read text from a text file. It is simpler than the Python read command.

```
READLINE(file, n)
```

Here are some notes about this pseudocode command:

- **file**: instead of `file` put the name of the text file. You should use the name of a file that already exists. You will read the contents of this file into your program.
- **n**: instead of the letter `n` write the line of the file. The contents of that line will be copied into the computer's memory.

Store in a variable

The `READLINE` command reads one line from a text file. You will normally store this text as a variable. The complete command will look like this.

```
variable ← READLINE(file, n)
```

Example

You should keep a record of the contents of any text file. That will help you understand the `READLINE` command. Here is an example of `READLINE`. It refers to the file `Password.txt`, which we looked at earlier.

```
Password = READLINE(Password.txt, 3)

ATTEMPT ← USERINPUT

IF ATTEMPT = Password THEN

        OUTPUT "Correct Password"

ENDIF
```

Can you work out what this pseudocode algorithm does?

Learning activity

Write a pseudocode algorithm that saves your name, address and phone number to a text file. Write several lines of text. Keep track of the contents of the text file.

Test yourself

1. Write the pseudocode command that lets the user input a username and stores this value in line 1 of a text file. Choose any name you like for the file.

2. Write a pseudocode command that uses a loop to input four users' names and stores them one after the other in a text file.

3. Write a pseudocode command that reads line 1 of `Password.txt` and displays it on the screen.

4. Write a pseudocode command that overwrites line 3 of `password.txt` with the value `Station99`.

Extension activity

A teacher has a class of 30 students. She wants to store the names of these students in a text file. Write a pseudocode algorithm with a loop in it. Every time the loop repeats a name is added to a text file.

Write a second pseudocode algorithm that reads every line of the file and prints out the names of the students.

Syllabus reference

3.2.10 Subroutines (procedures and functions)

Understand the concept of subroutines.

Explain the advantages of using subroutines.

Additional information

Students should know that a subroutine is a named "out of line" block of code that may be executed (called) by simply writing its name in a program statement.

2.3 Subroutines

Introduction to subroutines

> ### Introduction
>
> This section introduces a new type of programming. You will learn to use subroutines in your programs. Subroutines are blocks of code. Each subroutine has a name. If you use the name in your code, all the stored commands will be carried out.

Subroutine

A subroutine is a block of code. Each subroutine is given a name. The code in the subroutine is typically stored outside of the main program, usually at the top of the file. The code in the subroutine is carried out if the name of the subroutine appears in the main program. This is referred to as 'calling' the subroutine. There are two main types of subroutine:

- A **procedure** is a subroutine that carries out actions.
- A **function** is a subroutine that returns (makes) a new value.

You will learn to write procedures and functions in Python.

Define and call

When programmers use subroutines in a program they must do two things:

- **Define:** defining a subroutine means writing the code. Every subroutine has a name. The name should remind you of what the subroutine does.
- **Call:** calling a subroutine means putting the name of the subroutine in your code. The computer will carry out the stored commands.

A subroutine is defined in one part of the program. It is called in a different part of the program. The code is not carried out when the subroutine is defined. It is carried out when the subroutine is called.

Why use subroutines?

Once you have defined a subroutine you can call it many times. You can call the subroutine more than once in the same program. You can copy a useful subroutine into a new program. Common subroutines have been used and tested many times. They are reliable. A programmer might type the same block of code many times. It is better to type the code once and save it as a subroutine. Then the programmer can call the subroutine instead of typing the commands again. Using subroutines has many advantages for a programmer:

- Programs are shorter, quicker to write and have less repetition.
- Each subroutine can be tested independently before being included in the main program.
- Subroutines from previous programs can be reused, reducing the risk of errors.

- The code is more readable.
- Use of subroutines helps with teamwork, as each subroutine can be given to a different team member to develop.

Programming that uses subroutines is called **procedural programming** or **structured programming**. Find out more features of structured programming on page 86.

Readability

When you define a subroutine, you choose a name for it. You should choose a name that reminds you what the subroutine does. This is helpful when you call the subroutine. Using helpful names also makes your program more readable. The reader will see the name of a subroutine instead of a long block of code.

Teamwork

Using subroutines helps with teamwork. Writing a big program is too much work for one person. Instead the program can be broken up into subroutines. Each subroutine can be written by a different programmer. This means each member of the team has a separate task. All the programmers know exactly what they must do. Breaking a big task into subroutines means the program is finished much more quickly. It means every programmer in the team is kept busy. It makes it easier to share the work.

Predefined subroutines

Some subroutines are provided as part of standard program code. In Python, these subroutines are called 'predefined functions'. You do not have to define these subroutines. You can just use them in your code.

The names of predefined functions are shown in purple in IDLE. Here are some predefined Python functions you have used:

```
print()
input()
int()
```

Code libraries

Programmers may want to reuse a useful subroutine in a new program. That saves time. Using tried and tested code reduces the risk of error. A group of useful subroutines can be stored together in a file. A file that stores useful subroutines is called a module. A collection of modules is called a code library.

Programmers will share good subroutines. They let other programmers use the subroutines they wrote. Some code libraries are open to all programmers. In the next section you will use subroutines made by other programmers.

Syllabus reference

3.2.9 Random number generation in a programming language

Be able to use random number generation.

Additional information

Students will be expected to use random number generation within their computer programs.

Random numbers

Introduction

You have learned that subroutines are a way of saving useful code. Useful subroutines are stored in files called modules. In this section you will import a module. The module holds subroutines made by other programmers. This module will let you make and use random numbers

Import a module

Python programmers make useful subroutines. Programmers store their subroutines in modules. Some programmers share their modules with other programmers. We may use the subroutines they made. To do this we must import the module where the subroutines are stored. Importing the module lets us use all the subroutines from the module. The command to import a module is the word "import", then the name of the module. In this section you will import the `random` module.

```
import random
```

This command must go at the start of the program. We must import the module before we use the subroutines.

Random numbers

If something is random it means you cannot predict it. There is no pattern. Random numbers are useful in programming. For example, in games, programmers use random numbers to make the games more interesting. Events will be less predictable.

Random numbers are also useful in code systems and in maths.

Extension

The Python random module makes numbers we call pseudo-random. That means they are almost random. They are not quite purely random. They are certainly good enough for most purposes where random numbers are needed.

Randint

We will use a subroutine stored in the random module. This subroutine is called `randint`. The subroutine will make a random integer.

To call the subroutine we enter the name of the subroutine in our code.

```
random.randint()
```

This command means "call the subroutine randint from the module random".

We must also tell the computer the range to use. That means the minimum and maximum values for the random number generator. For example, this command will make a number between 1 and 100:

```
random.randint(1, 100)
```

We will store the random number. We can store it as a variable. In this example, the random number is stored as a variable called `number`

```
number = random.randint(1, 100)
```

This is the completed code.

Test the function

To test the random number generator, run the code and see whether the numbers it makes seem random. Do they vary in an unpredictable way?

Try this code and see what results you get.

```
import random
number = random.randint(1,100)
print(number)
```

Each time you run this program you will get a different random number between 1 and 100.

Save your program

Before you run a program, you must save it. Do not give your program the name "random". This may confuse Python, because `random` is the name of the module. You may get an error that stops Python from working. If you ever see an error like this, delete or rename your most recent program.

Test yourself

These questions relate to this example of Python code:

```
example = random.randint(0,9)
```

1. In this code what is the data type of the variable?

2. Could this code ever generate the value 0?

3. What line of code must you include before this command?

4. Write a program where the user inputs minimum and maximum values before generating a random number within that range.

Learning activity

You wrote a program that generated random numbers. Put the code inside a `for` loop. Generate ten random numbers. Check to see whether they seem random. Try changing the minimum and maximum values.

You should not put `import random` inside the loop. That command only needs to happen once.

Extension activity

You wrote a program that generated ten random numbers and printed them out. Change your code so that this happens:

- The program generates 1000 numbers between 1 and 10.

- The program does not print out each random number.

- Instead the program counts how often each number comes up.

- At the end of the program it will print out how many 1s there are, how many 2s, etc.

Syllabus reference

3.2.2 Programming concepts

Use, understand and know how the following statement type can be combined in programs: subroutine (procedures and functions).

Additional information

Students should be able to write programs using these statement types. They should be able to interpret algorithms that include these statement types.

3.2.10 Subroutines (procedures and functions)

Understand the concept of subroutines.

3.2.12 Robust and secure programming

Be able to write simple authentication routines.

Introduction

In the last section you used a subroutine called `randint`. You did not define this subroutine. You imported it into your program. In this section you will define subroutines. Then you can call the subroutines in your code.

Define a procedure

There are two types of subroutine: procedures and functions. Procedures carry out commands. Functions create new values. In this section you will define a new procedure. It will run a password login system.

Login using a `while` loop

This program uses a `while` loop to check a passcode.

```
passcode = input("enter your passcode: ")
while passcode != "6729":
        passcode = input("enter your passcode: ")
```

Unless the user enters the right passcode, the program locks into an endless loop. You can enter and run this code now to check what it does.

Login procedure

You can turn the login code into a procedure.

```
def login():
        passcode = input("enter your passcode: ")
        while passcode != "6729":
                passcode = input("enter your passcode: ")
```

You have turned the program into a procedure by adding a new first line. This is called the header. Here are some points to remember:

- The header starts with the word `def`. This is short for define. The rest of the code defines the subroutine.
- After `def` put the name of the procedure. Always choose a name that reminds you of the purpose of a procedure. In this example we have called the procedure `login`.
- The header ends with two brackets and a colon.

After the header comes all the other code. This code is indented. It is inside the procedure.

If you run this program now, it won't do anything. The code is now stored inside the procedure definition. It will not be carried out unless you call the procedure.

Call the procedure

To call the procedure you just put the name of the procedure and the brackets inside your code.

```
login()
```

This command is not indented. It is not part of the procedure. It is part of the main program. This command calls the login procedure. The computer will carry out all the commands in the login procedure.

Make this change and run the program to see how it works.

Make a procedure

Define a procedure that displays a welcome to the user who has logged in. Here is a simple example, but you can make a better one.

```
def welcome():
        print("================")
        print("  Welcome")
        print("================")
```

Call the `welcome` procedure after the `login` procedure. Your main program now looks like this:

```
login()
welcome()
```

Why do we call the two procedures in this order?

Advantages

Defining and calling procedures seems like a lot of extra work. However, remember that procedural programming has advantages, for example for teamwork and readability. Look back at page 75 to remind yourself. As procedures are so useful in programming, every programmer should learn how to use them.

Test yourself

1. Welcome and login are procedures. They are not functions. Why is that?

2. A programmer defined the two procedures you saw on this page. Here is the main program. What is the error in this code?

```
login
welcome
```

3. A programmer made two subroutines. He called them procedure1 and procedure2. Why was this poor programming practice?

4. Explain the difference between defining and calling a procedure.

Learning activity

Follow the instructions on this page to make a program with a login procedure and a welcome procedure.

Extension activity

Create a subroutine called `diceroll` that prints out a random number from 1 to 6. Write a main program that calls this subroutine inside a `for` loop.

Syllabus reference

3.2.10 Subroutines (procedures and functions)

Describe the use of parameters to pass data within programs.

Additional information

Students should be able to describe how data is passed to a subroutine using parameters.

Parameters

Introduction

You have learned that procedures store commands. When the procedure is called, the commands are carried out. In this section you will learn about parameters. A parameter is a value that you can add when you call a procedure. A parameter changes what the procedure does. In this way, you can make one procedure do many different tasks

Draw a line

Here is a very simple procedure. It draws a line on the screen. The line is made of 40 dashes in a row.

```
def line():
    print("-"*40)
```

This procedure always does the same thing. The line is always the same length. You call the procedure with this command:

```
line()
```

Include a parameter in the procedure definition

Every procedure name is followed by brackets. You can put extra values – called parameters – inside the brackets. A parameter will change what the procedure does.

Here is the `line()` procedure, but this time it has a parameter:

```
def line(length):
    print("-"*length)
```

We have called the parameter `length`. You can use any name. It is best to use a name that reminds you of what the parameter is for. In this example, `length` is an integer value. It tells the computer how many dashes to draw.

If `length` holds a small value, then the computer will draw a small line. If `length` holds a large value, then the computer will draw a long line.

Call the procedure with a parameter

Now, when you call the procedure you can include a number. Here is a program that calls the `line()` procedure three times:

```
def line(length):
    print("-"*length)
line(10)
line(80)
line(2)
```

Each time, the procedure is called with a different parameter. Try entering this program and seeing how the parameters change the action of the procedure.

If you use a parameter that is not an integer you will get an error.

Underline procedure

Here is a procedure called `underline()`. When `underline` is called in the program, a text string is passed to the procedure as a parameter. The procedure prints out the text, plus a line underneath the text. This procedure uses the `line()` procedure you have already made.

```
def underline(word):
    print(word)
    line(len(word))
```

In this example the procedure is called. The parameter is the word `"Welcome"`.

```
underline("Welcome")
```

A maths procedure

This procedure will split any value in half, and print out the result. It uses the arithmetic operators // and %. For a reminder about integer division look back to page 20.

```
def halve(number):
    result = number//2
    remainder = ""
    if number%2 == 1:
        remainder = "and a half"
    print(result, remainder)
halve(13)
halve(16)
halve(1011)
```

Learning activity

Make all the procedures shown in this section: `line`, `underline`, `halve` and `vertical`. Call each procedure from the main program like this:

```
line(50)
underline("Log In")
halve(90)
vertical("Welcome")
```

Test yourself

Try making this procedure and calling it with different parameters.

These questions relate to this procedure:

```
def makesquare(text):
    textlength = len(text)
    for i in range(textlength):
        print(text)
```

1. What is the name of the procedure?

2. What is the name of the parameter?

3. Give the command to call this procedure with the parameter `"HOTEL"`.

4. What would be the output of this procedure with that parameter?

Extension activity

In the learning activity you made a program that called the three procedures. Change the programs so that they accept the user's input. The user's input is passed to the procedure as the parameter. Run the program. Enter different values.

Syllabus reference

3.2.10 Subroutines (procedures and functions)

Students should be able to use subroutines that require more than one parameter.

Multiple parameters

Introduction

You have learned how to use a parameter. A parameter changes the action of a procedure. In this section you will learn to call a procedure with more than one parameter.

More than one parameter

We can define and call a procedure that uses more than one parameter:

- **Define the procedure:** the parameter names go inside the brackets. The names are separated by commas.
- **Call the procedure:** the parameter values go inside the brackets. The number of parameters must be the same as in the procedure definition.

The parameters must appear in the same order in both places.

Vertical line

This procedure prints a vertical line of characters.

```
def vertical(height):
    for i in range(height):
        print("|")
```

When we call the procedure, we must give the height of the line. It must be a number value. This value will be sent as a parameter. Here are some examples:

```
vertical(20)

vertical(4)

vertical(60)
```

Write this procedure. Below the procedure write a main program. In this program, call the procedure several times. You must use an integer value to call the procedure. If you use a different data type, you will get an error.

Line with two parameters

We can change the procedure so that as well as the height of the line we give the symbol that we want to use.

```
def vertical(height, symbol):
    for i in range(height):
        print(symbol)
```

Now when we call the procedure we can give the height and the symbol.

```
vertical(20, "#")
```

Look at the order they appear in the procedure definition. Whenever we call the procedure we must put the parameters in the right order. That means it must match the order of parameters in the procedure definition. If you give the parameters in the wrong order you will get an error. Try this example:

```
vertical("*",50)
```

You will see an error message.

Remainder division

The numbers in a division sum are called the dividend and the divisor. For example, in this sum:

```
16/5
```

16 is the dividend and 5 is the divisor.

Here is a procedure that shows the result of integer division, plus a remainder:

```
def remainder(dividend,divisor):
        print(dividend//divisor,"remainder",dividend%
        divisor)
```

To call this procedure we must provide two parameters. One is the dividend. One is the divisor.

```
remainder(16,5)
```

The result of this code will be:

```
3 remainder 1
```

We must make sure we give the parameters in the right order.

Box

This program defines and calls a procedure that draws a box on the screen.

```
def box(width, height):
        print(" ","-"*width)
        for i in range(height):
                print("|"," "*width,"|")
        print(" ","-"*width)
box(10,5)
```

Enter this program as shown. Then try calling the procedure with different parameters.

Summary

To use parameters, follow these rules:

1. When you define a procedure, put the names of parameters inside the brackets.
2. You then use the parameters like variables inside the procedure.
3. When you call the procedure, you must put values inside the brackets.

The values inside the brackets must match the parameters of the procedure:

- the same number of parameters
- the same data type(s)
- in the same order.

Test yourself

Here are four commands that call the `box()` procedure shown on this page. In each case say why the command would cause an error.

```
box("*",10)
box(9)
box(3.3,8.2)
box(10,10,10)
```

Learning activity

Copy the example programs shown on this page. Test them by calling the procedures with different data values.

Extension activity

Write a procedure that takes two numbers and shows what percentage one is of the other.

Syllabus reference

3.2.10 Subroutines (procedures and functions)

Use subroutines that return values to the calling routine.

Additional information

Students should be able to describe how data is passed out of a subroutine using return values.

Functions and returned values

Introduction

You have learned to write procedures. Procedures are subroutines. There is a second type of subroutine: a function. A function is a subroutine that creates a new value and returns it to the main program. In this section you will learn to write and use functions.

Local variables

Many of the procedures that you have made create new values. Values that are made inside a procedure are called local variables. A local variable only holds its value when a procedure is running. As soon as the procedure is over, the value is lost. Local variables are a helpful feature of programming languages. Using local variables reduces the risk of program error. It makes teamwork easier. However, sometimes we need to save a value after a procedure is finished. To stop a value being lost, we must return the value to the main program.

Example – random strength

In a computer game, characters have attributes such as strength and speed. When you start the game attributes are set at random. This procedure simulates the throw of dice to set the strength of a character.

```
import random
def strength(dice):
        result = 0
        for i in range(dice):
                throw = random.randint(1,6)
                result = result + throw
        print("your strength is",result)
```

This command calls the `strength` procedure with a parameter of 3. It simulates the throw of three dice.

```
strength(3)
```

Try typing in this program. If you run it a few times you will see that it generates different strength values within the range 3–18. These are the maximum and minimum values you can obtain with three dice. You can also change the parameter. If you change it to 4 it will simulate the throw of four dice.

However, there is a problem. The result is stored in a variable called `result`. We need to use that value in the game, but `result` is a local variable. You have learned that local variables are lost from the computer's memory when a procedure ends.

How can we fix this problem?

Return a value

We need to change the procedure so that the value of the variable is not lost. We must tell the procedure to return the value to the main program. We change the procedure like this (see the bold type below).

```
def strength(dice):
    result = 0
    for i in range(dice):
        throw = random.randint(1,6)
        result = result + throw
    return result
```

There is a special name for a subroutine that returns a value. It is called a function. If a subroutine has the word `return` in it, then you know it is a function.

Capture the returned value

The main program must capture the returned value. It will capture it in a variable. We will then be able to use the value in the main program.

Here is the main program showing this change. We have captured the returned value in a variable called `hero`. This represents the strength of the hero of the game.

```
hero = strength(3)
```

Battle game

Here is the completed main program. The hero battles a monster. Whoever has the greatest strength will win.

```
hero = strength(3)
monster = strength(3)
if hero > monster:
    print("the hero wins")
if monster > hero:
    print("the monster wins")
if monster == hero:
    print("it was a draw")
```

Put together the function called `strength` and the main program shown on this page. You now have a very simple battle game. Try playing it a few times.

Learning activity

Create the simple battle game shown on this page. Try playing the game a few times. How often does the hero win?

Test yourself

These questions relate to this line of code.

`score = battle(4)`

It is taken from a program you have not looked at before. However, you should be able to answer the questions using your knowledge of programming.

1. What is the name of the function in this example code?
2. What is the value of the parameter?
3. What is the variable that captures the returned value?
4. How do you know this is an example of a function rather than a procedure?

Extension activity

Extend the battle game by adding extra features. For example, the hero and monster might have strength, speed and cunning. Set these values at random. Display the values and let the hero choose which of the three he will use in battle. Students who have progressed very fast in programming can extend the battle game so that the hero has a range of choices and weapons to help with battling the monster. The only limit is your imagination.

Syllabus reference

3.2.11 Structured programming

Describe the structured approach to programming

Additional information

Students should be able to describe the structured approach to programming including modularised programming;

clear, well-documented interfaces (local variables, parameters); and return values.

2.4 # Structured programming

The structured approach to programming

Introduction

Structured programming is a way of developing programs. Programmers break large programming problems into parts and develop the parts separately. You have learned to write programs that use subroutines. Now you will learn how programmers use these features in their programming practice.

Modular programming

Modular programming means breaking a big program into parts. These parts are called subroutines. A subroutine is a named block of code. When you enter the name of a subroutine in the program, all the code in the subroutine is carried out. You can use the subroutine many times in the same program.

A subroutine might be defined within your program. You can also save the subroutine in a separate module. These modules are stored in code libraries. You can reuse the stored subroutines in new programs.

You have learned that there are two types of subroutine: procedures and functions. A procedure carries out a task. A function creates a new value that is returned to the main program.

Variables in modular programming

A variable is created when it is first given a value. If a variable is created in the main program it is a global variable. You can use global variables anywhere in your program. You can use a global variable inside a subroutine. This is bad practice. To write good modular programs you should avoid global variables. What if you want to share values between the main program and a subroutine? Use local variables, parameters and returned values. Here are some details:

- **Local variable:** if a variable is created inside a subroutine it is a local variable. Local variables are held in memory while the subroutine is running. When the subroutine ends, the local variable is lost from memory. It cannot be used outside of the subroutine.

- **Parameter:** sometimes you need to use a value from the main program in a subroutine. To do this you use a parameter. Every subroutine name ends with two brackets. A parameter goes inside the brackets. The value is passed from the main program to the subroutine. Both functions and procedures can have a parameter. They can have more than one parameter.

- **Returned value:** sometimes you need to use a value from a subroutine in the main program. The subroutine ends with `return` and a value. The value is passed back to the main program. A subroutine that returns a value is called a function.

Example

Here is the definition of a function called `convert`. This function converts a value in miles per hour into a value in kilometres per second. The function definition includes a parameter and a returned value.

Parameter

```
def convert(mph):
    seconds   = 3600    # seconds in an hour
    kilometres = 1.6    # kilometres in a mile
    kps = mph/seconds * kilometres
    return kps
```

Returned value

The parameter is `mph`. This value is passed from the main program.

The returned value is `kps`. This value is created by the function. It is returned to the main program.

Interface

When you call a function from the main program you must use a variable to capture the returned value. The formula has this general structure:

```
variable = function
```

In the following example the variable is `result`. The function is `convert`.

Parameter

```
result = convert(70)
```

Captures the returned value

The function `convert` needs a parameter. We know that because the function definition has a parameter in it. In this example the value `70` is the parameter. It can be any value. The connection between the main program and a subroutine is called the interface. By using parameters and returned values we can carefully control which values are passed between the main program and the subroutine.

By using sensible names for subroutines, variables, parameters and returned values we make our code easy to read and understand.

Learning activity

Write a report on the main features of structured programming, using these headings:

- Define a procedure
- Define a function
- Parameter
- Returned value
- Call a procedure
- Call a function

Test yourself

Here is an example of a subroutine called `gofaster`

```
def gofaster():
    speed = speed + 10
```

1. Is `gofaster` a function or a procedure?

2. Write the line that would call the subroutine `gofaster`.

3. In this subroutine speed is a global variable. Rewrite the subroutine so that `speed` is passed to the subroutine as a parameter and returned to the main program.

4. Write the command in the main program that would call the subroutine `gofaster` with the value `40` as a parameter, and save the returned value as a variable called `speed`.

Extension activity

Improve your report. Add screen shots of code you wrote. The screen shot should match the description. For example, if you wrote about parameters, include a screen shot of a procedure that you wrote that used parameters.

Advantages of the structured approach

Introduction

You have learned the features of the structured approach to programming. A program is broken down into procedures. Parameters and returned values are used to link procedures to the main program. In this section you will learn the advantages of programming in this way.

The structured approach

Using a structured approach to programming involves two activities:

- **Decomposition** – this is breaking a large task into smaller tasks, and solving each one with a subroutine.
- **Composition** – this is putting the subroutines together to make a complete program.

Both decomposition and composition have advantages for the programmer.

Decomposition

A program has to solve a problem. The first task of the programmer is to break the problem into smaller problems. Then the programmer writes a subroutine to solve each of the small problems.

For example, a young programmer decided to make a program to remind him what homework he has to hand in each day. The software had to:

- let the user input details of homework
- store homework details in a text file
- find today's date
- load the homework details from the text file
- look through the homework details to find today's date
- display details of homework due today.

If any of those features were missing, the program would not do its job. Breaking the homework program into smaller sub-problems is an example of decomposition.

Further subdivision

The programmer has broken the task into subtasks. Next he looks at the subtasks. He might decompose some of the subtasks. The process of decomposition continues until the tasks cannot be broken down any further. Each task is as small as it can be. When decomposition is completed each task will represent one computer action, carrying out one process or producing one new output.

Now each part can be written as a subroutine. The subroutine will carry out the single task. Writing a subroutine is easier than writing the whole program.

Composition

Next the subroutines must be fitted together to make the finished program. This is called composition.

The programmer connects subroutines to the main program using the structured approach. Code in the main program calls the subroutines one by one. Values pass between the subroutine and the main program:

- The program sends values to the subroutine as parameters.
- The subroutine sends values back to the main program as returned values.

The result is a structured program. It has a short main program. The main program calls a series of subroutines.

Summary of advantages

The structured approach has many advantages for programmers. These are reasons why this method is widely used:

- **Easier problem solving:** the programmer breaks a big task into smaller tasks. Each of the smaller tasks is an easier problem to solve.
- **Team work:** the different tasks can be split between the members of a team. The work is shared. The task is finished more quickly.
- **Readability:** the main program is short. It is a series of calls to subroutines. The subroutines should be given names that explain what they do. This means the main program is easy to read and understand.
- **Reusability:** subroutines made for one program can be reused in other programs. This makes the task of the programmer much easier.
- **Reliability:** subroutines can be tested and debugged before they are joined to make the main program. This reduces the chance of errors in the program.

Test yourself

1. Which comes first, composition or decomposition? Explain your answer.

2. A programmer has broken a problem into the smallest possible tasks. What is the next step?

3. Explain why the use of subroutines makes a program less likely to have errors in it.

4. How does the main program pass a value to a subroutine?

Learning activity

A teacher wanted to make a program to take a class register and print out absence statistics. Decompose this program into subroutines.

Extension activity

On the previous page a homework application is decomposed into subroutines. Write one or more of the subroutines. Test the subroutines with suitable input data.

For extra stretch and challenge, create the program in full.

> ### Introduction
>
> You have learned to write Python programs that use procedures and functions. Pseudocode algorithms can have procedures and functions. In this section you will learn to make procedures and functions in pseudocode.

Procedure or function?

In pseudocode, you must decide whether a subroutine is a procedure or a function. Remember the key difference between them. A function returns a value. A procedure does not return a value.

Define a procedure

Here is a Python procedure. It has one parameter.

```
def line(length):
        print("-"*length)
```

Here is the same procedure in pseudocode. It is almost the same.

```
SUBROUTINE line(length)
        OUTPUT "-" * length
ENDSUBROUTINE
```

The start and end of the procedure are marked by the commands SUBROUTINE and ENDSUBROUTINE. The commands are in capitals.

Call a procedure

When we call a procedure we give the name of the procedure, followed by two brackets. Any parameters go inside the brackets.

For example, this Python code calls the procedure `line()`. It draws a line of 70 characters.

```
line(70)
```

The pseudocode command is the same.

```
line(70)
```

You know how to define and call procedures in Python. You will be able to understand Pseudocode algorithms that define and call procedures.

Define a function

A function is like a procedure except it returns a value. For example, this function divides a value by two. The value is sent as a parameter. It is returned as a return value.

```
def half(value):
        value = value/2
        return value
```

Here is a pseudocode function that does the same thing.

```
SUBROUTINE half(value):
        value ← value/2
        RETURN value
ENDSUBROUTINE
```

Call a function

A function creates a new value. When you call a function you typically capture the returned value in a variable.

For example, a programmer called the `half` function. She sent the parameter 70 to the function. She stored the new value in a variable called `result`.

```
result = half(70)
```

The command in pseudocode is almost the same. Remember that pseudocode uses an arrow instead of an equals sign.

```
result ← half(70)
```

Example

Here is a pseudocode function called `login`. It returns a value to the main program.

```
SUBROUTINE login()
        password ← ""
        count ← 0
        WHILE password ≠ "tt5566"
                password ← USERINPUT
                count ← count+1
        ENDWHILE
        RETURN count
ENDSUBROUTINE
```

The main program calls the function like this:

```
attempts ← login()
OUTPUT attempts
```

What value is returned by this function? What is the right password?

Learning activity

The pseudocode function `login()` is shown on this page. Write a Python program that matches this pseudocode algorithm.

Test yourself

1. Which line in the `login()` function shows that it is a function not a procedure?

2. Rewrite the `login` function as a procedure that does not return a value.

3. Why don't we use a counter-controlled loop in this function?

4. Rewrite the `login` function using a REPEAT loop instead of a WHILE loop.

Extension activity

Choose any program you have written that uses procedures or functions. Write a pseudocode algorithm to match the program you chose.

Syllabus reference

3.2.12 Robust and secure programming

Be able to write simple data validation routines.

Be able to write simple authentication routines.

Additional information

Students should be able to use data validation techniques to write simple routines that check the validity of data being entered by a user. Examples of these simple data validation routines are: checking whether an entered string has a minimum length, checking whether a string is empty.

Students should also be able to write a simple authentication routine that uses a username and password.

2.5 Robust programming

Data validation

Introduction

You have learned to use validation to check data input. Bad data input can stop a program from working. In this section you will learn more ways to check the user's input.

Data checks

When users run a program they enter input data. If they enter bad data the program will go wrong. Data of the wrong type might crash the program. Numbers that are too big or too small will produce incorrect results. Programmers can add commands to check input data. This protects the program from bad data that might make it crash. One way to check data input is through validation.

Validation

Validation means making sure that data is valid. Valid data makes sense, and matches the needs of the program. To make sure input is valid it is checked using rules. These rules are also called validation criteria.

Programmers add commands to check input against the validation criteria. If the input does not match the criteria it is not used in the program.

Validation checks

There are many different types of validation check. Here are three examples:

- **Range checks** are used with numerical variables. The number must be within a valid range. For example, a teacher may need to enter the age of a student at a secondary school where the age could not be below 11 or above 18 years.
- **Length checks** are used mainly with text variables, particularly code numbers. The right number of characters must be entered. For example, a mobile phone number may need to have exactly 11 digits.
- **Type checks** can be used with all variables. You have learned that every variable must have a data type. A type check makes sure that input is of the right data type. For example, if you are entering an age it must be a number value, if you are entering a name it must be made of letters of the alphabet, and so on.

We can turn these checks into logical tests.

Selection or repetition?

What if the input fails the logical test? How can we stop invalid data being used in the program?

- **Selection:** we can use the logical test in an `if… else…` structure. If the data does not pass the logical test an error message will appear.
- **Repetition:** we can use the logical test in a `while` loop. The loop will repeat until the data passes the logical test.

You will see both examples in this section.

Example

There are many different ways of making validation checks in Python and in other programming languages. We will look at some examples.

Program 1 is a Python program that has a range check. The user inputs how much money she wants to take out of her bank account. If the value is below 0, the number is rejected.

```
## WORKED EXAMPLE
# Range check

Balance = 1000.00
Money = input("How much money do you want from your bank account: ")
Money = float(Money)

if Money < 0:
    print("You cannot withdraw less than 0")
else:
    print(Money, " has been withdrawn from your account")
    Balance = Balance - Money

print(Balance, " remains in your account.")
```

Program 2 is the same program with extra range checks built in. This program uses `elif`.

```
## WORKED EXAMPLE
# Range check

Balance = 1000.00
Money = input("How much money do you want from your bank account: ")
Money = float(Money)

if Money < 0:
    print("You cannot withdraw less than 0")
elif Money > Balance:
    print("You do not have that much money")
elif Money > 250.00:
    print("You cannot withdraw more than $250.00 a day")
else:
    print(Money, " has been withdrawn from your account")
    Balance = Balance - Money

print(Balance, " remains in your account.")
```

Program 3 repeats the input until the data is in the right range.

```
## WORKED EXAMPLE
# Range check

Age = input("How old are you: ")
Age = int(Age)

while Age < 0:
    print("You cannot be less than 0")
    Age = input("How old are you: ")
    Age = int(Age)

print("Age data accepted")
```

Test yourself

1. What variables are used in program 1 and what are their data types?

2. What range checks are used in program 2?

3. What is the error message in program 3?

4. Describe the three types of validation check you have learned.

Extension activity

Write a program that asks the user to choose a new password. The program will loop until the password is at least 10 characters in length.

Learning activity

Enter all three Python programs shown on this page and try them out to see what happens. What happens if you enter a value that breaks the validation criteria?

Syllabus reference

3.2.12 Robust and secure programming

Be able to write simple data validation routines.

Be able to write simple authentication routines.

Additional information

Students should be able to use data validation techniques to write simple routines that check the validity of data being entered by a user. Examples of these simple data validation routines are: checking whether an entered string has a minimum length, checking whether a string is empty.

Students should also be able to write a simple authentication routine that uses a username and password.

Secure programming

Introduction

You have learned to use validation to check data input. Bad data input can stop a program from working. In this section you will learn more ways to check the user's input.

Check the length of a string

On page 90 you learned the function `len()`. Using this function you can find the length of any string. In this example the length of the string is stored in a variable called `stringlength`:

```
example = input("Enter an example string")
stringlength = len(example)
```

You can use this function to make a logical test. This test result is True if the example text is longer than eight characters.

```
len(example) > 8
```

We can use this logical test in an `if… else` structure. Here is a program that lets you change a password to a new value.

```
password = "adminpass"
newpassword = input("enter the new password ")
if len(newpassword) > 8:
        password = newpassword
        print("password changed")
else:
        print("the password is too short")
```

If the new password is longer than eight characters, the password is changed to the new value. If the length of the password is too short, the password does not change.

Check whether a string is empty

Users type input data. Sometimes users make a mistake. They might press the Enter key without typing anything. That will make the program go wrong.

If a user presses Enter without typing anything the variable has no characters in it. The string length is 0. We say the string is empty. This test checks whether a string is empty:

```
len(example) == 0
```

We can use this test in a `while` loop. In this program the user enters a choice from a menu. If the string is empty, the loop will repeat. It will keep repeating until the string is not empty.

```
selection = input("enter your selection from the menu ")
while len(selection) == 0:
        selection = input("please try again")
```

Check password

When we log in to a network or a website we often give a password. The right password is stored in the program. We can make a logical test to check whether the user's input matches the right password. We can use the logical test in a selection structure.

In this example the right password is "Asteroid". If the user enters the right password a procedure called menu() will run.

```
password = input("enter the password ")
if password == "Asteroid":
        menu()
```

We can also use the logical test in a while loop structure. In this example the program will loop if the user enters the wrong password.

```
password = input("enter the password ")
while password != "Asteroid":
        password = input("try again ")
```

Check username and password

When we log in we sometimes have to give a username as well as a password. We can use a nested if structure to check the username and then check the password.

```
username = input("enter user name ")
if username == "admin"
        password = input("enter password ")
        if password == "Asteroid":
                menu()
```

Find out more about the nested if structure on page 36. We could also use a nested while loop structure. Find out more about nested loops on page 48.

Extension – if the username is in the list

The operator in tells us whether a value is in a list. Here is an example of a logical test. The test result is True.

```
if "cat" in ["horse", "cat", "mouse", "rabbit"]:
```

Some programs might have a list of valid usernames. This program checks whether the username is in the list of allowed names.

```
userlist = ["bob", "sal", "admin"]
username = input("enter user name ")
if username in userlist:
        password = input("enter password ")
        if password == "Asteroid":
                menu()
```

Syllabus reference

3.2.12 Robust and secure programming

Be able to select suitable test data that covers normal (typical), boundary (extreme) and erroneous data.

Be able to justify the choice of test data.

Testing

Introduction

Testing a program means trying it out. A programmer will always test a program to make sure it works properly. If there are problems or errors they will be fixed. In this section you will learn about how to design good tests with suitable test data.

Input and output

A completed program that runs on a computer is an example of software. Software has input and output:

- Input is the data the user enters into the computer.
- Output is the result the computer gives to the user.

The user needs the output of the software. That is why people buy software. Programmers must know what the output should be. They must make software that produces the right output.

Testing

Before software is passed to the client it must be tested. To test software you:

- try out different inputs to the software
- check what output you get.

The output you get should match the output the user wants.

If the output matches what the user wants, the software has passed the test. If the output does not match what the user wants, the software has failed the test. The programmer must fix the software. Programmers will plan a whole series of tests. They will record every test and what the results are. They will analyse test results to make sure the software is working properly.

Test data

To test software you must input data. That is called the **test data**. To carry out a full range of tests you must try many different types of test data. As a rule, you should try three different types of test data:

- **Normal data:** this is the normal input that you would expect users to enter when they use the software in real life. You must make sure that in normal use the software works as expected and accepts the input. Normal data is also called typical data.
- **Boundary data:** test the limits of your software by entering large or small numbers that are at the upper and lower limits of the acceptable range. Boundary data is at the boundary of what the program will accept. Some boundary data will be accepted by the program (it is within the boundary) and some boundary data will produce an error or error message (it is outside the boundary).
- **Erroneous data:** this is data that should not be entered, for example when a user enters letters instead of numbers, or presses the Enter key at the

wrong time. We use these tests because users sometimes make mistakes and we must check what happens when they do. The best result is for the data to be rejected and an error message to be shown.

Example

A programmer made a program to add up the bill in a coffee shop. The user enters the cost of drinks and the software shows the total amount. The program was tested. Here are some of the values that were input as test data:

- the prices of two ordinary cups of coffee
- a very big order with 100 different coffees
- the number 1,000,000
- letters of the alphabet instead of numbers.

Can you work out which of these are normal, extreme and erroneous data?

Test yourself

1. What is test data: the input, the program code or the output?

2. Explain why programmers test a program before they pass it to the client.

3. An input prompt says "enter a four digit number". The test data was the letter "X". Explain why.

4. An input prompt was "enter your age". The test data was "999". Explain why.

5. A test produced the expected results. What does that tell the programmer?

6. A test produced output that was different from what the client wanted. What must the programmer do?

Learning activity

A voice recognition program records samples of human speech and shows the words as text on the screen. What are the inputs and outputs of this software?

Design some tests for this program. Say what test data you would use, and what results you expect.

Extension activity

Write a program to match the example on this page. It will be used in a coffee shop to add up the bill. Your program should let users choose how many coffees they want and it should output the bill. For extra stretch and challenge let users choose between three types of coffee with different prices.

Add validation routines to check the user enters valid data.

Run a series of tests on the program and report on the results.

3.1 Interpret algorithms

Algorithms and programs

Introduction

You have learned to write computer programs using the Python programming language. An algorithm is a sequence of steps that can be used to solve a problem. Algorithms can be used to show the logic of a computer program. In this chapter, you will learn about algorithms.

Computable problems

Not all problems can be solved by computers. A problem that can be solved by computers has these features:

- The problem is clearly stated.
- The solution is clearly stated.
- There are logical steps that can get us from the problem to the solution.

Sometimes it is easy to work out the solution. In other cases, it can be difficult. An algorithm is a sequence of steps that can be followed to complete a task. The algorithm sets out the logical steps required to get us from a problem to a solution. The algorithm might be lengthy or complex.

A computer program is an implementation of an algorithm. An algorithm is not a computer program. An algorithm is not linked to any particular programming language.

Solving a computable problem

A computer processes data by carrying out two actions:

- **Calculation** is working out the result of arithmetic processes.
- **Logic** is finding the result of True/False tests.

The logical steps to get from a problem to a solution must be computable processes. That means they must be calculations or logical comparisons.

The processes can be organised in three different ways:

- **Sequence** is the order in which the processes must be carried out.
- **Selection** is choosing between two different processes based on a logical test.
- **Repetition** is repeating a process many times.

The solution to a computable problem can be expressed using these three structures. Later in this chapter you will see some solutions to common computing problems. Sometimes there is more than one solution to the same problem. You will compare different solutions to the same problem, to see which is best. Find out more on pages 124–126.

Representing algorithms

Once we have found the solution to the problem we can express it as an algorithm. An algorithm sets out:

- what calculations and logical comparisons to carry out
- the sequence in which to carry out the processes
- when to use selection and repetition.

There is more than one way to represent an algorithm. In this book, you have seen two methods:

- flowcharts – see page 10
- pseudocode – see page 12.

The same algorithm can be set out in either way. They are two different ways to express the same logical process.

Implementing an algorithm

An algorithm sets out the steps to solve a problem. We need to carry out the steps to get the solution. Carrying out the steps is called implementing the algorithm. This is how it can be done:

- We can carry out the steps ourselves. For example, we could work out the calculations in our head. If an algorithm is short with only a few steps a person can find the result without a computer.
- If the algorithm has a lot of steps, or very difficult calculations, it is better to use a computer. The computer works faster and more accurately. We will get a solution sooner and with fewer errors.

Remember that implementing the algorithm is what gets the solution. Until we implement the algorithm we will not have the result.

Programming languages

A programming language is a way to implement an algorithm on a computer. A program tells the computer to carry out the logical steps. The program sets out instructions in a way that the computer can understand. When we run the program the computer carries out the instructions.

There are many different programming languages. They use different ways to set out the instructions to implement an algorithm.

Find out more about programming languages on page 190.

Find out more about programming languages on page 190.

Learning activity

Here is a flowchart that sets out an algorithm.

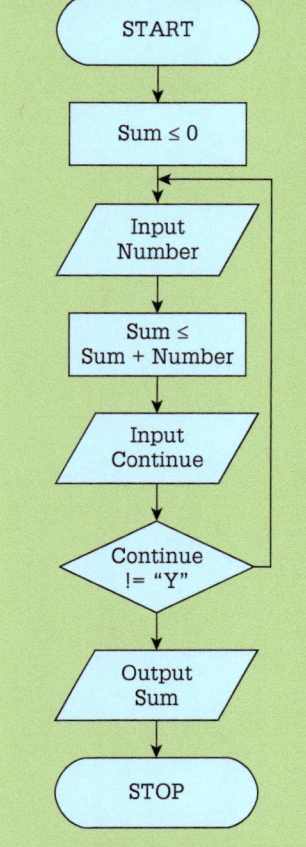

Copy this flowchart. Identify the places where it shows:

- calculation
- logical comparison
- repetition.

What problem is solved by this algorithm?

Test yourself

1. An algorithm can include calculations. What operators do we use to express calculations?
2. An algorithm can include logical tests. What operators do we use in logical tests?
3. An algorithm can include repetition. What are the two types of loop we can use?
4. What is the difference between an algorithm and a computer program?

Extension activity

The flowchart represents an algorithm. Implement this algorithm in Python.

Abstraction

Introduction

You have learned that an algorithm sets out the steps to solve a problem. When we set out an algorithm we remove unnecessary details from the problem. This is called abstraction. In this section you will learn more about abstraction.

Reusable algorithms

The algorithm on page 99 sets out the logical steps to solve a problem. It shows how to add up a series of values to give a total. We could use this algorithm to solve many different real-life problems, for example:

- adding up the total cost of shopping at a till
- adding up the daily output of a factory
- adding up the number of particles released by radioactive material.

Although these problems are very different, we could use a similar algorithm to solve them. The underlying structure is the same. The algorithm loops. New data is entered, and the algorithm adds each new value to the total. The details of what values to add together are not important. The algorithm works for all similar problems.

Many problems have a common underlying structure. An algorithm made to solve one problem can be used to solve another.

Abstraction

Abstraction is the process of removing unnecessary detail from a problem. Abstraction is a way of showing the underlying structure of something.

A map is an example of abstraction.

A map simplifies the details of a place. A map does not show the houses or the people who live there. A map that showed all the details would be too complex. It would take too long to make. Instead a map uses abstraction. It shows the relationship and structure of the place. It includes the facts you need. It leaves out the facts you don't need.

This calculation is an abstraction.

2 + 2 = 4

The calculation does not say what items we are adding together. Adding two items to another two items always makes four items. The abstraction leaves out the details. Abstraction makes it easier to solve the problem.

What are "unnecessary" details?

Abstraction means removing unnecessary details, but how can we decide what details are necessary or unnecessary? It depends on the problem we need to solve.

If our problem is to store objects made by a factory, then the size of the objects is very important. If the problem is to count how many objects there are, then the size of the objects is not so important.

Abstraction helps us to see that different problems have the same structure. The problems can have the same solution because they are similar. An algorithm made to solve one problem can be used for a different problem.

Advantages of abstraction

Programmers use abstraction when they create an algorithm. Abstraction has several advantages:

- **It simplifies the task:** if you include all the details of a problem the task is very complicated. Abstraction lets us remove most of the details. Now the problem is easier to understand and easier to solve.

- **It clarifies logical processes:** algorithms are based on a small range of processes and structures. You learned about these in the last section. If we remove unnecessary details it is easier to see the logical processes and calculations of an algorithm.

- **It helps with reusability:** you have seen that many different problems share the same basic structure. A programmer can use one algorithm for many problems. This saves work and time.

Test yourself

1. Abstraction means removing unnecessary details. Explain in your own words how we know which details are necessary or unnecessary.

2. Explain how abstraction helps with reusability.

3. A programmer was asked to write a program to work out the average weight of apples in an orchard. What details can she leave out of the algorithm? What details would she include?

4. In this book, so far you have learned two ways to set out the logical structure of an algorithm. What are they?

Learning activity

Here is a pseudocode algorithm:

```
A ← USERINPUT

B ← USERINPUT

WHILE A ≠ B

        B ← USERINPUT

ENDWHILE
```

What is the purpose of this algorithm? Give an example of a real-life application of this abstract algorithm.

Extension activity

Write a Python program that matches the algorithm you looked at in the learning activity.

Syllabus reference

3.1.1 Representing algorithms

Determine the purpose of simple algorithms.

Additional information

Students should be able to use visual inspection to determine how simple algorithms work and what their purpose is.

Purpose of an algorithm

Introduction

You have learned how algorithms are made and used. In this section, you will learn how to analyse and understand an algorithm.

Purpose of an algorithm

You have learned that an algorithm takes data and processes it to produce information. For example, the flowchart on page 99 took a series of numbers as input. The output was the sum (total) of the numbers. The purpose of an algorithm is to turn input data into output information. To describe the purpose of an algorithm you must describe the relationship between input and output values.

In this section you will learn some methods for understanding the purpose of an algorithm, including:

- spotting familiar algorithms
- naming conventions
- what calculations are used
- the structure of the algorithm
- using a trace table.

You may recognise a familiar algorithm from your learning activities. Learning to recognise these common algorithms will make you a better programmer.

Naming conventions

A well-designed program or algorithm will have sensible variable names. The name of the variable will tell you its purpose and help you to understand the algorithm. For example, a variable could be called `Largest` or `Sum`. Variable names help you to understand what each algorithm does.

However, variable names do not always give you all the information you need. For this reason, you need to look at other features of the algorithm.

Calculations

Algorithms nearly always include calculations. In pseudocode, calculations use the arrow symbol to assign a calculated value to a variable. For example:

```
Sum ← Sum + Number
```

Calculations are a key way that data is transformed into information. Look at the calculations in the algorithm. Which arithmetic operators are used? Describe the calculations in words. This will help you to understand the purpose of the algorithm.

Structure

Look at the structure of the algorithm. There are two important structural features to look at:

- Are there any `IF` structures?
- Are there any loops?

Describe in words the structure of the algorithm. This will help you understand what it does.

IF structures

Look at the IF structure of the algorithm. Answer the following questions.

1. What is the logical test?
2. What actions are carried out if the test result is True?
3. What actions are carried out if the test result is False?

Loop structures

Look at the loop in the algorithm. Answer the following questions.

1. Is it a counter-controlled or a condition-controlled loop?
2. What actions are carried out inside the loop?
3. What is the exit condition of the loop?

Trace tables

A final way to discover the purpose of an algorithm is to use a **trace table**. You will learn more about trace tables in the next section.

Test yourself

1. How will naming conventions help you understand an algorithm?
2. What symbol is used in pseudocode to assign a value to a variable?
3. A pseudocode loop begins with FOR. What is the exit condition of the loop?
4. Explain two ways in which logical tests are used in algorithms.

Learning activity

This algorithm uses a pseudocode operation called MOD. MOD gives you the remainder of an integer division. It is like the % operator in Python – see page 21.

```
Even ← 0

FOR i ← 1 TO 5

        Number ← USERINPUT

        Remainder ← Number MOD 2

        IF Remainder = 0 THEN

                Even ← Even + 1

        ENDIF

ENDFOR

OUTPUT Even
```

Explain in your own words the operation and purpose of this algorithm.

Extension activity

Create a Python program to match this algorithm.

Syllabus reference

3.1.1 Representing algorithms

Determine the purpose of simple algorithms.

Additional information

Students should be able to use trace tables to determine how simple algorithms work and what their purpose is.

Trace tables

Introduction

To find out the purpose of an algorithm you can use a trace table. In this section you will learn how to use a trace table to find out how an algorithm works.

Test an algorithm

You have learned that algorithms are used to set out the logic of a program. An algorithm is made before the programmer starts to write code. It is a good idea to test the algorithm before you start to write the code. This section explains how you can test an algorithm.

An algorithm is not software. You cannot run it on a computer to see what happens. Instead you use a trace table. A trace table records the values of each variable in an algorithm. This is how it works:

- The table has a column for each variable in the algorithm.
- The table has a row for every line of the algorithm.
- You go through an algorithm line by line.
- You record the value of each variable at every line.

Example

Here is a pseudocode algorithm for a simple program that carries out an addition or subtraction sum. It uses the IF structure. When you make a trace table, start by numbering every line of the algorithm.

```
1. Num1 ← USERINPUT

2. Num2 ← USERINPUT

3. OUTPUT "Enter plus or minus"

4. PlusMinus ← USERINPUT

5. IF PlusMinus = "+" THEN

    6. Answer ← Num1 + Num2

7. ELSE

    8. Answer ← Num1 - Num2

9. ENDIF

10. OUTPUT Answer
```

Start the trace table

There are four variables in this algorithm. They are Num1, Num2, PlusMinus and Answer. We make a trace table with a column for every variable.

Line	Num1	Num2	PlusMinus	Answer
1				
2				
3				
4				

Choose test data

Just as when you are testing a program, to test an algorithm you must choose test data. The test data will be the input to the algorithm. In this example we will choose the test data:

20

15

+

Count through the lines

Now you count through the lines of the algorithm. At each line you show the values of the different variables: if a value is entered into a variable, it stays in that variable for all the lines that follow. The value in a variable column only changes if the algorithm changes it. Here are the details:

- Line 1: user input is assigned to variable Num1. Look at the test data. The first value is 20, so put 20 in the "Num1" column of the trace table.
- Line 2: user input is assigned to variable Num2. The test data is 15. This goes in the "Num2" column of the trace table.
- Line 3: this is an output line. There are no changes to variables.
- Line 4: user input is a plus or minus sign. Our test data is + and that goes into the "PlusMinus" column of the trace table.

This is what our trace table looks like so far.

Line	Num1	Num2	PlusMinus	Answer
1	20			
2	20	15		
3	20	15		
4	20	15	+	

Complete the trace table

The next line of the algorithm is line 5. This line has a logical test. The test is:

```
PlusMinus = "+"
```

The test result is true, so the algorithm moves to line 6:

```
Answer ← Num1 + Num2
```

Adding Num1 to Num 2 makes 35. The value 35 is assigned to the variable Answer. The algorithm finishes with line 10, which is an output line. The value of the variable Answer will be output on the screen.

The completed trace table looks like this.

Line	Num1	Num2	PlusMinus	Answer
1	20			
2	20	15		
3	20	15		
4	20	15	+	
5	20	15	+	
6	20	15	+	35
10	20	15	+	35

What is the output of this algorithm?

Test yourself

1. Complete this sentence: The trace table has a column for each... .
2. What should be entered into each row of a trace table?
3. Explain two ways in which a value can be assigned to a variable.
4. A trace table normally counts down line by line – but not always. Why not?

Learning activity

Create two trace tables for the algorithm shown on this page. Use these sets of test data:

20, 30, –

–19, –15, +

Extension activity

Create a Python program to match this algorithm. Test it using the same test data. See whether the results match your trace table.

Syllabus reference

3.1.1 Representing algorithms

Determine the purpose of simple algorithms.

Additional information

Students should be able to use trace tables and visual inspection to determine how simple algorithms work and what their purpose is.

Trace tables with loops

Introduction

You have learned to make a trace table to test the outcome of an algorithm. In this section you will learn to make a trace table for an algorithm that has a loop in it.

Example

Here is the algorithm we will test using a trace table. The lines are numbered to help us make the trace table.

```
1. A ← 0

2. B ← "Y"

3. WHILE B = "Y"

4.        C ← USERINPUT

5.        IF C > A THEN

6.              A ← C

7.        ENDIF

8.        B ← USERINPUT

9. ENDWHILE

10.OUTPUT A
```

Can you tell the purpose of this algorithm? The variable names will not give you any clues.

To investigate the algorithm we will make a trace table. This algorithm has a loop so lines are repeated. The trace table could get very long. To make the trace table shorter we will only include lines where a value is assigned to a variable.

Test data

Data is input to the variable C in line 4 and the variable B at line 8. We will test the algorithm by entering the following test data:

```
C = 10

B = "Y"

C = 5

B = "N"
```

Now we will make a trace table using these values.

Begin the trace table

The algorithm has three variables called A, B and C. This table shows their values up to line 5 of the algorithm.

Line	A	B	C
1	0		
2	0	Y	
4	0	Y	10

Line 5 has an IF command with the logical test C > A. Looking at the trace table we see the result of the test is True. That means line 6 is carried out. In line 6 the value of variable C is assigned to variable A.

Line	A	B	C
1	0		
2	0	Y	
4	0	Y	10
6	10	Y	10

At line 8 the value Y is assigned to variable B. The test result at the top of the WHILE loop is True, and this means the loop repeats, going back to line 3. The completed trace table looks like this.

Line	A	B	C
1	0		
2	0	Y	
4	0	Y	10
6	10	Y	10
8	10	Y	10
4	10	Y	5
8	10	N	5

Line 10 is the output line. The output result is 10.

Test yourself

1. How does the user stop the WHILE loop in this algorithm?

2. In your own words explain what happens if the result of the logical test in line 5 is True.

3. What is the purpose of this algorithm?

4. Suggest suitable names for the three variables instead of A, B and C.

Learning activity

Create a trace table for the algorithm shown on this page. Use the test data below. What is the output?

50, Y, 20, Y, 99, Y, 55, N

Extension activity

Turn any Python program you have made into a pseudocode algorithm. Make a trace table for this algorithm. Use any suitable test data.

Search algorithms

Linear search

> ### Introduction
>
> You have learned what algorithms are. In this section you will look at some examples of algorithms and evaluate how they work. You will look at the linear search algorithm.

Searching

You have learned that data can be stored in a structure called an array or list. You have learned these structures can be linear or 2-D. If you need a reminder go back to pages 62–63.

This short program uses the operator `in`. This operator is used to make a logical test. It is used to compare an item with a list. The test result is True if the item is in the list.

```python
searchlist = ["x","m","a","d","q"]
searchitem = input("enter a letter: ")

if searchitem in searchlist:
    print("the item is in the list")
else:
    print("the item is not in the list")
```

This is an example of searching for an item in a list. In this example the program searches for a value input by the user. Try making this short program and running it. Try it with different input values.

Boolean data type

In the Python program on this page the variable 'foundit' is used to record whether an item has been found in a list. This variable can have the values True or False. True and False are Python keywords.

Foundit is a Booolean variable. A Boolean variable can only hold the values True or False. Those are the only values that are needed in this program.

Linear search

Can we find whether an item is in a list without using the `in` operator? A simple way to do it is to count through each item in the list. The program tests each item to see whether it matches the search item. If the program gets to the end of the list without finding a match, then the item is not in the list.

Counting through the list like this is called a linear search. We can carry out a linear search using a `for` loop. Here is an example of a Python program that does that:

```python
searchlist = ["x", "m", "a","d","q"]
listlength = len(searchlist)
searchitem = input("enter a letter: ")

foundit = False

for i in range(listlength):
    if searchlist[i] == searchitem:
        foundit = True

if foundit == True:
    print("the item is in the list")
else:
    print("the item is not in the list")
```

These are the key features of this program:

- A Boolean variable called `foundit` is set to False at the start of the loop.
- If any item in the list matches the search letter, `foundit` is set to True.

What result do you want?

The previous program was a simple algorithm to search for an item in a list. It produces a Boolean value: True or False. The value is True if the item is in the list.

We can adapt the search algorithm to return an integer. The search could tell you the index number of the item in the list. Here is an example of a Python program that searches for an item and tells you that item's position value in a list:

```python
searchlist = ["x","m","a","d","q"]
searchitem = input("enter a letter: ")
foundit   = -1
listlength = len(searchlist)

for i in range(listlength):
    if searchlist[i] == searchitem:
        foundit = i

if foundit > -1:
    print("the item is in the list")
    print("at position ",foundit)
else:
    print("the item is not in the list")
```

Can you see the differences from the previous program? These are the key points:

- `foundit` is an integer instead of a Boolean value.
- If the item is not found, the variable `foundit` has the value –1.

In the rest of this work on search algorithms we will concentrate on Boolean Yes/No results. Remember that it is easy to alter any search algorithm to produce an index number instead.

Pseudocode version

Pseudocode is a way of showing a search algorithm that is not linked to any particular language. Here is the linear search algorithm in pseudocode. In pseudocode we count to listlength minus 1.

```
searchlist ← ["x","m","a","d","q"]

searchitem ← USERINPUT

foundit ← False

listlength ← LEN(searchlist)

FOR i ← 0 TO listlength(listlength - 1)

        IF searchlist[i] = searchitem

            foundit ← True

        ENDIF

ENDFOR
```

The linear search algorithm can be implemented in any programming language. It produces a Boolean True/False value.

Test yourself

1. The Python `in` operator is used to make a logical test. When is the test result True?

2. The `foundit` variable always has the value False at the start of a search. When does it change to the value True?

3. Can the `foundit` variable have the value False at the end of a search? Explain why.

4. The linear search algorithm can be adapted to produce an integer value. What does the integer value tell you?

Learning activity

There are three example Python programs in this section. Enter each program and test it using suitable test values. Write a program that searches for an integer in a list of integers.

Extension activity

What results do you get from a search algorithm if an item appears more than once on the list?

Create an algorithm that identifies how many times an item appears in a list.

Syllabus reference

3.1.3 Searching algorithms

Understand and explain how the linear search algorithm works.

Additional information

Students should know the mechanics of the algorithm.

3.2.10 Subroutines (procedures and functions)

Use subroutines that return values to the calling routine.

Additional information

Students should be able to describe how data is passed out of a subroutine using return values.

Search function

Introduction

You have looked at logical statements written as English sentences. You have learned how to write a program that carries out a linear search. In this section you will learn how to turn that program into a function that returns the result of the search as a value to the main program. This function can be applied to any search task.

What is a function?

A function is a subroutine that returns a value. Values are passed between the main program and a function:

- Values are passed to the function as one or more parameters.
- The function returns a value.
- The returned value is captured by a variable in the main program.

You can learn more about functions, parameters and returned values on pages 84–85.

In this section you will create a function that carries out a linear search. Here are some details:

- The parameters are the search list and the search item.
- The returned value is a Boolean True/False value.

If the item is found, the function returns the value True. If the item is not found the function returns the value False.

Define the linear search function

The linear search function can look for any item in any list. The search list and the search item are parameters. Here is the first line of the linear search function.

```
def linear(searchlist,searchitem):
```

Inside the function we put the lines of the search algorithm. Those are the commands you learned in the previous section.

```
def linear(searchlist,searchitem):
    for item in searchlist:
        if item == searchitem:
            return True
    return False
```

The value True is returned to the main program if the item is found. Remember that the word `return` stops the function. The search will stop when the item is found.

If the item is not found, the loop will end without returning a value. The final line returns the value False. That line is only carried out if the loop has finished without finding the item.

Call the search function

To call the linear search function, we put the name of the function in our main program. We must provide two parameters: a search list and a search item.

The function `linear` returns a Boolean value. We add a variable to capture the returned value. This variable will hold the value True or False.

Here is an example program that uses the linear search function. In this example, the returned value is captured by a variable called `result`.

```
mylist = [100,70,11,21,4,19]
number = input("enter a number ")
number = int(number)

found  = linear(mylist,number)

if found:
    print("the number is in the list")
else:
    print("the number is not in the list")
```

Advantages of using a search function

You can write the search commands in your main program. Or you can use a search function. It is better to use a search function. There are several advantages:

- It makes the main program shorter and easier to read.
- When the function finds the item, it stops. That means the program runs more quickly.
- Once you have written the search function you can use it in lots of different programs, saving work and time.
- If you find a better search function you can copy it into the program, and call that function instead.

In the rest of this book we will look at search functions that return Boolean values.

Test yourself

These questions refer to this line of code taken from a main program.

```
result = linear(biglist, myvalue)
```

1. The linear search function returns a value. What is the data type of this value?

2. In this command what is the name of the variable that captures the returned value?

3. In this example what are the names of the parameters passed to the linear function?

4. What are the data types of these parameters?

5. If myvalue is not in biglist what is the value of the variable result?

Learning activity

Work in Python. Create the linear search function shown in this program.

Write a program that creates a list of the students in your class. The user enters a student's name. The program says whether the student is in your class. Use the linear search function you made.

Extension activity

Adapt the program you made in the learning activity. Add a `while` loop to the main program so the user can keep entering names. The program will search the student list for each name. The program will stop if the user types "exit".

Syllabus reference

3.1.2 Efficiency of algorithms

Understand that more than one algorithm can be used to solve the same problem.

3.1.3 Searching algorithms

Understand and explain how the binary search algorithm works.

Additional information

Students should know the mechanics of the algorithm.

Search a sorted list

Introduction

You have learned to create a search function. It uses the linear search. The linear search is not the quickest way to find an item in a list. If a list is sorted into order, you can use a binary search. In this section you will see how a binary search finds an item in a list.

Sorted lists

Some lists are sorted into order. A list might be sorted in alphabetical or numerical order. It depends on the type of items in the list.

This list is not sorted.

```
mylist = [12,3,24,5,6,9,10,99,20]
```

This list has the same items, but the items are in sorted order.

```
mylist = [3,5,6,9,10,12,20,24,99]
```

It is faster for the computer to find an item in a sorted list. We can use a quicker search method. It is called a binary search.

Sorting a list

Python has a command to sort a list. You put the word sort after the name of the list, then two brackets. Here is the command to sort a list called `mylist`.

```
mylist.sort()
```

In the next sections you will learn other ways to sort a list.

Search a sorted list

Imagine you are reading a book. You want to find Chapter 5. One way to do it is to read through every page of the book until you get to Chapter 5. This is like a linear search. In a linear search the computer looks at the first item in the list. Then it looks at the next item. The computer looks at every item in order and stops when it reaches the right value.

There is a quicker way. You can open the book in the middle (it doesn't have to be the exact middle). What chapter do you see? Here are your options:

- If you are at Chapter 5 you have found the item you want.
- If the chapter number is larger than 5, look further back in the book.
- If the chapter number is smaller than 5, look further towards the end of the book.

Your search will be twice as fast because you have divided the book into two. You don't even need to stop there. You can repeat the binary search method. You can keep halving the search until you have found the item you want.

Example

Here is a sorted list. Each element in the list has an index number. Numbers begin at 0. We will search this list for number 24.

First search

The list starts at element 0. The list stops at element 8. Element 4 is the midpoint. When we check element 4 we see it has value 10.

Index	0	1	2	3	4	5	6	7	8
Data	3	5	6	9	10	12	20	24	99
					MID				
						Search this half			

Second search

Element 4 has a value smaller than the value we are looking for, so we will search from the midpoint upwards. We will search from element 5 to element 8. The midpoint of this new shorter list is element 6. When we check element 6 we see it has the value 20.

Index	0	1	2	3	4	5	6	7	8
Data	3	5	6	9	10	12	20	24	99
							MID		
								Search this half	

Final search

Element 6 has a value smaller than the value we are looking for, so we search above this midpoint. The new search list is element 7 and element 8 only. The midpoint of this list is element 7. Element 7 has the value 24.

Index	0	1	2	3	4	5	6	7	8
Data	3	5	6	9	10	12	20	24	99
								MID	

The midpoint matches the item we are looking for so the search can stop.

Binary search

In the next section you will implement the binary search method.

Test yourself

1. You are looking for the word "granite" in a dictionary. You open the book in the middle and see the word "marble". Do you search before or after this page?

The following questions regard a list that has 20 elements.

2. What is the index number of the first element in the list? What is the index number of the last element of the list?

3. What is the index number of the midpoint of the list?

4. If we split it in half, and then in half again, how many elements are in the new list?

Extension activity

Try the search game using cards that are not sorted into order. Explain in your own words why the binary search does not work on a list that is not sorted.

Learning activity

Play a search game with a partner. One of you is the hider; the other is the seeker.

1. The hider uses some blank cards and writes a number on each one.

2. The hider places the number cards face down in sorted order.

3. The hider gives the seeker a number value and challenges the seeker to find the card with that number on it.

4. The seeker is only allowed to turn the cards over one at a time. What is the smallest number of cards the seeker can turn over, before he or she finds the right card?

If the finder uses the binary search, he or she is likely to find the number more quickly. Try both types of search.

Implement the binary search algorithm

> ## Introduction
>
> You have learned why a binary search is quicker than a linear search. In this section you will learn how to implement the binary search in Python. You will also learn how to write the binary search algorithm in pseudocode.

Define the binary search function

We will define the binary search function. The header of the function looks like this:

```
def binsearch(searchlist, searchitem):
```

The function is called `binsearch` and it takes two parameters:

- `searchlist`: this is the list we need to search through.
- `searchitem`: this is the item we need to find in the list.

Start and stop values

The binary search will repeat many times. Each time it splits the list in two. The list keeps getting smaller.

The first binary search will look through the whole list, so we must set the start and stop values for the search. Remember the first element in the list is 0.

```
start = 0
stop = len(searchlist)-1
```

The last element always has a number 1 less than the length of the list.

`while loop`

The binary search will use a `while` loop. What is the exit condition? The binary search will stop if the list cannot be split any more.

This command will make the loop repeat while the start value is smaller than, or equal to, the stop value.

```
while start <= stop:
```

Find the midpoint

Now we will add the commands that go inside the loop. Remember that these commands are indented. First we find the midpoint between the start and stop values. To do this, add the start and stop values together, and divide by 2.

The midpoint must be an integer value, so convert to integer. It doesn't matter if this means it is not the exact midpoint.

```
mid = (stop+start)/2
mid = int(mid)
```

Now we check whether the midpoint matches the search item. If it does, the search can stop.

```
if searchitem == searchlist[mid]:
        return True
```

If the midpoint is not the search item

If the midpoint is not the search item, we will continue the search. We reset the start and stop values. We move them closer together:

- If `searchitem` is smaller than the midpoint we will stop at midpoint – 1.
- If `searchitem` is bigger than the midpoint we will start at midpoint + 1.

Here are the commands:

```
if searchitem < searchlist[mid]:
        stop = mid - 1
else:
        start = mid + 1
```

The loop will repeat, using these new start and stop values.

If the item is not in the list

If the loop stops but we haven't found the item, then it is not in the list. Our final command is outside the loop. It returns the value False.

```
return False
```

This command is only carried out if the binary search has been through the whole list and not found the item.

Test yourself

1. Write one line of program code. It will call the function `binsearch`. It will search a list called `biglist` for the value 7.

The following questions contain logical tests. When are the test results True?

2. `searchitem < searchlist[mid]`

3. `searchlist[0] == searchitem`

4. `searchitem == searchlist[mid]`

Learning activity

Put together the commands shown in this section to create a complete binary search function. Write a simple program that calls the binary search function to make sure it works.

Extension activity

Test the binary search function by using it with many different lists and search items. Record your results.

Syllabus reference

3.1.2 Efficiency of algorithms

Understand that more than one algorithm can be used to solve the same problem.

Compare the efficiency of algorithms explaining how some algorithms are more efficient than others in solving the same problem.

3.1.3 Searching algorithms

Understand and explain how the binary search algorithm works.

Additional information

Students should know the mechanics of the algorithm.

Compare and contrast linear and binary search algorithms.

Additional information

Students should know the advantages and disadvantages of both algorithms.

Compare search algorithms

Introduction

You have learned that there are two ways to search a list to find an item. One way is the linear search. The other way is the binary search. Each of the two methods has advantages and disadvantages.

More than one algorithm

There are two common ways to search a list. The linear search looks through every item. The binary search keeps splitting the list in two until it finds the right value.

Both of these algorithms do the same task. But they do it in different ways. Often you can solve the same problem in more than one way. The different solutions have advantages and disadvantages.

Linear search

One way to write an algorithm is by using pseudocode. The linear search function can be written in pseudocode. In this example the parameters are called array and item.

```
FUNCTION linear(array, item)
    length = LEN(array)
    FOR i ← 0 TO length-1
        IF array[i] = item
            RETURN True
        ENDIF
    RETURN False
ENDFUNCTION
```

This pseudocode algorithm can be implemented in any programming language.

Binary search

Here is the binary search function in pseudocode. The parameters are called array and item.

```
FUNCTION binary(array, item)
    start ← 0
    stop ← len(array)-1
    WHILE start <= stop:
        mid ← (stop+start)/2
        mid ← INT(mid)
        IF item = array[mid] THEN
            RETURN True
        ENDIF
```

```
        IF item < array[mid] THEN
                stop ← mid - 1
        ELSE
                start ← mid + 1
        ENDIF
    ENDWHILE
    RETURN False
ENDFUNCTION
```

How long will it take?

You have seen that two algorithms can do the same job. When programmers are choosing which algorithm to use they want to know which one does the job the fastest.

When we do a search we might be lucky. We might find the search item immediately – the item might be in the first place we look. However, we cannot rely on luck. To be safe, programmers often think about the longest time it could take. What if we have to search the whole list to find the item? How long will that take? Of course it depends how long the list is.

We will call the length of the list n.

In a linear search, we might have to look at every element in the list to find the item we want. We multiply the time it takes to look at one element, by the number of elements.

In a binary search we keep dividing the list in two. The number of items we have to look at is much smaller than n. This search takes less time.

Advantages and disadvantages

The binary search has a clear advantage over the linear search. It is much quicker because it keeps dividing the list in half. This difference is particularly important if the computer is searching through a very big list, for example a list of all the user names on a social media site that has millions of users.

The disadvantage of the binary search is that it does not work if the list is not sorted. Sometimes it is not practical to sort a list. For example, if sorting it would take a very long time, or the list is constantly changing. In this case we must use the slower linear search method.

This table summarises the advantages and disadvantages of the two search methods.

	Advantages	Disadvantages
Linear search	It works on any list	It is slower than a binary search
Binary search	It is faster than a linear search	It only works with a sorted list

Extension activity

Make a trace table to show the action of the binary search algorithm. Use the same test values as in the previous activity.

If you have time, test the algorithms with other test data.

Test yourself

1. What is a good reason for using a linear search to find an item in a list?

2. What is a good reason to use a binary search to find an item in a list?

3. An array has 20 elements. You do a linear search for an item. In the worst case, how many operations would this take?

4. "A good programmer only needs to know one algorithm for a task." Is this true? Explain your answer.

Learning activity

On page 107 you learned how to make a trace table for an algorithm. Make a trace table to show the action of the linear search algorithm. Use these test values.

```
array = [12,16,22,34,
        60,77,151]

item = 60
```

117

3.3 Sort algorithms

Sorting a list

Introduction

You have learned how different algorithms can be used to search for an item in a list. In this section you will learn how different algorithms are used to sort a list into order.

What is sorting?

Any list can be sorted. Sorting means rearranging the elements of the list. Sorting puts the elements in order.

Some lists have elements that are numbers. Sorting puts the elements in numerical order. Some lists have elements that are strings. Sorting puts the elements in alphabetical order. In Python a list can have elements of different data types. Sorting does not always work well in this case.

Python has more than one sort command. You learned one command on page 112.

```
mylist.sort()
```

What are sort algorithms?

You can sort in Python with a single command. In this section you will learn to write algorithms that sort the list by rearranging the items one by one. This will help you to understand how sorting works.

You have learned that there can be more than one algorithm to do the same task. In this section you will learn two sort algorithms:

- the bubble sort
- the merge sort.

These algorithms both have the effect of reorganising a list or array. The two algorithms work differently. The bubble sort is easier to write, but it takes longer for the computer to sort a list using the bubble sort. A programmer would use a different sort algorithm to sort a long list.

The bubble sort

The bubble sort works by swapping pairs of items. Here is a description of what you do when you use a bubble sort:

- Start at the first element of the list.
- Go through the elements one by one.
- Check each element against the element that follows it.
- If the next element is smaller, swap the two elements.
- When you get to the end of the list go back to the start and do it again.
- Keep repeating the process until there are no more swaps.

Try the bubble sort in class

You can act out the bubble sort in class. Students will represent the different elements of the list. To represent the list students can stand in a line or sit on chairs. Sitting on chairs makes the list clearer to see, but it takes a bit longer to organise.

Students can sort themselves in any order. You might decide to sort in name order. Or you can give each student a card with a number on it, then sort by number value.

As in pseudocode and Python, we will start numbering our list at 0. Here are the instructions:

- All the students stand in a line. All students must know what their position number is, starting at 0. All students must know what their sort value is.
- Start with student at position 0 in the list.
- The student in position 0 turns to the student at position 1. The two students compare values. Who has the bigger value?
- If the student in position 0 has a bigger value than the student in position 1, then the two students swap places.
- Now move on to the student in position 1. The student at position 1 compares values with the student in position 2. If student 1 has a bigger value, these two students swap places.
- Carry on comparing and swapping until you get to the last position in the list.
- Now go back to position 0 at the top of the list. Repeat the whole process.
- Keep repeating the process until there are no more swaps. Now the list is sorted.

Remember that the computer can only carry out one process at a time. You cannot have lots of different swaps happening at the same time. Each student must keep still until it is that person's turn to move.

Swap two items

You can see that you have to be able to swap two items for the bubble sort. Every sort algorithm uses swapping.

In Python it is easy to swap the value of two items, for example two elements of a list. Here is the command to swap the values `x` and `y`:

```
x,y = y,x
```

This command will swap the values of `mylist[0]` and `mylist[1]`.

```
mylist[0], mylist[1] = mylist[1],mylist[0]
```

Learning activity

Carry out the bubble sort on a line of students.

Test yourself

Here is a list. It is not sorted.

Position	0	1	2	3	4
Value	16	10	4	7	1

A programmer used the bubble sort to sort this list.

1. What was the first swap that happened? What was the second swap that happened?

2. The sort algorithm starts at the first position and moves down to the end of the list. This is one "pass" of the sort. Show what the list will look like after one pass.

3. What did the list look like after the bubble sort was finished?

Extension activity

If you feel confident, write a Python program to implement the bubble sort. The right answer is on the next page – but try making the program before you look.

Syllabus reference

3.1.4 Sorting algorithms

Understand and explain how the bubble sort algorithm works.

Additional information

Students should know the mechanics of the algorithm.

Students will be expected to know the version of the algorithm that uses two nested loops, with the outer loop being indefinitely controlled by a condition that tests whether any swaps were made; and the inner loop being controlled definitely.

Bubble sort

Introduction

You have learned what sorting is. You have learned what a bubble sort is. In this section you will write the algorithm for a bubble sort. You will write the algorithm in pseudocode.

You will also see a Python program that implements the bubble sort algorithm. You can copy the Python example, and try it out as we go.

Make a sort function

Here is a short example program. We can use a program like this to test any sort function.

```python
def bubblesort(sample):
    return sample


sample = [16,10,4,7,1]
print("unsorted list")
print(sample)

newlist = bubblesort(sample)
print("sorted list")
print(newlist)
```

In this example program the function is called `bubblesort`. The list is called `sample`.

The function does not do anything yet. If you run the program the sample list is not sorted. We will now add commands to the bubble sort function.

One comparison

A bubble sort uses comparisons. Each element is compared to the next element in the list. If the first is bigger, the two elements swap. We will add one command to the bubble sort function. The new command will compare the first two elements of the example list.

```python
def bubblesort(sample):
    if sample[0] > sample[1]:
        sample[0],sample[1] = sample[1],sample[0]
    return sample
```

One pass

This program does one comparison. We will change it to count through the whole list. This is called one pass. We will use the for loop to count through every element of the list. We must stop one before the end of the list.

Here is a program which implements one pass of the bubble sort:

```
def bubblesort(sample):
    stop = len(sample)-1
    for i in range(stop):
        if sample[i] > sample[i+1]:
            sample[i],sample[i+1] = sample[i+1],sample[i]
    return sample
```

The `if` statement is nested inside the `for` loop.

Keep passing

The bubble sort does one pass. We will change it so it keeps passing. The bubble sort keeps passing through the list until there are no more swaps.

We don't know how many times the sort algorithm will need to pass through the list. So we will use a `while` loop, not a `for` loop. The `while` loop will stop when there are no more swaps. Or – putting it the other way – it will loop if there is a swap.

We will use a Boolean (True/False) variable to record whether there is a swap or not. Here is how we do it:

- Before the `while` loop begins we set the variable 'swap' to True – that is so the loop will start
- The loop will repeat 'while swap == True'
- We set 'swap' to False - because no swaps have happened yet in this pass
- If there is a swap then we set the variable 'swap' to True.

If the computer passes through the list and there are no swaps, then the while loop will stop, and the sort will be over.

Here is the finished bubble sort with all these features in place:

```
def bubblesort(sample):
    stop = len(sample)-1
    swap = True
    while swap == True:
        swap = False
        for i in range(stop):
            if sample[i] > sample [i+1]:
                sample[i], sample[i+1] = sample[i+1], sample[i]
                swap = True
    return sample
```

Learning activity

1. Create a bubble sort function.

2. Put the function inside a program and test it to see whether it sorts properly every time.

3. Repeat the test with lists of different sizes.

Extension activity

We do not know in advance how many times the bubble sort will need to pass through the list. It depends how mixed up the list is to start with. The maximum number of passes happens if the list is in reverse order. For example:

```
[12,11,10,9,8,7]
```

How many passes would it take to sort this list? What is the relationship between the number of passes and the number of elements in a list?

Test yourself

Here is a line from a bubble sort algorithm in pseudocode.

```
IF sample[i] > sample[i+1] THEN
```

1. Explain in your own words what the logical test is.

2. What will the bubble sort function do if the logical test is True?

3. Why does each pass of the `for` loop stop one before the end of the list? Why doesn't it go to the very last element in the list?

4. The bubble sort keeps passing through the list. We don't know how many times it will need to pass through the list. How does the computer decide when to stop sorting the list?

Syllabus reference

3.1.4 Sorting algorithms

Understand and explain how the merge sort algorithm works.

Additional information

Students should know the mechanics of the recursive version of the algorithm. It will be sufficient for students to explain this algorithm in prose, they will not be expected to be able to write pseudocode for it.

Students should be able to demonstrate how a merge sort would be performed on a given set of data.

Merge sort

Introduction

You have learned about the bubble sort. This is a simple algorithm to sort a list. In this section you will learn about an alternative to the bubble sort. This is called the merge sort.

The bubble sort is slow

Using the bubble sort is quite a slow way to sort a list. The sort must pass through the list many times. It only stops when there are no more swaps. Even though a computer goes very fast, a bubble sort can take several minutes. It will take even longer with a long list.

For this reason, programmers have invented other, faster, ways to sort lists. One way is the merge sort.

The merge function

The merge sort makes use of the merge function. The merge function takes two short lists and merges them together to make one big list. You can act this function out in class.

Pick 12 students and organise them into two short lines. Make sure each line stands in order. You can choose any sort order. You might decide to sort in alphabetical order of names. Or you can give each student a card with a number on it, then sort by number value. Here are the instructions:

- The two students at the front of each line compare values.
- The one with the smallest value leaves the line and starts a new line in a new part of the classroom.
- The students at the front of the two lines compare values again. The one with the smallest value goes to the end of the new line.
- Keep comparing values until one of the lines is empty. Any remaining students join the end of the new line in the same order.
- In this way you end up with one sorted line.
- Compare this to the bubble sort – instead of several passes the whole merge is completed in one pass.

Limitations of the merge function

The merge function on its own cannot be used for most sorting tasks. The merge function only works if you already have two sorted lists.

Usually programmers need to sort one list that isn't sorted already. For this reason, programmers rarely use the merge function on its own.

Split and merge

We can adapt the merge function to work on one big list. Here is how we do it:

- Split the list repeatedly until you are left with lots of tiny lists, with only one element in each list.

- Merge them into lists of two.
- Now merge the lists of two into lists of four.
- Continue until the whole list is merged together into one sorted list.

Expert programmers can write programs to do this task. For now, you will just act out the sort in class.

Try the merge sort in class

You can act out the merge sort in class. Remember that each student should be given a value. Use the values to sort the line. This is what to do:

- Form a single line of students – not in any sorted order.
- Each student turns to the student next to him or her.
- Form a little sorted line of just two people – smallest value first.
- Now each line of two turns to the line next to them.
- Use the merge function to merge the two lines to make a line of four.
- Keep merging lines until all the students are merged into one long line. It should be in sorted order.

Try it in other ways

If it isn't convenient to act out the merge sort using a line of students, try it in other ways. You can sort a pack of cards or a set of names on cards. Any list or collection or line can be sorted in this way. The merge sort method is much quicker than the bubble sort method.

Test yourself

1. Why can't we use the merge function on its own for most sorting tasks?

2. You have learned two sort methods. Which is quicker?

3. The merge sort begins by splitting a list into lots of tiny lists. How long are these lists?

4. Why does the merge function start by splitting a list into lots of tiny lists?

Learning activity

Try out the merge sort using any of the methods described on this page.

Extension activity

Write a Python program that merges two short sorted lists to create one longer sorted list. This is the basis of the merge sort.

Syllabus reference

3.1.2 Efficiency of algorithms

Understand that more than one algorithm can be used to solve the same problem.

Compare the efficiency of algorithms explaining how some algorithms are more efficient than others in solving the same problem.

Additional information

Students should refer to time efficiency.

3.1.4 Sorting algorithms

Compare and contrast merge sort and bubble sort algorithms.

Additional information

Students should know the advantages and disadvantages of both algorithms.

Compare sort algorithms

Introduction

You have learned about two sort algorithms. One is the bubble sort. One is the merge sort. Each algorithm has advantages and disadvantages. In this section you will compare the two algorithms.

Which algorithm to choose?

A programmer may need to write a program to sort a list. Different ways of sorting have different advantages. The programmer will compare the advantages and disadvantages of different methods of sorting and then pick the right algorithm.

Some algorithms make programs that run quickly. Some algorithms make programs that run slowly. The speed difference can be very important if you need to sort a very big list. For example, think of social media sites. Many of them have many millions of users. Sorting a list of users might take a very long time.

How long will it take to sort a list?

When the computer sorts a list, it carries out different actions. Each of these actions takes some time. Each action is very quick, but the time adds up if there are a lot of elements in the list. The amount of time it takes to sort a list depends on how many elements there are in the list. We use the letter n to mean the number of elements in the list.

How long it will take to sort a list also depends on how mixed up the list is. If a list is almost in order it might be quick to sort. If the list items are very mixed up it might take longer to sort. For this reason we often think of the worst case. That is, we think about how many operations the computer will have to perform if the list is very mixed up.

Speed of the bubble sort

How many actions must the computer carry out for the bubble sort? Remember that we use n to stand for how many elements there are in the list.

With each pass of the bubble sort the computer looks at each element in the list. That means each pass takes n actions.

The number of passes will vary. If the list is very mixed up the bubble sort could take n passes.

The maximum time taken by the bubble sort is n times by n.

We can also write that value as n*n or n².

Speed of the merge sort

The merge sort splits the list in two over and over until each list has one element. It works like this:

● Splitting a list of n elements takes fewer than n passes. We call the number log(n). This number is always quite a lot smaller than n.

- Once the list has been split down we use the merge function to merge the small lists into one big list. Each element is copied once, so that takes n operations.

The maximum number of operations is n times by `log(n)`. This is a much smaller number than n*n, so the merge sort is quicker than the bubble sort.

Storage requirement

A merge sort has a disadvantage that may be important in some programming tasks. As it splits the list into lots of sublists, the merge sort uses up more space in the computer memory than the bubble sort.

	Advantages	Disadvantages
Bubble sort	It is easy to write	It is slower than a merge sort – only use it on a short list
Merge sort	It is faster than a bubble sort – it can be used on any size of list	It is harder to write than a bubble sort Uses more storage space

Extension – what this means for programmers

We can work out how long it will take to sort a list with a million names in it. Let's say that the computer can do 10 million operations in a second:

- A bubble sort takes n*n operations. That could take thousands of seconds. In other words, it could take an hour or more to complete the sort.

- A merge sort takes n*log(n) operations. That might be less than a second.

The merge sort is much faster.

Test yourself

1. A programmer needs to sort a list of 10 million bank customers. What sort algorithm would the programmer use?

2. A teacher needed to sort a list of 50 pupils. Would the bubble sort be suitable for this task?

3. The speed of a sort algorithm depends on the size of n. What does n stand for?

4. As well as n, what other feature of a list affects the time it takes to sort it?

Learning activity

Write a short report for trainee programmers. Explain the difference between the merge and bubble sort algorithms. Tell the trainees when they should choose each algorithm. Explain the advantages of each one.

Extension activity

Investigate how the merge sort algorithm is implemented in Python.

Syllabus reference

3.1.2 Efficiency of algorithms

Understand that more than one algorithm can be used to solve the same problem.

Compare the efficiency of algorithms explaining how some algorithms are more efficient than others in solving the same problem.

Additional information

Students should refer to time efficiency.

3.1.4 Sorting algorithms

Compare and contrast merge sort and bubble sort algorithms.

Additional information

Students should know the advantages and disadvantages of both algorithms.

Graphing time efficiency

Introduction

You have learned that you can use more than one algorithm to do a task. For example there is more than one search algorithm, and there is more than one sort algorithm. Some algorithms are more efficient than others. We can use graphs to show and compare the efficiency of different algorithms.

Worst case timing

The amount of time it will take to search or sort a list depends on how big the list is. Remember that we use n to stand for how many elements there are in the list.

The amount of time it takes also depends on how the list is organised. Imagine that a computer is looking for an item in a list using the serial search. The item might be the very first item in the list. Then the computer will find it after one operation. The item might be the last in the list. Then the computer will find it after n operations. The same algorithm works more quickly in one case than another.

Or imagine if a list is already nearly sorted, and another list is all jumbled up. Sorting the first list could be much quicker, even though you use the same algorithm in both cases.

For this reason programmers sometimes compare algorithm efficiency by thinking about the worst case. They think about what happens if the list is completely jumbled up, or if the item you want is at the very end of the list. If an algorithm works well in the worst case, then it must be a good algorithm.

Graphing time efficiency

A convenient way to show the efficiency of an algorithm is to show how time (t) increases as the number of items (n) increases. In all these examples we will think about worst case timing.

Linear search

The linear search algorithm looks at every item in a list. In the worst case it will look at every item. So the amount of time is directly in proportion to the number of items. This is called a linear relationship and the graph looks like this.

Binary search

Binary search is quicker than a linear search. The time taken (t) increases more slowly in relation to the number of items (n). That is because the list is divided in half each time.

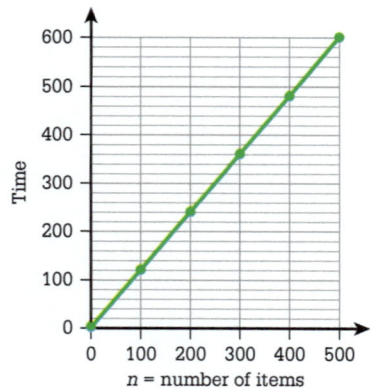

↑ Linear search algorithm

The relationship between t and n is shown in the next graph. This is called a logarithmic relationship. The line showing time increases more slowly than the linear search. That means the search is quicker.

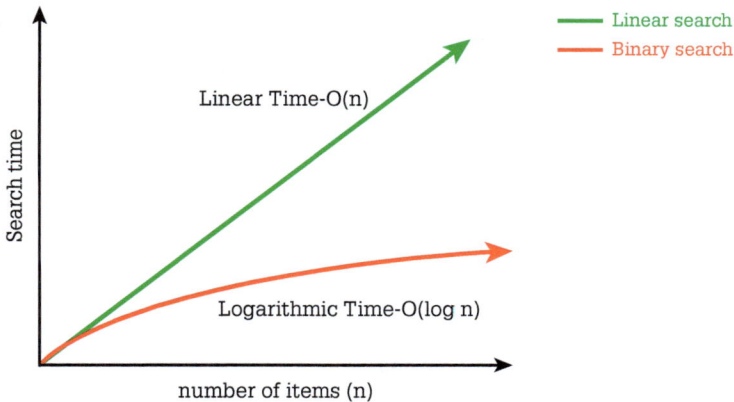

↑ Comparing linear and binary search

Bubble sort

The worst case time taken by the bubble sort is n ✗ n or n². So if a list has 4 items, a bubble sort can take 16 operations (worst case). If the list has 10 items it will take 100 operations, and so on.

This means the line showing time climbs very steeply. The bubble sort takes a long time to sort a big list. It is not practical. This graph shows that relationship.

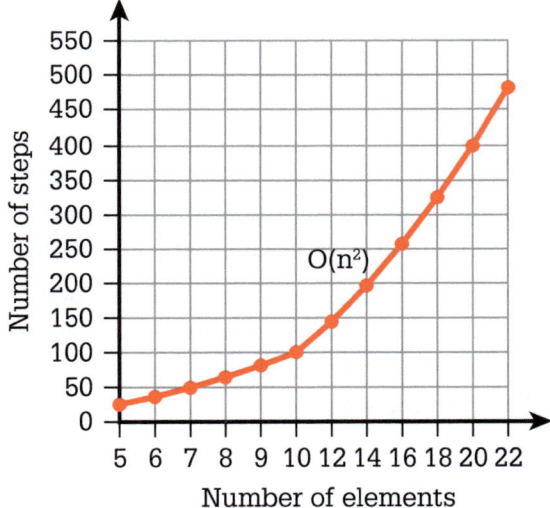

Merge sort

The merge sort is quicker than the bubble sort. The time (t) increases more slowly than it does in a bubble sort. The next graph compares the speed of the two algorithms.

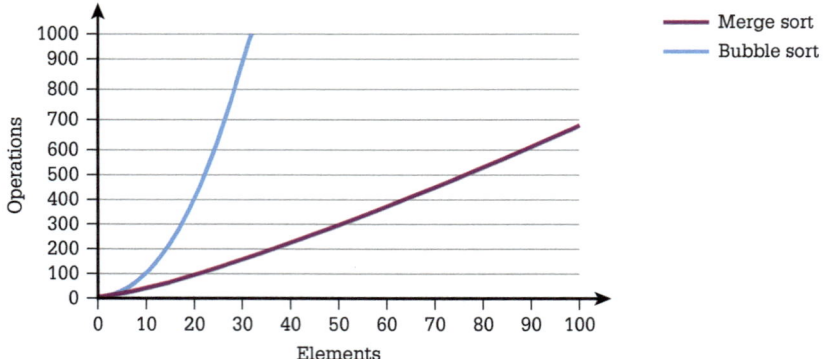

⬆ Comparing worst case sort times

Optimising time efficiency

Programmers sometimes make changes to an algorithm to improve its efficiency. This is called optimising.

For example here is a Python function which carries out the bubble sort. You have seen this before.

```python
def bubblesort(sample):
    stop = len(sample)-1
    swap = True
    while swap == True:
        swap = False
        for i in range(stop):
            if sample[i] > sample [i+1]:
                sample[i], sample[i+1] = sample[i+1], sample[i]
                swap = True
    return sample
```

At the centre of the algorithm is a `for` loop. It goes through the entire list from 0 to the stop value each time. This takes a long time, especially if the list is long.

But actually the algorithm does not need to look through the whole list each time. If the last item in the list is out of place, the first run through will have caught it. In fact we can reduce the number of swaps needed by one each time. Here is an optimised version of the bubble sort:

```python
def bubblesort(sample):
    stop = len(sample)
    swap = True
    while swap == True:
        # reduce stop by 1 each time
        stop = stop-1

        swap = False
        for i in range(stop):
            if sample[i] > sample [i+1]:
                sample[i], sample[i+1] = sample[i+1], sample[i]
                swap = True

    return sample
```

Can you see the change?

In fact we can optimise the bubble sort even further. After every pass, all elements after the last swap are sorted, and do not need to be checked again. Let's make that change.

```python
def bubblesort(sample):
    stop = len(sample)-1
    swap = True
    while swap == True:
        swap = False
        for i in range(stop):
            if sample[i] > sample [i+1]:
                sample[i], sample[i+1] = sample[i+1], sample[i]
                swap = True
                stop = i ## NEW COMMAND
    return sample
```

Try this algorithm and check that it sorts a list correctly. This change can decrease the number of comparison the algorithm has to do by up to 50% – a big improvement in time efficiency.

Extension – Big O

Programmers call the worst case speed of an algorithm its big O value. The big O value shows the relationship between the number of items and the time taken by the algorithm.

Algorithm	Time increases by…	Relationship	Speed comparison
Binary search	$\log(n)$	Logarithmic	fastest
Linear search	n	Linear	
Merge sort	$n \bullet \log(n)$		
Bubble sort	$n \bullet n$	Polynomial	slowest

Test yourself

1. A computer carries out a linear search to find an item. What is the worst place the item could be, in terms of the time it takes?

2. A list has n items. What is the worst time it could take to sort the list using the bubble sort? Give your answer as an equation using the number n.

3. A linear search takes n operations. A binary search takes log(n) operations. Which is quicker?

4. Two lists are exactly the same size, but one takes longer to sort using the bubble sort. Why might that be?

Learning activity

Draw four graphs showing the relationship between the number of items in a list and the speed of the four algorithms you have learned: bubble sort, merge sort, binary search and linear search.

Extension activity

Research other sort algorithms – such as Insertion sort and Quick sort. What are the worst case speeds for these algorithms? What else can you find out about how to implement these algorithms?

Syllabus reference

3.3.1 Number bases

Understand that computers use binary to represent all data and instructions.

Additional information

Students should be familiar with the idea that a bit pattern could represent different types of data including text, image, sound and integer.

4.1 Binary systems

Binary data

> ### Introduction
>
> In this section you will learn what a computer does. You will learn why computers use binary data.

What is a computer?

A computer is an electronic machine for processing data. "Data" is a general term for facts and figures. All types of data can be processed by a computer. Computers can work with:

- numbers
- words
- images
- sounds
- video
- physical processes.

All of these types of data can be stored inside a computer. The computer processes the data. That means it turns the data into something more useful. The useful output of the computer is often called information.

Data is processed to make useful information

A computer processes data to make useful information. Computers are made by people, to be useful to people. There is no point in using a computer unless it does something you want to do.

➡ A flashlight can be in one of two states – either on or off

Inside the computer

Inside every computer is a processor. The processor stores and processes data. The processor stores the data using electrical switches that can either be on or off. A switch that is on will conduct electricity. A switch that is off will not carry an electric signal.

"Binary" means anything that can be in one of two different states. A switch that can be on or off is binary. There are exactly two choices – no more, no less. The data inside a computer is stored in a binary format.

A computer can process data of many different kinds, but each different type of data must be turned into binary before a computer can process it.

Representing data and instructions

All data in the computer must be turned into a pattern of on/off signals. In Chapter 5 – starting on page 152 – you will find out more about how different types of data are stored in the computer.

You have written programs to control the computer. When you run a program all the instructions are converted to binary numbers. On page 188 you will learn more about how instructions are converted to binary numbers.

Describing binary data

When we want to show binary data we write it as a "binary number": that is, a number made of 1s and 0s. We can also call this base 2. For example:

```
0 1 0 0 1 1 1 0
```

If you opened up a computer and looked in the processor you would not see 1s and 0s. That is just a convenient way of representing the on and off electrical signals.

Test yourself

1. The computer does not have little 1s and 0s inside its memory. Why do we sometimes represent computer data in that form?

2. Explain in your own words why data must be converted to binary form when it is input to a computer.

3. On the previous page a flashlight is given as an example of something that is binary (has two different states). Think of another example, from outside computer science.

4. Why are computers useful?

Learning activity

In this section five different types of data are mentioned: numbers, words, images, sounds and video. Search on the Internet for a short example of each type of data. Store a sample of each type of data in your own storage area of the computer system.

Extension activity

In a table show the storage space taken up by each of the samples you have found. Which type of data takes up the most space?

Syllabus reference

3.3.3 Units of information

Know that:

- a bit is the fundamental unit of information
- a bit is either a 0 or a 1
- "b" represents bit
- a byte is a group of eight bits
- "B" represents byte.

Know that quantities of bytes can be described using prefixes.

Know the names, symbols and corresponding values for the decimal prefixes:

- kilo – 1 kB is 1000 bytes
- mega – 1 MB is 1000 kilobytes
- giga – 1 GB is 1000 megabytes
- tera – 1 TB is 1000 gigabytes.

Bits and bytes

Introduction

You have learned that data is held in the computer in binary form. In this section you will learn how the size of computer memory is measured as the amount of binary data it can hold.

Bits

Binary numbers are made up of the digits 1 and 0. We abbreviate the term "binary digit" to "bit". Therefore, in computer science, one bit is a 0 or a 1.

One bit is the smallest piece of computer memory. A bit represents a single on/off switch inside the computer's electronic memory.

We can measure the size of part of the computer's electronic memory by saying how many bits it contains. We put the letter "b" (in lower case) after the number. This shows the number stands for a number of bits. For example, a group of 32 bits would be written as 32b.

Bytes

Inside the computer, on/off bits are organised into groups of eight. A group of eight bits is called a byte. A byte is enough memory to store a single letter of the alphabet.

We can measure the total capacity of an area of computer memory or storage. We usually give the answer as a number of bytes. We put the letter "B" (in upper case) after the number to show it stands for a number of bytes. For example, a group of 32 bits is the same as 4 bytes. We would write that as 4B.

To convert bits to bytes, just divide the number of bits by 8.

Writing binary numbers

We usually write binary numbers in groups of eight bits. That matches the way a computer organises bits. If the number is less than eight bits long, we put extra 0s on the left of the digits to make it up to eight bits. For example, the binary number 1 1 0 1 would be represented by this byte:

00001101

Measuring memory

The area of the computer processor that stores data as on/off electrical signals is called the memory (random-access memory or RAM). We measure the size of RAM by how many bytes it can hold.

Storage devices keep data using non-electronic on/off signals. We measure storage by how many bytes it can hold. We measure memory and storage in units called kilobytes, megabytes, gigabytes and terabytes.

Name of the unit	How many bytes	Symbol for the unit	Typical storage
kilobyte	1000 bytes	kB	half a page of plain text = 1KB
megabyte	1000 kilobytes	MB	A photo = 2–4 MB
gigabyte	1000 megabytes	GB	A movie = 1 or 2 GB
terabyte	1000 gigabytes	TB	1 terabyte would hold about 17,000 hours of music or 500 hours of movies

When computers are advertised they often say how many bytes of **RAM** there are in the computer.

How many bytes?

As you can see from the table, each unit is 1000 times larger than the one before. For example a megabyte is 1000 kilobytes. In the past, people sometimes defined these units differently. Each one was 1024 times bigger than the last. This way of calculating sizes is not the standard method any longer.

Extension – RAM and computer speed

The computer processor makes changes to the data in **RAM**. That is called processing the data. It is very quick and easy for the processor to access the contents of **RAM**. The processing will be quick.

If there isn't enough room in **RAM**, then some of the data must be stored outside of **RAM**. It is slower for the processor to access this data. That means the computer will go more slowly. Adding more **RAM** to a computer will usually help it process data more quickly.

Test yourself

1. Explain the difference between a bit and a byte.

2. A storage area holds 250 bytes. How many bits is that?

3. Roughly how many pictures could be stored using 1 gigabyte of data?

4. How many KB are there in a TB?

Learning activity

Using magazines and the Internet, collect adverts for computers currently for sale. What does each advert say about the computer? How big is the RAM?

Extension activity

Research what other factors, as well as the size of RAM, affect the speed of a computer processor.

Syllabus reference

3.3.1 Number bases

Understand the following number bases: decimal (base 10), binary (base 2).

Binary and decimal

Introduction

You have learned that a computer stores data as binary numbers. In this section you will compare binary to decimal (our normal number system).

The decimal system

The number system that you are familiar with in everyday life uses ten different digits. Every number that exists can be represented using these ten digits:

0 1 2 3 4 5 6 7 8 9

How do we represent every number, using just ten digits? The answer is we use the position of a digit to change its meaning. Look at these numbers:

702

720

207

Each of these decimal numbers uses the digit 2. In the first case 2 means two. In the next example 2 means twenty. In the final example 2 means two hundred. The difference is the position of the digit in the number.

Position value in base 10

It is easy to work out the value of a digit in a decimal number. Start at the right of a number. The digit on the right stands for single units. As we move to the left each digit has a value that is ten times bigger. Here is an example – the decimal number 720.

1000 (thousands)	100 (hundreds)	10 (tens)	1 (units)
0	7	2	0

In this example we have seven hundreds, two tens and no units. That is the meaning of 720 in decimal.

We call this numbering system "base ten" because decimal has ten digits, and each position is ten times greater than the next.

The binary system

Binary numbers are made of the binary digits 1 and 0 (also called bits). Every number that exists can be represented using just 1s and 0s. As with the decimal system, the position of the bit tells you its value. Start at the right of a number. The bit on the right stands for single units. As we move to the left each bit has a value that is two times bigger. Here is an example – the binary number 0 1 0 1.

8 (eights)	4 (fours)	2 (twos)	1 (units)
0	1	0	1

In this example we have no eights, one four, no twos and one unit. Adding the values together makes 5. Therefore, the number 0 1 0 1 in binary has the same value as the number 5 in decimal.

Talking about binary numbers

When you talk about binary numbers, never use decimal words. If you see the binary number 1 0 do not call it ten. 1 0 has the value two in binary. To avoid confusion with decimal numbers we would normally say "the binary number one oh"

To say the binary number 1 0 1 we do not say "one hundred and one". It is called "one zero one" or "one oh one".

Extension – the invention of the decimal system

The decimal number system that we use today was developed in India, probably in the 3rd century BCE (2300 years ago). It was better for doing complex maths than any other number system that existed at that time. This number system was adopted in the Arabic world, and spread beyond India. Around 850 CE, the Persian mathematician Al-Khwarizmi and the Arab mathematician Al-Kindi wrote books that explained the decimal number system. Later, Europeans learned this system from Arabic mathematicians. In Europe, decimal digits are still sometimes called Arabic numerals.

Extension – the invention of the binary system

Binary number systems were developed much later than the decimal system. A German philosopher called Gottfried Leibniz set out the idea of binary numbers, made with 1s and 0s, in 1679. In the 19th century, a British mathematician called Ada Lovelace wrote notes about how binary numbers could be used in digital processing. This work influenced the development of computers that make use of binary data.

Test yourself

1. What features of the decimal number system make it base ten?

2. Explain why a digit such as 9 can hold many different values in a decimal number.

3. How many bits are there in the binary number 0010?

4. In the binary number 0010 what value does the 1 stand for?

Learning activity

Complete this table by replacing the question marks with number values. Remember that each value is twice as big as the one before.

?	?	?	?	8	4	2	1
0	0	1	0	0	1	0	1

Extension activity

Find out more about the history of different number systems. Write a report on the development of either the decimal or binary number systems.

Syllabus reference

3.3.2 Converting between number bases

Understand how binary can be used to represent whole numbers.

Additional information

Students must be able to represent decimal values between 0 and 255 in binary.

> ## Introduction
>
> You have learned about binary and decimal numbers. In this section you will learn how to count in binary and how this compares to counting in decimal.

Counting in decimal

To count up from zero in decimal numbers you start at 0. You count in the "units" column. The digit in the "units" column gets 1 bigger each time:

        00

        01

        02

When you get to 9, you have run out of digits:

        09

How can you add more? You return the "units" column back to 0, and add 1 to the next column along. In decimal that is the "tens" column:

        10

You then start again, counting upwards in the "units" column. When you reach 9:

        19

You reset the units column to 0 and add 1 in the "tens" column:

        20

In this way you can count up to any number using decimal.

Counting in binary

When you count in binary it is the same. Start with 0:

        0

Then add 1:

        1

You have used 0 and 1 and there are no more binary digits. Therefore, you return the "units" column to 0, and add 1 in the column to the left:

        10

Continue to count. Add 1 in the "unit" column:

        11

Now you have run out of digits in both columns, so you reset them both to 0, and add a 1 in the column to the left:

        100

In this way you can count up to any number in binary. However, the numbers can get quite long. A larger number can have a long series of bits.

Learning activity

A group of eight students stand in a row for this activity. The rest of the class can watch. Later, everyone will get a turn to take part. The teacher is going to count up in the normal way. The eight students are going to act out binary counting.

⬆ Students taking art in the "Binary counting" activity

Each student represents one of the bits in a byte. In this picture each student has a card that represents his or her "position value". The position on the right represents units, the next position represents twos and so on.

Remember that each bit can have one of two values. The students must show the value of their bit. In this picture the students turn their cards round. If the card is facing outward, so you can see the value, it stands for a number 1. If the card is turned back, so you can only see the blank back, it stands for a number 0.

Other classes have done this count activity in different ways – see "Variations" below.

The student on the right stands for units. This student has the most work to do. Every time the teacher counts, this student has to turn his or her card around. If you are this student, you have to follow these rules:

- If your card is 0 turn it to show 1.

- If your card is 1 turn it to show 0. Signal to the student on your right (for example nod, or tap the student's shoulder).

- The other students don't move. They wait and watch the person to their left. If you are one of these students and the person to your left signals to you:

  – If your card is 0 turn it to show 1.

  – If your card is 1 turn it to show 0. Signal to the person on your right.

If you follow these rules carefully you can count through every binary number from 0 to 255.

Variations

You could ask the eight students to use a row of chairs. As well as turning cards around, students stand up to represent 1 and sit down to represent 0. Or students could each have a flashlight that they turn on and off.

Anything that can be in two states can be used to represent binary numbers. Be imaginative.

Syllabus reference

3.3.2 Converting between number bases

Be able to convert in both directions between binary and decimal.

Convert between binary and decimal

Introduction

You have learned about binary and decimal numbers. In this section you will learn how to turn binary numbers into decimal form. You will learn how to turn decimal numbers into binary.

Position values

You have seen that the value of a bit in a binary number depends on the position of the bit in the number. This table shows the position value of the eight bits that make up a byte.

128	64	32	16	8	4	2	1

To convert a binary number to decimal you write the number into a table like this one. Make sure the number ends in the column on the right. Any empty columns should be at the left of the table. Put a 0 in any empty column.

Here is an example – the binary number 11010.

128	64	32	16	8	4	2	1
0	0	0	1	1	0	1	0

To turn this number into a decimal number:

- find all the columns that have a 1 in them
- add the column values together.

The columns are 16, 8 and 2:

        16 + 8 + 2 = 26

This shows that the binary number 11010 is the decimal number 26.

Converting decimal to binary

There is more than one way to convert decimal numbers to binary. You will learn a method that uses the position values table. Start with the decimal number you want to convert. For example, let us convert the number 40 to binary.

Look at the table of position values. What is the largest value you can subtract from 40 (without making a minus number)? The largest value you can subtract is 32, so you write a 1 in the "32" column.

128	64	32	16	8	4	2	1
		1					

Now take away the value. In this example 40 – 32 = 8.

What is the next largest value you can take away? It is 8, so you write a 1 in the "8" column.

128	64	32	16	8	4	2	1
		1		1			

8 – 8 = 0, so the conversion is complete. Write a 0 in every other column.

128	64	32	16	8	4	2	1
0	0	1	0	1	0	0	0

This shows that 40 in decimal is 00101000 in binary.

Simplify the process

To simplify the process, complete all the subtractions and then transfer the values to the position table. For example, let's convert the decimal number 99 to binary:

```
99 – 64 = 35
35 – 32 = 3
3 – 2 = 1
1 – 1 = 0
```

Now mark the numbers you have taken away in the position table. Write 0 in all the other columns.

128	64	32	16	8	4	2	1
0	1	1	0	0	0	1	1

This shows that 99 in decimal is 01100011 in binary.

Test yourself

1. Convert these eight-bit binary numbers to decimal:

```
0 0 0 1 1 0 0 1

0 1 0 1 0 0 0 0

1 0 0 1 0 0 1 1

1 1 1 1 1 1 1 1
```

2. Convert these decimal numbers to eight-bit binary numbers:

```
31

55

70

101
```

Learning activity

Write a handout or a presentation to teach young learners how to convert between decimal and binary.

Extension activity

Here is a challenging activity for confident programmers. Write a Python program where the user inputs any denary (decimal) number from 0 to 255 and the program output is the equivalent binary number.

Syllabus reference

3.3.1 Number bases

Understand the following number base: hexadecimal (base 16).

3.3.2 Converting between number bases

Understand how hexadecimal can be used to represent whole numbers.

Additional information

Students must be able to represent decimal values between 0 and 255 in hexadecimal.

Be able to convert in both directions between: binary and decimal; binary and hexadecimal.

4.2 Hexadecimal

What is hexadecimal?

Introduction

You have learned about the binary and decimal number systems. In this section you will learn about the hexadecimal number system. It is based on the number 16.

Hexadecimal digits

You have learned that binary numbers are made using two digits (0 and 1). We can also call this base 2. Decimal uses ten different digits. We can also call it base 10. Hexadecimal is a number system that uses 16 different digits, which is why we can also call it base 16.

The 16 hexadecimal digits are:

```
0 1 2 3 4 5 6 7 8 9 A B C D E F
```

These 16 digits stand for the numbers 0 to 15. Digits 0 to 9 are just the same as decimal. The next six digits stand for the numbers 10 to 15:

```
A means 10

B means 11

C means 12

D means 13

E means 14

F means 15
```

Be careful – hexadecimal numbers do not always have letters in them: letters are used in some hexadecimal numbers, but not all.

Position values

Just as with binary and decimal numbers, hexadecimal digits have different values in different positions. Many of the hexadecimal numbers you will look at have just two digits. As with all numbers, the right-hand column stands for units (1s). As hexadecimal is base 16, the next column is 16 times greater in value. Digits in the second column stand for 16s.

16 (sixteens)	1 (units)

Let's look at one example. Here is the hexadecimal number 2B.

16 (sixteens)	1 (units)
2	B

There is a 2 in the 16s column. This has the value:

```
2 × 16 = 32
```

There is a B in the units columns. In the hexadecimal system, B stands for 11.

    11 x 1 = 11

Adding the two values together we have:

    32 + 11 = 43

Therefore, hexadecimal number 2B means 43 in decimal.

Convert hexadecimal to decimal

By using this method we can convert any two-digit hexadecimal number to decimal. You multiply the digit in the left-hand column by 16. Then you add the value of the digit in the right-hand column.

Here is another example.

16 (sixteens)	1 (units)
7	C

Remember that in hexadecimal notation, C stands for 12, so the answer is:

    7 x 16 = 112

    112 + 12 = 124

Convert decimal to hexadecimal

We can use this method in reverse to convert decimal to hexadecimal. Divide the decimal number by 16. If it doesn't go exactly, use the value up to the decimal point. Don't round it up, just ignore the fractional part. This is how to record it:

- The result goes in the 16s column.

- The remainder goes in the units column.

For example, to convert 59 to hexadecimal:

    58 / 16 = 3 remainder 10

    10 is A in hexadecimal.

    The answer is therefore 3A.

16 (sixteens)	1 (units)
3	A

Test yourself

1. Convert the hexadecimal value B4 to decimal.

2. Convert the decimal number 100 to hexadecimal.

3. What is the largest value hexadecimal digit?

4. What is the largest value hexadecimal number you can write with two digits? What is its decimal value?

Learning activity

Work in a team. Write a quiz about decimal and hexadecimal conversions. Make sure you work out the right answer to every question. Then challenge another team in the class to answer your questions.

Extension activity

Investigate the value of larger hexadecimal numbers. What is the value of the largest number you can write with four hexadecimal digits?

Syllabus reference

3.3.2 Converting between number bases

Be able to convert in both directions between binary and hexadecimal.

Hexadecimal and binary

Introduction
You have learned to convert between hexadecimal and decimal numbers. In this section you will learn how to convert between hexadecimal and binary numbers. It is much easier than decimal conversion.

Exact match

On pages 136–137 you learned how to count up in binary. There is an exact match between the first 16 binary numbers and the 16 hexadecimal digits.

Hexadecimal	Binary
0	0000
1	0001
2	0010
3	0011
4	0100
5	0101
6	0110
7	0111
8	1000
9	1001
A	1010
B	1011
C	1100
D	1101
E	1110
F	1111

You can use this table to convert between hexadecimal and binary. Every number converts exactly. There are no subtractions or remainders to worry about.

Match and convert hexadecimal

It is very easy to use the table above to turn hexadecimal into binary. For example, think of the hexadecimal number A1B7. Refer to the table and simply write in the matching four-bit binary number under each digit.

A	1	B	7
1010	0001	1011	0111

This shows that the answer in binary is 1010 0001 1011 0111. By using the table you can get the answer in a few seconds. You don't need to covert either number to a decimal value.

Match and convert binary

Using the table of matching numbers, you can convert any binary number to hexadecimal.

First put the bits into groups of four. If the bits don't divide equally into fours, then add some 0s at the start of the number. For example, take the binary number 1010111001100. There are 13 bits in this number. We have to add three 0s at the start, then we can arrange the bits into four groups of four bits:

        0001 0101 1100 1100

Next use the table to turn each group of four bits into a hexadecimal digit.

0001	0101	1100	1100
1	5	C	C

The answer in hexadecimal is therefore 15CC.

Make the conversion table

Sometimes you need to convert between hexadecimal and binary, but you don't have the conversion table. It is easy to make it for yourself:

- Write the first 16 hexadecimal numbers from 0 to F, down the page, each on a new line.
- Count the first 16 binary numbers from 0000 to 1111, writing them down the page next to their hexadecimal equivalent.

When you get used to this conversion, you'll find you don't even need the table: you'll be able to do the conversion in your head.

Extension – "nibble"

When you do binary to hexadecimal conversion you put the bits into groups of four. There are eight bits in a byte, so four bits is half a byte. Computer scientists use the word "nibble" or "nybble" to mean a four-bit binary number. Can you guess why they chose that word?

Test yourself

1. Convert the hexadecimal number ABCD to binary.
2. Convert the binary number 1010 1111 1010 0000 to hexadecimal.
3. Convert your age to binary and hexadecimal.
4. Explain why it is more convenient to use hexadecimal than decimal for people who need to work with binary values.

Learning activity

Create a large and colourful version of the table that matches hexadecimal and binary numbers.

Extension activity

Write a Python program that lets the user input a two-digit hexadecimal number and outputs the equivalent binary number. HINT: use `elif`.

How hexadecimal is used

Introduction

You have learned that it is very easy to convert binary numbers directly to hexadecimal. For this reason, hexadecimal is used in many computer activities. In this section you will learn about some of them.

Binary data

Every item of data or information inside the computer is held in binary form. Everything within the computer has to be a binary number. That includes:

- text (letters and other characters)
- colours
- sounds
- software instructions.

The computer uses different coding systems to turn all the different types of data into binary numbers. When human users work with this binary data they almost always use hexadecimal instead.

Why do we use hexadecimal?

Binary numbers are very useful in computer science, but they have disadvantages:

- It is hard for people to read and understand binary numbers.
- When you write a binary number it is easy to make a mistake.
- It is hard to spot and fix errors in binary numbers.
- Writing a binary number takes a lot of space.

People wanted numbers that were easier to understand and work with than binary numbers. Decimal notation wasn't suitable because converting binary to decimal is difficult. Hexadecimal notation was chosen for these reasons:

- It is very easy to turn hexadecimal into binary.
- It is very easy to turn binary into hexadecimal.
- Hexadecimal is much easier to read than binary.
- Hexadecimal numbers take up less space than binary numbers.

Using hexadecimal notation is an easy way to work with binary numbers.

Main memory and the registers

Data in the computer memory is made of bits. The bits are arranged in bytes. Every location in memory has its own address. Memory addresses are binary numbers. Therefore, everything about the computer's memory can be represented by binary numbers. The data that is stored is binary. The address where it is stored is binary. We use hexadecimal to make it easier to read and write this information.

Colours

Nowadays the most common way to store colour information is using a system called 24-bit colour. Every colour is made of a mix of red, green and blue. Three bytes of data are used. One byte stores the amount of red, another byte stores the amount of green and the third stores the amount of blue. By mixing the three primary colours together in different proportions, over 16 million different colours can be made. Red, green and blue are each represented as a two-digit hexadecimal. The entire colour combination is therefore represented as a 6-digit hexadecimal number. The picture shows an example of one of these.

⬆ Using hexadecimal values we can define the full range of 24-bit colour choices

Machine code and assembly language

Machine code is a number code system that turns all software instructions into binary numbers. Programmers who write in machine code almost always turn these numbers into hexadecimal. We can also represent machine code instructions using a simple word code called assembly language.

Programmers writing programs in assembly language use hexadecimal to represent binary data and binary addresses. This makes it much easier to write machine code and assembly language. It also makes it easier to debug (fix errors). Error messages are often displayed using a hexadecimal code.

Find out more about machine code and assembly language on pages 188–189

Test yourself

1. Why is the colour system that uses red, green and blue called 24-bit colour?

2. Why do programmers use hexadecimal instead of decimal to represent binary codes?

3. Apart from colours, identify two different types of information that are stored in the computer using binary codes.

4. What is an error message and how does it help with debugging?

Learning activity

Carry out Internet research to find out what colours are represented by these three hexadecimal colour codes:

```
#FF0000

#00FF00

#0000FF
```

Extension activity

Make a colour table matching a range of hexadecimal colour codes to the matching shade of colour. You can make this electronically. If you want to, you can print it and use it for classroom display.

4.3 Binary arithmetic

Binary addition

Introduction

You have learned how all data is stored in binary form inside the computer. In this section you will learn how to do simple maths using binary numbers. This is how data is processed inside the computer. First you will learn about adding binary numbers together.

Inside the computer

All data is stored and processed inside the computer. The computer processes the data in two ways. They are:

- arithmetic – doing calculations
- logic – doing logical comparisons and deductions.

In this section you will learn about how the computer does calculations. To find out about logical processing turn to Chapter 7, pages 212–224.

The four rules of binary addition

To add any two binary numbers, you only need to learn these four rules.

```
0 + 0 = 0
0 + 1 = 1
1 + 1 = 0 and carry 1
1 + 1 + 1 = 1 and carry 1
```

These rules follow logically from the rules of binary counting that you learned on page 136.

Add two binary numbers

To add two binary numbers:

- put the numbers one above the other
- use the four rules of binary addition to add up each column.

Example

We will do this addition:

```
101100 + 1001110
```

Put the two numbers into a table. If the number is smaller than eight bits, remember to fill up on the left with 0.

Value 1	0	0	1	0	1	1	0	0
Value 2	0	1	0	0	1	1	1	0

Start at the right-hand column and add up the digits in the column using the four rules. We will put the result of each addition in the final row of the table. We will use the empty row for "carry" values.

The first (right-hand) column is 0 + 0. The second column is 0 + 1. We can fill in the answers in the bottom row.

Value 1	0	0	1	0	1	1	0	0
Value 2	0	1	0	0	1	1	1	0
Result							1	0

The third column is 1 + 1. The answer to this is 0 and carry 1. Here is how we put that into the table. The carry value goes into the next column along.

Value 1	0	0	1	0	1	1	0	0
Value 2	0	1	0	0	1	1	1	0
Carry					1			
Result						0	1	0

The next column is 1 + 1 + 1. The answer is 1 and carry 1.

Value 1	0	0	1	0	1	1	0	0
Value 2	0	1	0	0	1	1	1	0
Carry				1	1			
Result					1	0	1	0

Now you can continue with every column. Apply the four rules to each column and write in the results. Here is the completed table.

Value 1	0	0	1	0	1	1	0	0
Value 2	0	1	0	0	1	1	1	0
Carry				1	1			
Result	0	1	1	1	1	0	1	0

The bottom row gives us the answer to the addition.

```
00101100 + 01001110 = 01111010
```

Convert all three numbers into decimal and you will see that the answer is correct.

Learning activity

Make a poster for the classroom that sets out the four rules of binary addition.

Test yourself

Work out these binary additions.

1. 00110010 + 01010111
2. 01101110 + 01100110
3. 11011 + 11001111
4. 1011 + 01100100 + 01000001

Extension activity

Write a Python program that accepts two binary numbers and outputs the result of adding the two together using binary addition.

Syllabus reference

3.3.4 Binary arithmetic

Apply a binary shift to a binary number.

Describe situations where binary shifts can be used.

Additional information

Binary shifts can be used to perform simple multiplication by powers of 2.

Binary multiplication

Introduction

You have learned how to add together two or three binary numbers. Now you will learn to multiply two binary numbers.

Powers of two

A byte is made of eight bits. The eight bits represent a number. The bits get their value from their position in the byte. The position values of the eight bits are shown in this table.

128	64	32	16	8	4	2	1

Each column value is two times the value of the column before it. Each column value is a multiple of two.

```
2               = 2
2 x 2           = 4
2 x 2 x 2       = 8
2 x 2 x 2 x 2 = 16
```

We can also show these values as "powers of two".

```
2               = 2¹ or 2 to the power 1
2 x 2           = 2² or 2 to the power 2
2 x 2 x 2       = 2³ or 2 to the power 3
2 x 2 x 2 x 2 = 2⁴ or 2 to the power 4
```

This table shows the "powers of 2" for each binary value.

128	64	32	16	8	4	2	1
2^7	2^6	2^5	2^4	2^3	2^2	2^1	2^0

By mathematical convention we show 1 as 2^0.

Left-shift to multiply by 2

If we move any bit one column to the left it doubles in value. For example, this bit represents 16.

128	64	32	16	8	4	2	1
			1				

If we shift it to the left it now represents 32.

128	64	32	16	8	4	2	1
		1					

This is called a left-shift. We can use the left-shift to double the value of any binary number. We simply shift all the bits one space to the left.

For example, the binary number

```
11001
```

represents

    16 + 8 + 1 = 25

128	64	32	16	8	4	2	1
0	0	0	1	1	0	0	1

If we left-shift each bit in the number, it now looks like this. We fill in the right column with a 0.

128	64	32	16	8	4	2	1
0	0	1	1	0	0	1	0

The new number is:

    110010

that represents

    32 + 16 + 2 = 50

The number has doubled in value.

Multiply by other powers of 2

You have seen that the left-shift method multiplies a number by 2. We can use this method to multiply by any power of 2. For example, 8 is $2 \times 2 \times 2$. We can also write this as 2^3 or 2 to the power 3.

A shift three places to the left multiplies by 8, because 8 is 2 to the power 3.

Let's take the same number as before:

    11001 = 16 + 8 + 1 = 25

128	64	32	16	8	4	2	1
0	0	0	1	1	0	0	1

If we left shift each bit by three places, the result looks like this. As before, fill in the blank columns on the right with 0s.

128	64	32	16	8	4	2	1
1	1	0	0	1	0	0	0

The result is:

    11001000

Converting this to decimal we get:

    128 + 64 + 8 = 200

We see that 25 has become 200. 25 * 8 = 200. The left-shift has multiplied the original value by 8.

Writing binary multiplication

To show a binary multiplication we should write both numbers in binary form. Instead of writing the example calculation you just did as:

    11001 × 8

we should write:

    11001 × 1000

Writing both numbers in binary makes the left-shift method even easier. Count the number of 0s in the second number, and that tells you how many places to shift the first value to the left.

Syllabus reference

3.3.4 Binary arithmetic

Apply a binary shift to a binary number.

Describe situations where binary shifts can be used.

Additional information

Binary shifts can be used to perform simple division by powers of 2.

Binary division

Introduction

You have learned how to add and multiply binary numbers. Now you will learn how to divide binary numbers by powers of 2.

Right-shift

Each bit in a byte has a position value. If you shift a bit to the left it increases in value. It increases by a power of 2.

If you shift a bit to the right it decreases by a power of 2. For example, this bit represents 16.

128	64	32	16	8	4	2	1
			1				

If we shift it to the right by one column it has half the value.

128	64	32	16	8	4	2	1
				1			

Shifting a bit one column to the right divides the number by 2.

Divide by any power of 2

You can divide a binary number by any power of 2:

● Find what power of 2 you want to divide by.

● Shift the bits that many places to the right.

For example, eight is $2 \times 2 \times 2$. We can write this as 2^3 or 2 to the power 3. That means to divide by eight we shift the number to the right by three places.

For example, let's divide 01100000 by 8.

128	64	32	16	8	4	2	1
0	1	1	0	0	0	0	0

Shift every digit to the right by three places.

128	64	32	16	8	4	2	1
0	0	0	0	1	1	0	0

The answer is 00001100.

Underflow

Sometimes bits will be shifted so far to the right that some of the 1s are shifted out of the byte. The technical name for this is underflow.

Underflow may occur for example when the result of a division is not a whole number.

We are only working with whole binary numbers in this book. That means that you won't always get exactly the right answer to some division sums.

If we divide 12 by 8 the true result is 1 and a half. But the result of the binary shift would be 0000 0001.

Check your results

To check any binary division, convert both numbers to decimal. In this example the two numbers are:

        01100000 = 64 + 32 = 96

Dividing by 8 gives us:

        00001100 = 8 + 4 = 12

The sum is correct (96 divided by 8 is 12).

Writing binary division

When we write a binary division we write both numbers in binary form. Instead of writing

        01100000 ÷ 8

we write:

        01100000 ÷ 1000

This makes it easier to use the right-shift method. Simply count the number of 0s in the second number. This tells you how many columns to shift to the right.

Summary of binary multiplication and division

This table summarises the number of shifts you need when you divide or multiply any binary number by a power of 2.

I want to multiply or divide by:	As a power of 2	As a binary number	Shift by this many places
1	2^0	1	0
2	2^1	10	1
4	2^2	100	2
8	2^3	1000	3
16	2^4	10000	4
32	2^5	100000	5
64	2^6	1000000	6
128	2^7	10000000	7

Remember that if we want to multiply we shift to the left. The number gets bigger. If we want to divide we shift to the right. The number gets smaller.

Further binary calculations

There are other types of binary arithmetic not covered in this chapter. For example:

- binary subtraction
- multiplication and division by numbers that are not powers of 2
- working with numbers that are bigger than one byte.

If you continue to study computer science you will learn these additional methods. They are outside of the scope of this book.

Test yourself

Work out these binary divisions. Check your answers by converting each number and the result to its decimal value.

1.   00010100 ÷ 10

2.   11110000 ÷ 1000

3.   01011000 ÷ 100

4.   10110000 ÷ 10000

Learning activity

Work with a partner. Give your partner four binary divisions to do. When your partner gives you the answers, check the result by converting every number to decimal.

Extension activity – class project

Record a series of short videos on a phone or video camera showing how to do binary addition, multiplication and division.

Syllabus reference

3.3.5 Character encoding

Understand what a character set is and be able to describe this character encoding method: 7-bit ASCII.

Understand that character codes are commonly grouped and run in sequence within encoding tables.

Additional information

Students should be able to use a given character encoding table to: convert characters to character codes, convert character codes to characters.

3.3.8 Data compression

Be able to calculate the number of bits required to store a piece of uncompressed data in ASCII.

5.1 Character encoding

Character codes

> ### Introduction
>
> Computers work with all types of data, including numbers, text, images and sound. All these different types of data must be held in binary form inside the computer. When data is held in binary form it is called digital data. In this lesson you will learn how text characters are stored using a code called ASCII.

Digital data

"Digital" is used to refer to a value that can be represented in digits as a number of units. A digital value does not vary in a smooth curve, but can be represented by a series of distinct values. All data held inside a computer is digital because the values are held as a pattern of on/off switches. We can represent these values as binary numbers.

Text data

The computer stores text using a number code system. Every text character is given a code number. The first widely used system of text coding was called ASCII. ASCII stands for American Standard Code for Information Interchange. The first version of ASCII was produced in the USA in 1963.

ASCII has a code number for each of the common text characters on the standard American computer keyboard. There are different codes for upper-case and lower-case letters. There are codes for the other characters that can be typed on the keyboard such as punctuation.

ASCII codes

The ASCII code system is sequential. That means the number codes go up in number order. ASCII number codes can be represented as decimal, binary or hexadecimal values. The table shows the ASCII codes for some of the upper-case letters of the alphabet. The code numbers are show in decimal, binary and hexadecimal.

Character	Decimal	Binary	Hexadecimal
A	65	100 0001	41
B	66	100 0010	42
C	67	100 0011	43
D	68	100 0100	44
E	69	100 0101	45
F	70	100 0110	46
G	71	100 0111	47
H	72	100 1000	48
I	73	100 1001	49

A space between characters has the ASCII code 32. What is this in binary and hexadecimal?

ASCII characters are stored in sequence. If you know the code for the first item in the sequence you can work out the codes for the other characters:

- The decimal ASCII code for lower-case letter "a" is 97. Work out the ASCII codes for the other letters of the alphabet in decimal, binary and hexadecimal.

Numerical digits 0–9 also have sequential ASCII codes.

- The decimal ASCII code for digit 0 is 48. 1 in ASCII is 49. Work out the ASCII codes for the other digits in decimal, binary and hexadecimal.

Storage space

If you look at the table, you will see that each ASCII code is represented by a seven-bit binary number. This means ASCII has 128 different codes.

Every byte in the computer has eight bits. ASCII leaves one bit in each byte spare. This spare bit can be used for other purposes such as a parity bit. However, eight-bit versions of ASCII are also available. Eight-bit ASCII has more codes.

To find the storage space used by a text file:

- Find out how many characters are in the file. That includes spaces and punctuation marks.
- Find out the number of bits used by each ASCII code (typically 7 bits).
- Multiply the number of bits by the number of characters to give the total file size in bits.

Test yourself

1. Interpret this series of ASCII codes as a character string.

67 79 77 80 85 84 69 82 30 83 67 73 69 78 67 69

2. Interpret this series of binary ASCII codes as a character string.

1001011 1000101 1011001 1000010 1001111 1000001 1010010 1000100

3. Convert the two ASCII messages into hexadecimal.

4. A student wrote a history essay of 3000 words. The average word has five characters (including spaces and punctuation). How much storage space does the essay take up on the student's computer?

Learning activity

Create a complete ASCII table showing the decimal ASCII code for all the lower-case letters.

Extension activities

Extend the ASCII table of lower-case letters to include the binary and hexadecimal versions of all ASCII codes.

Find out the ASCII codes for a range of other keyboard characters such as comma, full stop and equals sign. Make a table of these other character codes.

Syllabus reference

3.3.5 Character encoding

Understand what a character set is and be able to describe the following character encoding method: Unicode.

Describe the purpose of Unicode and the advantages of Unicode over ASCII.

Know that Unicode uses the same codes as ASCII up to 127.

Additional information

Students should be able to explain the need for data representation of different alphabets and of special symbols allowing a far greater range of characters.

Unicode

Introduction

You have learned that **ASCII** code is used to represent standard keyboard characters in digital form. In this lesson you will learn about an extended code system called Unicode. Unicode adds extra codes to ASCII. Unicode can be used to represent other alphabets and special character sets.

The standard keyboard

The computer keyboard is the most common way to enter text characters into the computer. The standard computer keyboard was based on the typewriter. The typewriter was developed in the 19th century by people who used European writing. For this reason, standard computer keyboards use the European alphabet.

ASCII code represents the characters of the standard keyboard. It uses seven bits to represent each character. That means it can represent 128 characters.

Limitations of the standard keyboard

There are many characters that are not represented in standard ASCII.

- **Additional characters** – many European languages use variations on the standard alphabet. For example, many languages have characters with accents.

- **Other alphabets** – there are many alphabets in use in the world. Two of the most common are the Cyrillic alphabet used mainly in Russia, and the Arabic alphabet used in many other countries. There are other alphabets each used by millions of people.

- **Non-alphabet writing systems** – some writing systems such as Chinese and Japanese do not use alphabetic characters. Each word is represented by a distinctive symbol. These are called ideograms.

- **Non-text characters** – our messages often include non-text characters such as shapes and symbols. Many people use icons, emoticons or emojis to represent emotions and other concepts as small pictures.

People wanted to enter these characters into the computer. They wanted to store them and transmit them as messages. This meant ASCII was not good enough. Extra codes were needed.

Introduction of Unicode

ASCII has limitations as a character system. In the 1980s computer scientists began to develop an alternative to ASCII. This became a new character-coding system called Unicode. The aim of the Unicode system is to have a code for every character that might be needed on modern computer systems. That includes all alphabets, ideograms and other symbols.

The first 127 symbols of Unicode are the same as the characters of seven-bit ASCII. That means all ASCII messages can be read using the Unicode system.

Modern Unicode

The Internet has made it easier to communicate with people from different cultures and countries. It is important that computers can be used by people all over the world. Unicode is ideal for this purpose.

New versions of Unicode are released regularly, to keep up with suggestions and new characters that are invented. Modern Unicode represents more than 130 different writing systems. The Unicode Consortium is responsible for maintaining Unicode and allocating codes.

Unicode is now the standard for all computer systems, communications and Internet content. Version 9.0 of Unicode, released in 2016, has 128,237 different character codes.

Released	Unicode Version	Sample Character			
		B&W	Color	Code	Name
1991–10	1.0			U+270F	*pencil*
2008-10-01	5.2			U+2614	*umbrella with rain drops*
2010-10-11	6.0			U+1F60E	*smiling face with sunglasses*
2014-06-16	7.0			U+1F336	*hot pepper*

⬆ This table shows some common images and the hexadecimal code for each one

Extension – storage space

Unicode includes more codes than ASCII. To store longer code numbers takes more storage space. A Unicode file can use more than one byte of storage per character. This is likely to be the case if the file includes characters that are not part of the standard English language character set.

Test yourself

1. The letter "a" has the ASCII value 97. What is its value in Unicode?

2. What is the advantage of Unicode over ASCII as a way of representing text?

3. Unicode text can use more storage space than ASCII text. Explain why.

4. The growth of the Internet has made it even more important to replace ASCII by Unicode. Explain why.

Learning activity

Investigate some of the different alphabets and writing systems in use in the world today.

Do you know any writing systems as well as the standard European alphabet? Find out how one writing system other than the European alphabet is represented in Unicode.

Extension activity

This page shows a table of common emojis. Create an extended table showing a range of different emojis and their codes.

Syllabus reference

3.2.8 String handling operations in a programming language

Understand and be able to use string conversion operations:

- convert character to character code
- convert character code to character.

Converting text to characters

Introduction

You have learned that ASCII and Unicode represent all characters as numbers. Python includes commands that let us convert all characters into their equivalent code number. In this lesson you will learn how to do this.

Find character code values

Every letter or other character has a Unicode value. You can test this out in the Python shell.

The Python function `ord()` will tell you the Unicode value of any character. Put a character inside the brackets. The Unicode number value is created by the function.

Open the Python shell and enter this command.

```
ord("A")
```

The computer will show the value 65, which is the Unicode value of capital A. Try putting other characters and keyboard symbols inside the brackets. If you put more than one character inside the brackets you will get an error message.

Example

This Python program will take any character input by the user and show its ASCII code.

```python
character = input("enter a single character: ")
if len(character)>1:
    character = character[0]
print("the character",character)
print("has the ASCII value", ord(character))
```

If the user enters a string of more than one character, the computer will reduce it to the first character in the string.

ASCII or Unicode?

Python uses Unicode so it can process additional characters.

For the standard keyboard characters ASCII and Unicode values are identical.

Turn code values into characters

The Python function `chr()` will tell you the character that matches any Unicode number. Put any number value inside the brackets. The function will return the equivalent Unicode character.

Open the Python shell and enter this command:

```
chr(99)
```

The computer will show the character "c", which has the Unicode value 99. Try putting other whole numbers inside the brackets. If you put a number with a decimal point you will get an error message.

Example

This Python program will take a value input by the user and show the character which has that Unicode value.

```python
code = input("Enter a Unicode value: ")
code = int(code)
print("The Unicode value",code)
print("represents the character", chr(code))
```

The value entered by the user is converted to an integer. Then the integer is converted to an ASCII character.

If you enter a larger number, you will see characters matching some of the extended Unicode values.

```
Enter a Unicode value: 13312
The Unicode value 13312
represents the character 㐀
```

Test yourself

1. Write the Python command to show the ASCII code for the character %.

2. Write the Python command to show the character represented by the ASCII code 40.

3. What does this Python command do?

```
character = character[0]
```

4. Write a Python program that will accept an input of a string of several characters, and print out the ASCII value of each one.

Learning activity

Create the two programs shown on this page and test them to find the ASCII code values of a range of characters.

Extension activity

Create an extended program with a menu that will let users choose whether to convert ASCII numbers to characters or characters to ASCII numbers. Put this menu inside a loop so users can repeat this activity until they type X to exit the program.

Syllabus reference

3.3.6 Representing images

Understand what a pixel is and be able to describe how pixels relate to an image and the way images are displayed.

Describe the following for bitmaps: size in pixels, colour depth.

Describe how a bitmap represents an image using pixels and colour depth.

Describe using examples how the number of pixels and colour depth can affect the file size of a bitmap image.

Calculate bitmap image file sizes based on the number of pixels and colour depth.

Images

Bitmaps and pixels

> ### Introduction
>
> You have learned that text and numbers are held in binary form in the computer's memory. Starting in this section you will learn how images are stored.

Pictures and pixels

Images can be stored in the computer in digital form. A digital picture is composed of thousands or millions of tiny points. These are called pixels. Pixel is short for picture element. A pixel is the smallest editable part of a picture. That is, one pixel is the smallest possible dot that we can change. When the image is displayed in a computer screen each pixel is a point of light. When an image is printed, each pixel is a dot of ink.

A computer stores an image by storing the location and colour of every pixel in the image. Information about all the pixels in an image is called the bitmap.

Size of an image

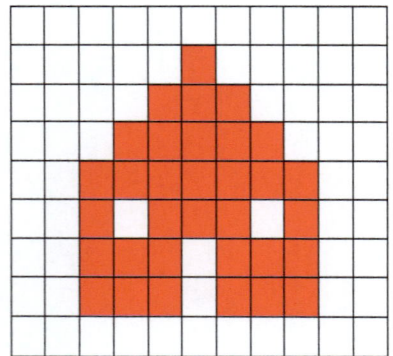

A bitmap represents an image as a grid of points. Here is a simple example. Of course, if this image were shown on the screen of your computer each point in the grid would be very small.

This image is 11 pixels wide and 9 pixels high. The image has 99 pixels.

$$11 \times 9 = 99$$

We can calculate the size of any image by multiplying the width in pixels, by the height in pixels.

"Monochrome" means using only one colour and white. To store an image in monochrome we can store each pixel using a single bit of data: 1 means colour, 0 means white.

Colour depth

Instead of storing an image in monochrome we can store it in colour. Every pixel is stored in the computer as a code number. The code number tells the computer what colour to make the pixel.

The colour depth of an image means the range of different colours that can be used in the image. An image with high colour depth can use a lot of colours. An image with low colour depth must be made of only a few colours.

These are features of an image with low colour depth:

- The colour code is a short number.
- The colour codes don't take up so much space.
- There are only a few colour codes.

An example of low colour depth is 256-colour. Each colour code uses only one byte, but there are only 256 different colour codes.

These are features of an image with high colour depth:

- The colour code is a long number, or made of several numbers added together.
- The colour codes take up more space.
- There are lots of different colour codes.

An example of high colour depth is 24-bit colour. Each colour code uses three bytes. There are more than 16 million different colour codes. Find out more about 24-bit colour on the next page.

How many bits?

In any coding system the range of values that can be stored is limited by the number of bits of storage available. You learned about binary numbers in chapter 4. A 4-bit binary number can store all the integers from 0 to 15 (16 different values). An 8-bit binary number can store all the integers from 0 to 255 (256 different values). So a 16-colour system would take 4 bits per pixel. A 256-colour range would take 8 bits.

File size

To find the file size of a bitmap image you multiply the number of pixels by the number of bytes used in the colour code.

The image of the house has 99 pixels (it is 11 pixels wide and 9 pixels high):

- If this image were stored using 256-colour, each pixel would use 8 bits. The total number of bits used by the image would be 99 multiplied by 8. That is 792 bits or 99 bytes.
- If this image were stored using 24-bit colour the storage requirement would be 24 multiplied by 99. This gives a total file size of 2376 bits or 287 bytes.

Test yourself

These questions are about an image 700 pixels wide and 900 pixels tall.

1. What is the size of the image in pixels?

2. If the image is made using 256 colours what is the file size of the image?

3. If the image is made using 24-bit colour what is the file size of the image?

4. Explain why a high colour depth makes a more realistic-looking image.

Learning activity

Make a 9 × 11 grid like the one shown. Use it to create a range of simple bitmap images. Make some images in colour and some images in black and white.

Extension activity

Explore the use of any graphics software that creates bitmap images. One example is MS Paint, which comes free as part of the Windows package.

Syllabus reference

3.3.6 Representing images

Describe, using examples, how the number of pixels and colour depth can affect the file size of a bitmap image.

Image quality and file size

Introduction

The file size of an image depends on how many pixels it contains. It also depends on how many bits are used to store the colour of each pixel. In this lesson you will learn how these factors combine to affect image quality and file size.

Image resolution

To measure the number of pixels in an image you measure the width of the image in pixels, and the height of the image in pixels. Then you multiply width by height.

An image will have more pixels if it is:

- a large image
- a high-resolution image.

High resolution means the pixels that make up the image are small. This means the image can be sharper with clear details. High-resolution images are better quality. However, because they have more pixels they have a larger file size.

Pixelation

If the pixels of an image are too large the image will look grainy and blurred. You will be able to see the dots that make up the image. We call this a pixelated image. Some people use the term "bitmapped" to describe this effect.

This effect can be produced if the image has low resolution. Pixelation gets worse if the image is made larger. Low-resolution images have fewer pixels, so they have a smaller file size.

RGB colour

Colour depth means the number of bits used to store colour information. Many modern images use 24-bit colour. This system uses three bytes for every pixel. Each byte can store a number from 0 to 255. Here are some details:

- The first byte stores the amount of red in the image. The number 0 means no red. The number 255 means maximum red.
- The second byte stores the amount of green in the image. The number 0 means no green. The number 255 means maximum green.
- The third byte stores the amount of blue in the image. The number 0 means no blue. The number 255 means maximum blue.

If all the values are set to 0 the colour is black. If all the values are set to 255 the combined colour is pure white.

Combining all possible values of red, blue and green makes this many colours:

$$256 \times 256 \times 256 = 16,777,216$$

⬆ This is an example of a high-resolution image

⬆ This is an example of a pixelated (bitmapped) image

⬆ Red green and blue light mix to make white light

The 24-bit **RGB** colour code can represent more than 16 million different colours. This gives a realistic image. The human eye can see about 10 million different colours.

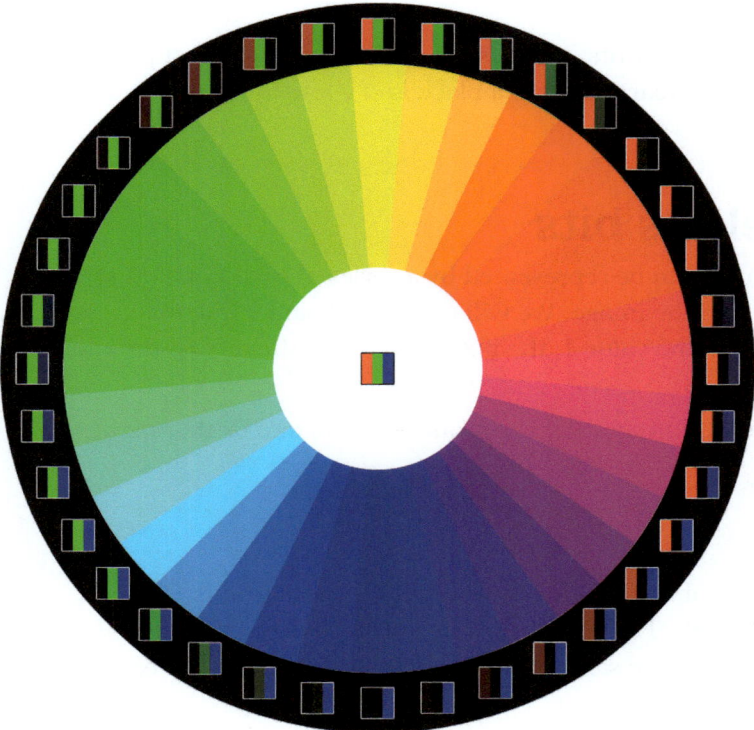

⬆ The colours made by using the red, green and blue light in each pixel at various intensities.

Notice that the colour depth does not tell you how many colours are used in the image. It tells you the range of available colours. A 24-bit colour code means a lot of colours are available, even if not all the colours are used.

Test yourself

1. What does high resolution mean? What is the advantage of a high-resolution image? What is the disadvantage?

2. In the RGB colour system if red, green and blue are set to maximum what is the colour that you see?

3. What is the advantage of high colour depth? What is the disadvantage?

4. What does pixelation mean? What can cause an image to be pixelated?

Learning activity

Using a search engine such as www.kiddle.co, find examples of high-resolution and low-resolution images on the Internet. Compare the difference in quality of these two types of image.

Extension activity

Load a high-resolution image into a graphics package. Save the image using different resolutions and colour settings. See what effect this has on file size.

Turn an image into binary

Syllabus reference

3.3.6 Representing images

Convert binary data into an image.

Additional information

Given a binary pattern that represents a bitmap, students should be able to draw the resulting image as a series of pixels.

Convert an image into binary data.

Additional information

Given a bitmap, students should be able to write down a bit pattern that represents the image.

Introduction

You have learned how a bitmap represents an image as a grid of pixels. In this lesson you will learn to store a black and white image using the bitmap system.

Store pixels as bits

A monochrome image can be represented by a series of bits. Each bit stands for one of the pixels in the image. We will use a black and white image as an example. If the bit has the value 1, the pixel is black. If the bit has the value 0, the pixel is white.

To store the image, we simply store the sequence of 1s and 0s that make the image.

Example

Here is an example of a monochrome image. The pixel grid is 11 pixels wide and 9 pixels high. The size of the pixel grid would be stored in the image file. Next to it is the same image, showing the bit value of each pixel.

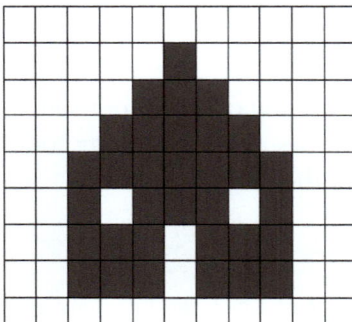

We can take the 1s and 0s out of the grid to make a sequence of bits.

0 0 0 0 0 0 0 0 0 0 0 0 0 0 0 0 0 1 0 0 0 0 0 0 0 0 0 1 1 1 0 0 0 0 0 0 0 1 1 1 1 1
0 0 0 0 0 1 1 1 1 1 1 1 0 0 0 0 1 0 1 1 1 0 1 0 0 0 0 1 1 1 0 1 1 1 0 0 0 0 1 1 1
0 1 1 1 0 0 0 0 0 0 0 0 0 0 0 0

Turn bits into pixels

The same method will turn a sequence of bits into a black and white image. Put the bit sequence into a pixel grid. If the bit is 0, the pixel is white. If the bit is 1, the pixel is black. As before, you must know the width and height of the pixel grid. This will be stored as part of the image file, along with the bit sequence.

Example

Here is a bit sequence. We are told this represents a monochrome image. The image is 13 pixels wide and 13 pixels high.

0000000000000000001110000000010011100000000
1000100000000111111110000000001110100000000
0111010000000001110100000000010100000000001
0100000000000101000000000000101000000000000
00000

The first step is to copy the bits into a 13×13 pixel grid. The next step is to replace the bits with black and white: 0 becomes white and 1 becomes black to see the completed image.

To convert a series of bits into an image, you will need to know:

- the size of the pixel grid (width and height)
- whether 1 stands for white or black – it could be either.

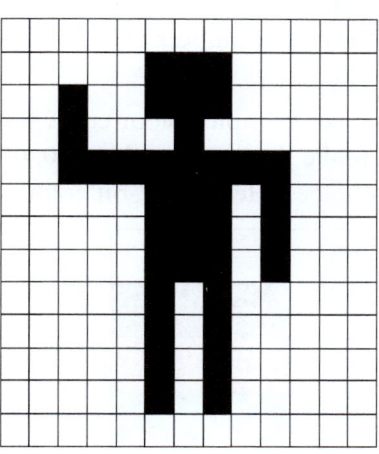

0	0	0	0	0	0	0	0	0	0	0	0	0
0	0	0	0	0	1	1	1	0	0	0	0	0
0	0	1	0	0	1	1	1	0	0	0	0	0
0	0	1	0	0	0	1	0	0	0	0	0	0
0	0	1	1	1	1	1	1	1	0	0	0	0
0	0	0	0	0	1	1	0	1	0	0	0	0
0	0	0	0	0	1	1	0	1	0	0	0	0
0	0	0	0	0	1	1	0	1	0	0	0	0
0	0	0	0	0	1	0	0	0	0	0	0	0
0	0	0	0	0	1	0	1	0	0	0	0	0
0	0	0	0	0	1	0	1	0	0	0	0	0
0	0	0	0	0	1	0	1	0	0	0	0	0
0	0	0	0	0	0	0	0	0	0	0	0	0

Colour images

Other images are in colour. Each pixel in the grid is stored as a byte, or even a series of bytes. The value of each byte represents a colour code. Find out more about turning a bitstream into a coloured image on the next page.

Learning activity

Work with a partner. You make a bitmap pixel grid on paper as shown here. Create a monochrome image by shading in some of the cells of the grid. Turn the image into a series of 1s and 0s. Pass these numbers to your partner. Tell your partner the size of the pixel grid. Ask your partner to turn the series of bits back into a monochrome image. Swap roles: you recreate your partner's image using the numbers you are given.

Extension activity

Given a sequence of n bits, how would you work out the size of the image it represents? Some values of n cannot be turned into a rectangular grid. Other values have multiple possible solutions.

Send your partner a sequence of bits without telling them the grid size. See if they can work out the correct dimensions of the image.

Test yourself

Turn this series of bits into a monochrome bitmap image. The pixel grid is 12 by 12.

000000000000011111111111001000000001001010111111
010010100001010010100101010100101011101010010000
001010011111111101000000000001001111111111110000
000000000

Syllabus reference

3.3.6 Representing images

Convert binary data into an image.

Additional information

Given a binary pattern that represents a bitmap, students should be able to draw the resulting image as a series of pixels.

Convert an image into binary data.

Additional information

Given a bitmap, students should be able to write down a bit pattern that represents the image.

Creating coloured images

Introduction

You have learned how a bitmap represents an image as a grid of pixels. You have learned how a black and white image can be presented as a sequence of 1s and 0s. A series of 1s and 0s is called a bitstream. It is also possible to store full colour images using a bitstream. You will learn how in this lesson.

Colour code

Before you can turn a bitstream into a colour image you must know the colour code system in use.

You have learned that colours are stored as code numbers. If the code numbers are long there are many colour choices, but each code takes a lot of bits. If the code numbers are short less storage is needed. But there are not so many colours.

Here is a very simple colour code. It uses only two bits per pixel. With two bits we can make the four numbers 00, 01, 10 and 11. That means we have four colour choices. Here is a 2-bit colour code based on these four code numbers.

Code	Colour
00	⬛
01	🟧
10	🟦
11	

A table like this that matches code numbers to colours is called a Colour Look-Up Table (CLUT) or a colour palette. Before you code or decode a bitmap image as a bitstream you must know the colour codes.

Turn a bit sequence into a colour image

To turn a bitstream into an image we must know the size of the image: how many pixels wide, and how many pixels high. We must know how many bits are used to store each colour code. Let us call that number n.

Then we count through the bit sequence:

- count the first n bits
- turn it into a number
- use the CLUT to find the colour that matches that number
- put that colour into the grid in position 1.

We count like this through the whole bit sequence. We put the right colour into every pixel of the image. Of course the computer can do this very fast.

Example

Here is an example of a tile design which uses a 7×7 grid of pixels. It uses the two-bit colour code table you saw earlier. The design is transmitted using a sequence of bits. Here are the first 14 bits in the sequence:

1110111011101110

We know each pixel is stored using two bits. So let us split the bits into groups of two:

11-10-11-10-11-10-11

Check the CLUT. 11 represents white, and 10 represents blue. So the first 7 pixels look like this.

The next 14 bits represent one blue pixel and six red pixels and look like this:

10-01-01-01-01-01-01

Here is the completed tile design. 7×7 = 49. It has 49 pixels. Each pixel uses two bits. So this image takes 98 bits of storage.

Turn a colour image into a bit sequence

We can also do this conversion in the other direction. We can turn a colour image into a sequence of bits.

- Check the colour of the first pixel in the image
- Look up that colour in the CLUT
- Add this binary number to the bit sequence

Repeat this process for every pixel in the image.

Example

Here is an example tile design using the 7×7 grid.

The first pixel is white, the next black and the third red. The three colour codes are 11, 00 and 01. Write the numbers in sequence:

11-00-01

Here is the complete bitstream for the first row of the image:

11000100110011

Syllabus reference

3.3.7 Representing sound

Understand that sound is analogue and that it must be converted to a digital form for storage and processing in a computer.

Understand that sound waves are sampled to create the digital version of sound. Understand that a sample is a measure of amplitude at a point in time.

Describe the digital representation of sound in terms of:

- sampling rate – that is, the number of samples taken in a second and is usually measured in hertz (1 Hertz = 1 sample per second)

- sample resolution – that is, the number of bits per sample.

Analogue sound

> ## Introduction
>
> You have learned how the computer holds numbers, characters and images. Starting in this section you will learn how the computer holds sound in digital form.

All sounds are formed by movements in the air. We call these movements sound waves. A sensitive mechanism in our ears is affected by the sound waves. We experience this as hearing the sounds.

Sound waves move like the waves you can see on water. The sound does not suddenly jump from one value to another. Instead it has continual smooth change. A value like this is called an analogue value. You can represent analogue values as a smooth curve. The signal can include any value in the range. A microphone can turn a sound into an 'wave' of electricity. But a computer has to store the sounds in a digital form. Digital recording involves the conversion of analogue sound to digital information.

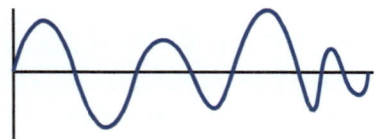

⬆ An analogue wave

Amplitude and frequency

There are two ways to measure the size of the sound waves:

- **Amplitude** is how tall the waves are on the graph. High amplitude waves reach a higher level on the graph. The amplitude tells you how loud the sounds are. High amplitude sounds are very loud.

- **Frequency** is how quickly the waves follow each other. High frequency waves are narrow and close together. The frequency tells you the pitch of the note. High-frequency sounds are high in pitch. Low-frequency sounds are low in pitch.

Digital recording

Inside the computer, values are not held in analogue form. All values inside the computer are made of 1s and 0s. The signal does not change smoothly. Instead it must jump from one number value to another. The values in between are not represented.

When a sound is recorded on the computer it must be converted from analogue to digital form.

The image shows how a smooth analogue wave is broken up into a series of digital values. A recording device measures the amplitude of the wave at regular intervals. The amplitude is stored as a digital value.

⬆ A digital recording

Sampling

The changing amplitude is measured thousands of times per second. This is called sampling. The more often the sample is taken the better the sound quality:

- If the sampling rate is high, many digital values are stored. More detail of the sound will be recorded. High-frequency sounds will be recorded. The digital recording will sound a lot like the original analogue sound.

- If the sampling rate is low, fewer digital values are recorded. There is less detail. Only lower frequencies are recorded. The digital recording does not sound so realistic.

However, a high sample rate has disadvantages. There are more digital values to store. The sound file is larger.

Hertz measurement

The sampling rate is measured in Hertz (abbreviated to Hz). 1 Hz means one sample per second. 1000 Hz means a thousand samples per second.

Test yourself

1. What is the name for a value that changes smoothly, and can have any value within a given range?
2. What is the name for a value that can only have certain set values, and not the values in between?
3. A digital recording turns the amplitude of a wave into a digital value. If the digital value is large, what does this tell us about the sound?
4. The points of highest amplitude can be close together or far apart. If the points of high amplitude are close together what does that tell us about the sound?
5. Explain why a high sampling rate means higher quality sound.

Learning activity

Draw a diagram to show sound waves. Mark the amplitude and frequency of the waves.

Extension activity

Investigate what a podcast is. Listen to an example of a podcast on the subject of technology. Write and record a sound file discussing audio formats.

Syllabus reference

3.3.7 Representing sound

Calculate sound file sizes based on the sampling rate and the sample resolution.

Additional information

File size (bits) = rate (Hz) × res × secs

rate = sampling rate (Hz)

res = sample resolution

secs = number of seconds.

Calculate file sizes

Introduction

You have learned that a digital recording is made by sampling analogue sound. In this lesson you will learn how the quality of a sound file is related to the file's size.

Sample rate

A digital recording is made by turning a smooth analogue wave into a series of number values. This is called sampling. A higher sample rate means higher-quality sound. Full CD-quality audio recordings have a sample rate of about 44,000 samples per second (44,000 Hz).

Sample resolution

The computer turns the amplitude of the wave into a number. The computer might use one byte (8 bits) or two bytes (16 bits) to store the amplitude.

A low-quality recording uses one byte (eight bits). One byte can make 256 different numbers. Each sample must use one of these 256 numbers. The amplitude might have to be rounded up or down to the nearest number. A narrower range of amplitudes can be recorded. When this happens, there is a loss of sound quality.

A high-quality recording uses 2 bytes (16 bits). Two bytes can make more than 65,000 different numbers. The numbers will be a close match to the real sound values. The recording will be high quality.

The number of bits used to record an amplitude is known as the bit depth or sample resolution.

Bit rate

The number of bits used to store one second of sound or video is called bit rate. The bit rate of a sound recording depends on:

- sample rate (number of times the sound value changes per second)
- bit depth (range of sound values available)
- number of channels (monophonic, stereophonic, quadrophonic – see "Extension" below).

We multiply these three values to give the bit rate.

High-quality sound and video has a high bit rate. For example, full CD-quality audio has these features.

Feature	Value
Sample rate	44,100 Hz
Sample resolution	16 bits per sample

The storage size for one second of one channel of high-quality audio is:

44,100 * 16 = 705,600 bits

Formats that use less storage provide lower-quality sound. CD quality is higher than MP3 quality. The lowest quality is used in landline phones. Imagine listening to music over the phone. The quality would be low.

File size

The bit rate tells you the number of bits per second. To find the file size multiply the bit rate by the number of seconds in the recording.

For example, one channel of high-quality audio uses 705,600 bits per second. One minute would be:

> 705600 * 60 = 42,336,000

To convert bits to bytes we divide by 8. (Bytes can also be converted to kilobytes, megabytes, etc.)

One minute of audio	
Bits	42,336,000 b
Bytes	5,292,000 B
Kilobytes	5,292 kB
Megabytes	5.29 MB

Extension – channels

Sound can be recorded using one or more channels:

- Sound recorded on a single channel is known as monophonic.
- Sound recorded on two channels is known as stereophonic.
- Sound recorded on four channels is known as quadrophonic.

Stereo or quadrophonic sound is more realistic than monophonic sound. We hear natural sound coming from different directions around us. Stereophonic and quadrophonic sounds reflect this. The more channels, the greater the file size – the bit rate is simply multiplied by the number of channels.

Test yourself

1. One minute of high-quality sound uses about 5 MB of storage. How much storage does one hour of high-quality sound use?

2. A low-quality recording has a sample resolution of eight bits per sample. It has a sample rate of 8,000 Hz. What is the bit rate?

3. In question 2 you calculated the bit rate of a low-quality recording. What is the size of a file storing one minute of sound at this bit rate?

4. Explain why a higher sample resolution gives a higher quality of sound.

Extension activity

Find examples of a song you like recorded in various different audio formats. For example listen to the same song on a CD and on an MP3 player. Can you tell the difference in sound quality? Does this affect your enjoyment of the music? Write a report on your findings.

Learning activity

Find a sound clip on the Internet – for example by searching for 'public domain sounds'. What is the length of the clip in seconds? What is the file size? From this information calculate the approximate bit rate.

Syllabus reference

3.3.8 Data compression

Explain what data compression is.

Understand why data may be compressed and that there are different ways to compress data.

Additional information

Students should understand that it is common for data to be compressed and should be able to explain why it may be necessary or desirable to compress data.

5.4 Compression

Why compression is important

> ### Introduction
>
> You have learned that digital files can be very large. Now you will learn about methods to reduce the size of digital files. Making a file smaller is called compression.

A computer stores text, audio, image and video data in digital format. The data files can be very large. These are the disadvantages of large files:

- They use a lot of the computer's electronic memory, making the computer work more slowly.
- They take up a lot of space in storage such as on a DVD or a flash drive.
- Large files are slow to send over the Internet.

Lossless or lossy?

There are many different compression methods. The different methods are described as lossless or lossy:

- **Lossless** compression reduces the size of a data file. There is no loss of data quality. Perfect lossless compression is hard to achieve.
- **Lossy** compression produces a bigger reduction, but data quality is reduced. Some of the detail of the file is lost.

Losing quality

There are a number of ways to compress a file. One way is to reduce the quality of the data.

The size of an image file depends on the number of pixels and the number of bytes used to store each pixel. The file size of an image can be reduced by:

- using low resolution – the image is made with fewer pixels
- reducing colour depth – fewer colours can be used.

Both methods reduce image quality. They are lossy compression methods.

Colour look-up table

In 24-bit colour there are 16 million possible colours. However, most images do not use all the colours.

The computer can compress an image by making a short list of colours. It only stores the colours it needs for that image. This short list is called a colour look-up table or a colour palette.

Each colour in the palette is given a short code. The computer stores the short codes in the image file in place of the 24-bit colour codes.

Compressed sound

The bit rate of a sound recording means the number of bits used to store one second of sound. Sound compression reduces the bit rate of the recording.

For example, by:

- using fewer channels (for example changing stereophonic to monophonic)
- having a lower sample rate (fewer samples per second)
- reducing sample resolution (using fewer bits to store each sample by removing higher and lower sounds).

Compressed video

Modern high definition TV (HDTV) uses a lot of storage space. Video compression means reducing the bit rate. To do this you can reduce:

- the number of audio channels
- the sample rate
- the image quality (for example the number of pixels per image).

Decompression

The computer can compress a data file. It must also be able to decompress the file. That means the computer must be able to restore the data file.

If lossless compression has been used the computer will be able to decompress the file in full. The decompressed file will have all the detail it originally had before compression.

If lossy compression has been used the computer will not be able to restore the file in full detail. Some detail and quality will be lost by compression.

Test yourself

1. What are the advantages and disadvantages of file compression?

2. In your own words, explain the difference between lossless and lossy compression.

3. A high-resolution image is made of lots of small pixels. What do you think are the advantages and disadvantages of high-resolution image files?

4. Describe how the file size of an audio recording might be reduced, and the likely effect on sound quality.

Learning activity

Take a photo or download one from the Internet. Copy the photo into a graphics package such as Microsoft Paint. Save the photo using several different file formats. See how the change in format affects the size of the file and the quality of the image.

Extension activity

Record a sound or video file. Use sound or video editing equipment to reduce the file size. What difference does it make to the quality?

Syllabus reference

3.3.8 Data compression

Explain how data can be compressed using run length encoding (RLE).

Additional information

Students should be familiar with the process of using frequency/data pairs to reduce the amount of data stored.

Represent data in RLE frequency/data pairs.

Additional information

Students could be given a bitmap representation and they would be expected to show the frequency and value pairs for each row. For example, 0000011100000011 would become 5 0 3 1 6 0 2 1

Run-length encoding

Introduction

You have learned that it is often necessary to compress a data file. One method of compression is called run-length encoding (RLE). In this section you will learn what RLE is. You will learn to compress data using RLE.

RLE

Many data files include a lot of repetition. RLE works by removing repetition in a data file.

Here is an example of part of an uncompressed data file. The data is shown as decimal numbers, but it could be data in any form.

> 19 19 19 19 18 18 18 18 18 18 19 19 19 19 19 19 19 19 18 18 18 18 18 18 18 18 18

We can simplify this sequence by saying how many times each value is repeated: 19 is repeated 4 times, then 18 is repeated 6 times, and so on. Here is the whole sequence.

Frequency	Value
4	19
6	18
8	19
9	18

The first number tells you the frequency. That is the number of times the value is repeated. The second number tells you the data value that is repeated.

This is an example of RLE. Storing the data using RLE would look like this:

> 4 19 6 18 8 19 9 18

Data compressed using RLE takes up less storage space. In a real data file, the sequences might be much longer than this example, perhaps with thousands of repetitions. The effects of RLE can be a very big reduction in file size.

Use of number bases

In the example above, the data and the number of repetitions are both shown as decimal numbers. Both values could be shown as binary, decimal or hexadecimal values. Remember that inside the computer, and in a stored computer file, all data is shown as a series of 1s and 0s. We use different number bases to display the data for human beings to understand.

Compress a bitstream

We can use the RLE method to compress a bitstream. A bitstream is a series of 1s and 0s. Here is an example of a bitstream:

> 0000001111100000000011111111111110000

We can compress this data using the RLE method.

Frequency	Value
6	0
5	1
8	0
12	1
4	0

Showing this as a data stream gives:

6 0 5 1 8 0 12 1 4 0

You will see that in this example the frequency is represented as a decimal number. The data is represented as a bit. This is one way of representing the compressed data.

Frequency–value pairs

RLE compresses data by removing repetition. The data is represented using pairs of numbers called frequency–value pairs. The first number represents the frequency – how many repetitions. The second value represents the value that is repeated.

Compress using RLE

To compress any data stream using RLE, use this method:

- Look at the first value in the data stream. Count how many times it is repeated.

- Write down the number of repetitions, followed by the value that is repeated. This is a frequency–value pair.

- Go on to the next value in the data stream and turn it into a frequency–value pair

- Continue until all the values in the data stream have been turned into frequency–value pairs.

The RLE file is the sequence of all the frequency–value pairs.

Test yourself

Represent each of these bitstreams using run length encoding. You may show the frequency value using decimal, followed by the value of the bit (1 or 0).

1. 00000000001100011111111111110000000000

2. 000001111111111110000000000001111111

3. 000000011110000000001100000000001111

4. 111111111110000000000001111111111000

Learning activity

On page 165 you represented bitmap images as a bitstream. Use RLE to convert your bitmap data into frequency–value pairs.

Extension activity

Share the RLE version of a bitmap with a partner. Convert the compressed bitstream from your partner into a bitmap image.

Syllabus reference

3.3.8 Data compression

Explain how data can be compressed using Huffman coding.

Additional information

Students should be familiar with the process of using a tree to represent the Huffman code.

Be able to interpret Huffman trees.

Additional information

Students should be able to interpret a given Huffman tree to determine the code used for a particular node within the tree.

Huffman coding

Introduction

You have learned that RLE stores data in frequency–value pairs. Each of the values is stored as a string of bits. In this lesson you will learn how values are coded in a process known as Huffman coding.

Representing values

You have learned that there are many ways to represent values as binary numbers. For example:

- Images use colour codes.
- Characters are recorded using ASCII or Unicode.
- Sound files store amplitude as a binary value.

High-quality data needs longer numbers. Using longer numbers allows a wider range of values. The data is more varied and precise. However, this leads to the problem that the data files are very large.

Huffman coding

One solution is to change the system of coding. Huffman coding is a way of coding data that uses less storage than other systems. Huffman coding uses a smaller code number to store values that appear more often. It uses longer code numbers to store values that appear less often.

Example – an image file

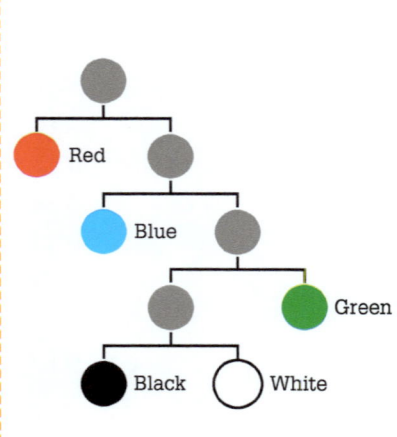

Let's take an example of an image file that had 272 pixels. The pixels were red, blue, green, black and white. Some colours were used more often than others, like this:

- red: 107 pixels
- blue: 75 pixels
- green: 60 pixels
- white: 20 pixels
- black: 10 pixels.

We can put these values into a Huffman tree. The Huffman tree is built from the data file. The arrangement of data values in the tree depends on the frequency of the data values in the file.

Huffman tree

Data values that appear more often in the file are higher up in the Huffman tree.

This example Huffman tree is made from the colour data listed above. Red is the most common colour, and it appears high in the tree. Black and white are the least common colours and they appear low down in the tree.

Find the Huffman code for a value

We can use a Huffman tree to find a binary code for any value in the tree. We do this by tracing a path from the top of the tree to the value we want. Here are the rules:

- Start at the top of the tree.
- Every time you take a **left** branch write a 0.
- Every time you take a **right** branch write a 1.
- Stop when you have got to the value you want

To find the Huffman code for red:

- Start at the top
- Take the left branch (0).

That is all you need to do. In this example, the code for red is 0.

In this data file red is a frequent value. Its code is very short.

Find the value from a Huffman code

You can also turn a binary code into a value. 1 means take the right branch. 0 means take the left branch.

For example, using the value 1101:

- Start at the top.
- Take the right branch (1).
- Take the right branch (1).
- Take the left branch (0).
- Take the right branch (1).

You have now reached the value you want. The value is: white. White is a less frequent value than other values. Its code is longer.

Saving space

The full 24-bit code for a colour value is stored only once. Colour codes are stored in a colour look-up table. Then each value in the table is given a short look-up code. The look-up code is used in the image file. The computer will use the Huffman system to allocate the look-up codes. The most frequent colours will be given the shortest codes.

Learning activity

Use a graphics package to copy the Huffman tree shown on this page. Or draw it neatly using pens.

Test yourself

Look at the example Huffman tree shown on the previous page.

1. Find the code for blue.

2. Find the code for green.

3. Find the code for black.

Extension activity

By multiplying the length of code for each colour by the colour frequency, find the total length in bits of the image file described on the previous page.

Syllabus reference

3.3.8 Data compression

Be able to build a Huffman tree.

Additional information

Students should be able to build a Huffman tree for a given string of data.

Build a Huffman tree

Introduction

In this lesson you will learn to build a Huffman tree from a set of data values.

The parts of a Huffman tree

Each connector in a Huffman tree is called a node. Each node has two branches coming out of it. In the examples in this book the nodes are shown as circles.

The top node in a Huffman tree is called the root. The end node of a branch is called a leaf. A leaf has no more branches coming out of it. The data values are stored in the leaf nodes. On this page they are shown as green circles.

Two rules of a Huffman tree

There are two rules when you make a Huffman tree:

- Values go in pairs.
- The more frequent value goes on the right.

If you remember these rules you will be able to make a Huffman tree.

Making a Huffman tree

You can make a Huffman tree from any data file with repeated values. Look through the file. Find out what values it contains. Count how often each value occurs in the file. That is the frequency. Put the values into a table with their frequencies.

Here is an example. A data file has five values in it. We will call them A, B, C, D and E. Here are the frequencies.

Value	Frequency
A	14
B	19
C	21
D	22
E	37

We start with the lowest frequency pair. In this case it is A and B. We take the pair of values from the table and put it into the tree. Put the lower frequency on the left. Add the frequencies together to create a parent node.

We take the two lowest frequencies out of the table. We replace them with the parent node. Put the values in order of frequency. Now the frequency list looks like this.

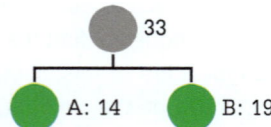

Value	Frequency
C	21
D	22
Parent	33
E	37

We create a pair from C and D. The parent node has the value 43.

Now the frequency list looks like this.

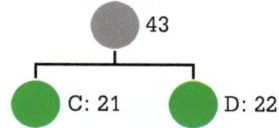

Value	Frequency
Parent	33
E	37
Parent	43

The lowest two frequencies are 33 and 37. These can be combined.

The table only has two values left.

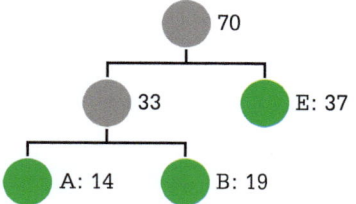

Value	Frequency
Parent	43
Parent	70

Completing the table by combining the two remaining nodes gives this pattern.

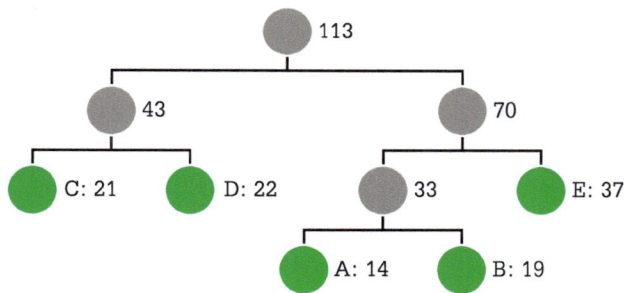

Test yourself

Answer these questions about the Huffman tree shown on this page.

1. What is the code for E?

2. What is the code for A?

3. What value has the code 00?

4. What value has the code 101?

Learning activity

On page 174 you saw a Huffman tree made from these values:

- red: 107 pixels
- green: 60 pixels
- black: 10 pixels.
- blue: 75 pixels
- white: 20 pixels

Use the method shown on this page to turn these values into a Huffman tree. It should match the example shown on page 174.

Extension activity

Draw a Huffman tree for these values and frequencies.

Value	Frequency
A	1000
B	500
C	100
D	50
E	20

Huffman compression

Syllabus reference

3.3.8 Data compression

Calculate the number of bits required to store a piece of data compressed using Huffman coding.

Additional information

Students should be able to build a Huffman tree for a given string of data and show how the string would be compressed using the tree.

Introduction

You have learned that a Huffman tree gives shorter codes to frequent data values. This makes a file smaller. Now you will learn how much you can compress a file using Huffman coding.

Colour look-up

Here is an example of a colour look-up table. The image has 272 pixels. Each colour is given a three-bit code. This table does not use Huffman coding. The colours are just numbered in order. We can find the size of the data file by multiplying the number of bits in the colour code by the frequency of each colour.

Colour	Code	Frequency	Number of bits
Red	000	107	3 * 107 = 321
Blue	001	75	3 * 75 = 225
Green	010	60	3 * 60 = 180
White	011	20	3 * 20 = 60
Black	100	10	3 * 10 = 30
TOTAL		272 pixels	816

The file takes 816 bits.

Use Huffman coding

We can build a Huffman tree from these values and frequencies. The Huffman tree looks like this.

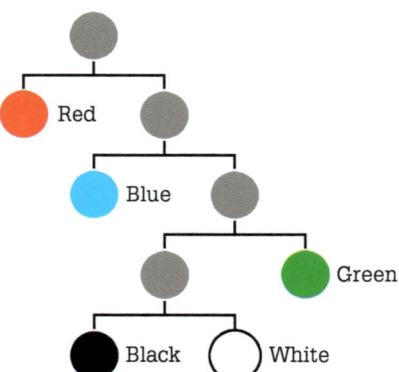

We can find the size of the data file by multiplying the number of bits in each colour code by the frequency of that colour.

Colour	Code	Frequency	Number of bits
Red	0	107	1 * 107 = 107
Blue	10	75	2 * 75 = 150
Green	111	60	3 * 60 = 180
White	1101	20	4 * 20 = 80
Black	1100	10	4 * 10 = 40
TOTAL			557 bits

The file takes 557 bits.

By using Huffman coding the file has reduced from 816 bits to 557 bits. This is a reduction of about 30 per cent of the original size of the file.

Larger compression

A file where some values are much more frequent than others will make a tall thin Huffman tree. A file like this can get a lot smaller with Huffman compression. Here is an example.

A file had 32,000 data values. It contained the digits 0 to 7, with different frequencies. We can store each value as a binary digit, as shown in this table. Each value uses three bits. The total file size is 96,000 bits.

Digit	Frequency	Binary digit	Number of bits	Total bits
0	19,650	000	3	58,950
1	150	001	3	450
2	11,000	010	3	33,000
3	300	011	3	900
4	70	100	3	210
5	20	101	3	60
6	10	110	3	30
7	800	111	3	2400
TOTAL	32,000			96,000

We can create a Huffman tree from these values. Using the Huffman tree creates the following codes. The more frequent values have smaller codes. The less frequent values have longer codes.

Digit	Frequency	Huffman code	Number of bits	Total bits
6	10	0000000	7	70
5	20	0000001	7	140
4	70	000001	6	420
1	150	00001	5	750
3	300	0001	4	1200
7	800	001	3	2400
2	11,000	01	2	22,000
0	19,650	1	1	19,650
TOTAL	32,000			46,630

The file has reduced from 96,000 bits to fewer than 47,000 bits. The file is less than half the size it was, with no loss of data quality.

Example – ASCII file

You will now see how Huffman code can greatly reduce the size of a text file, compared to normal 7-bit ASCII.

A file had 32,000 text characters. Each character was stored using 7-bit ASCII (see page 152 for more about ASCII). We multiply the number of characters by the storage needed for each one.

$32 \times 7 = 224$.

So the file required 224,000 bits of storage.

In Huffman code the more common characters are stored using shorter code numbers. The shortest code number is a single bit. One bit can store two values (1 or 0). Which characters are most common will depend on the language. In many languages the letters E and T are the two most common characters. In Huffman code these characters would be stored using the one bit code.

Two bits can store four codes (00, 01, 10 and 11). These codes will be used to store the next four most common characters. For example they might be A, I, O and N.

Here is a table of possible Huffman codes that might be used to encode text. In this example the text is all upper case. Text with a wider range of characters would use more Huffman codes.

Number of bits	Number of values	Used to encode
1	2	E T
2	4	AION
3	8	SHRDLU space and full stop characters
4	16	Remaining letters and punctuation
TOTAL	32 values	26 letters and 6 punctuation marks

The exact size of a file stored using these codes will depend on what proportion of the characters fall into the four code categories.

For example:

Number of bits	Proportion of text
1 (2 values)	15%
2 (4 values)	20%
3 (8 values)	35%
4 (16 values)	30%

Multiplying the percentage by the total gives us the number of characters in each category. For example E and T make up 15% of all characters. The file has 32,000 characters. 15% of 32,000 is 4,800.

The next table shows the results for all four rows:

Number of bits	Proportion of text	How many characters
1	15%	4,800
2	20%	6,400
3	35%	11,200
4	30%	9,600

Finally, we can multiply the number of characters by the amount of storage per character (1, 2, 3 or 4 bits) to give the total bits in each case:

Number of bits	Proportion of text	How many characters	Total storage
1	15%	4,800	4,800
2	20%	6,400	12,800
3	35%	11,200	33,600
4	30%	9,600	38,400
TOTAL	100%	32,000	89,600

To store these 32,000 characters takes 89,600 bits of storage using Huffman code. This value will depend on how many different characters occur in the file, and the frequency of each. You have to calculate the storage afresh in each case.

At the start of this section we calculated that an ASCII version of this file would take 224,000 bits. Subtracting one from the other gives us the difference in file size.

224,000 – 32,000 = 134,400

Using Huffman coding saves us 134,000 bits in this example.

Test yourself

These questions relate to this table of values, frequencies and Huffman codes.

Value	Frequency	7-bit ASCII code	Huffman code
A	2000	1000001	011
B	900	1000010	0101
C	3000	1000011	00
D	500	1000100	0100
E	7000	1000101	1

1. The file contains 13,400 characters. What is the total size of the file stored using seven-bit ASCII?

2. What is the total size of the file stored using Huffman codes?

3. What is the reduction in file size if Huffman coding is used?

Learning activity

Create a Huffman tree for the digit and frequency table shown on page 179.

Extension activity

Create the Huffman tree for the letter and frequency table shown in the "Test yourself" section.

Syllabus reference

3.4.1 Hardware and software

Define the terms "hardware" and "software" and understand the relationship between them.

6.1 Types of software

Hardware and software

Introduction

Every computer system is made of hardware and software. In this section you will learn the difference between hardware and software. Both are needed for a computer to function.

Input–processing–output

A computer is a machine for turning data into information. Data means facts and figures. Data is not organised or processed. The computer processes data. This turns it into useful information. Information that has been processed is organised and structured so that it is more useful to us. For example, numbers may be processed by carrying out calculations.

Digital devices

Computers are digital devices. All the data inside a computer is held in electronic switches. These switches can be on or off. All data must be converted into on/off signals. The data is held and processed in electronic form while the computer is running.

Hardware

- Hardware means the physical objects that make a computer system.
- Input devices convert data into digital signals that can be processed by the computer.
- The processor changes the digital signals to create useful information.
- Storage devices keep a record of the digital signals when they are not being processed.
- Output devices convert the digital signals inside the processor into a useful form outside the computer.

Sometimes all the different items of hardware are combined into a single object. A tablet includes input, processing, output and storage in one case. In some computer systems the devices are separate. For example, a desktop computer may have a wireless keyboard and a monitor connected by a wire.

Processing

A computer processes data to make information. The data is held inside the computer in the form of electronic signals. The data is processed by changing the electronic signals. This happens inside a part of the computer called the processor. The processor is at the centre of the computer system. It is an electronic device. It transforms data into information by changing the electronic signals in regular and organised ways.

The computer processor is also known as the central processing unit or CPU. You can learn more about how the processor holds and changes electronic data on pages 194–203.

Storage

Secondary storage, sometimes called permanent storage or permanent memory, is storage outside the CPU. The data in secondary storage is not lost when the computer is switched off. However, access to secondary storage is much slower than access to storage within the CPU. Most secondary storage uses magnetic or optical media, or semiconductor flash memory. You can learn more about storage on pages 204–210.

Software

The actions of the CPU are controlled by instructions. The instructions are held as binary code numbers. Where do the instructions come from? They come from software – every software file is a collection of instruction codes. To use software you must load it and run it. Here is how it works:

- **Loading software:** when you start software, all the instruction codes in the software file are copied from secondary storage into storage within the processor (random access memory: RAM).
- **Running software:** when the instructions are in RAM, the processor fetches them one at a time and carries them out.

All software is created by computer programmers. They write programs that control the computer's actions. In the next sections you will learn more about software.

Test yourself

1. The touchscreen of a tablet computer works as both an input and an output device. Explain how it is used for input and how it is used for output.

2. What is the difference between loading and running software?

3. What input devices are included in the design of a typical mobile phone?

4. When you listen to a music track on an MP3 player, what output device is used?

Learning activity

Work with a partner. Use a digital camera or smartphone to take a photo of an input device. Record a short description of how the device works.

Extension activity

Research the development of the self-driving car. What hardware and software systems are in place to make cars that can avoid obstacles and arrive at a destination?

Syllabus reference

3.4.3 Software classification

Explain what is meant by: application software, system software. Give examples of both types of software.

System and application software

Introduction

In this section you will learn about software – the instructions that tell the computer what actions to carry out. There are two types of software:

- application software
- system software.

How software is made

Software is created by programmers. A programmer would very rarely write the binary instruction codes the processor needs. In almost all cases a programmer writes a computer program using a high level programming language. When the program has been written, it can be converted into binary instruction codes that the processor can deal with.

Application software

Application software is any software that carries out useful work for us. Most of the software you might buy or use with a computer is application software, for example:

- a word processor on your school computer
- the email software on your laptop at home
- a game on a games console.

A modern computer typically shows the available applications (apps) as icons. Those are small images. Each image stands for a different file of instruction codes. When you click on an icon the software is loaded and starts to run.

↑ These icons represent different apps

System software

As well as application software, every computer needs system software. This is the software that enables the computer to work properly. The instructions in system software help the processor to control and organise the whole computer system.

In modern computers most of the system software that the processor needs is collected together into one big software system. This is called the operating system. When the computer is turned on, the first action of the processor is to load the operating system into its electronic memory. The operating system stays in the computer memory all the time the computer is switched on. The operating system runs in the background to make the computer work properly.

Operating systems

Different companies make different operating systems. Here are some examples:

- **Microsoft Windows** is the most widely used operating system in the world. Most laptop and desktop computers use Windows.

- **macOS** is the operating system used with Apple computers. Software designed for Apple computers cannot run on other computers.

- **Linux** is a free operating system. It can be more technically complicated to use than Windows or macOS. It is favoured by many computer experts.

- **Android** is an operating system used on many mobile devices such as tablets and smartphones. Apps written for Android devices will not run on devices that use a different operating system.

↑ There are many different operating systems made by different companies

Compatibility

System software runs the computer. It controls what software can be loaded and run on the computer. The choice of operating system affects all the other software choices you make. When you buy software, you need to know the software will run with your operating system.

If a software application can be used by an operating system we say it is compatible with that operating system.

Test yourself

1. What is an icon, and what happens when you click on an icon with the mouse, or touch an icon on the screen of a mobile device?

2. What is the operating system used on the computer at your school or college?

3. What is the last software application you used? Explain what that application does.

4. Why do you need to know what operating system your computer uses before you buy any application software?

Learning activity

Investigate any computer system that you have access to. It might be your computer at school or at home, or a tablet or smartphone you use.

Make a list of the applications that are available on the computer. If there are a lot, list the first ten you can find. Explain what each one does and why you think it would be valued by the people who use the computer. If you can, take a screen shot or image of the screen that shows the icons of the available applications.

Extension activity

Write a short review of any software application, explaining what it does. Note its good and bad features.

Syllabus reference

3.4.3 Software classification

Understand the need for, and functions of, operating systems (OS) and utility programs. Understand that the OS handles management of:

- processor(s)
- memory
- I/O devices
- applications
- security.

Operating systems and utilities

Introduction

You have learned that system software controls the operation of a computer system. In this section you will learn about some of the jobs that system software does.

Controlling the processor

When the computer is running, software instructions are passed to the processor. The computer carries out the instructions one at a time. One processing unit can only carry out one instruction at a time. The operating system controls the order in which instructions are carried out. There are different ways to do this:

- Single-tasking: a single-tasking operating system can only run one program at a time. When the program is finished another one can begin.
- Multi-tasking: a multi-tasking operating system can run more than one program at the same time. The operating system swaps quickly between the different programs. It must keep track of the process of each program.

Managing memory

Every computer has active electronic memory. You have learned that the active electronic memory linked to the processor memory is also called random access memory (RAM). Data stored in RAM can be used quickly by the processor.

Each program is given an area in RAM. This area will store the program instructions and the data used by the program. The operating system makes sure each program uses the right memory area. It makes sure the different areas of memory don't get mixed up.

To speed up the computer, the data not in use might be stored on a disk. This will free up memory for other programs. This is called swapping.

Managing storage

Storage means the permanent storage attached to the computer. Data in storage is slower for the processor to access. Data and instructions are stored in files. Files are given file names and stored in folders. This helps users to find the file they need. The operating system manages this process by finding free space in storage for each file. It must make sure that each file is stored in a different location, which does not overlap with any other file. Sometimes a file may be split between several different storage areas. The operation system manages this entire process.

Input and output

When you use software, data must flow between the processor and the different input and output devices which are linked to the computer. For example data will be input via the keyboard and output to the monitor. This data flow is managed by the operating system.

A device driver is a type of system software. It lets the processor send signals to and from devices such as the keyboard and screen. Nowadays operating systems include the drivers for most types of hardware. The operating system will identify new hardware when you plug it in. It will find the right device driver and load the software.

Running applications

The operating system allows you to load and run application software. The data and instructions that each application needs are loaded into RAM. Each application is given a share of the processor time. Each application is connected to input and output devices. The operating system ensures each application has the resources – storage space and processor time – which it needs to do its work.

System security

Security is an important topic in computer science. You will learn more about security in Chapter 9. One of the jobs of an operating system is to keep the data on the computer secure. This may include the use of passwords and user logins.

Utilities

Sometimes you need extra system software features. These may not be included in your operating system. You can buy special systems software to do extra tasks. These smaller system files are called utilities.

Here are some examples of utilities:

- virus checks
- software to find and fix faults in the computer
- drivers for unusual hardware items
- software to improve system performance.

Test yourself

1. One of the jobs of the operating system is to manage how files are stored. Explain in more detail what the operating system does to manage file storage.

2. When an application is running the operating system manages the resources needed by the application. What are these resources?

3. I bought a new mouse but I didn't need to buy new software to go with it. Why not?

4. Why might you need utility software, when you have an operating system already installed on your computer?

Learning activity

Do an Internet search to find examples of utility software. Write a list of the utilities you found and briefly describe what each one does.

Extension activity

Do an Internet search to find examples of reviews of operating systems. Pick two operating systems and read what people have said about them. Write a report comparing the two operating systems.

Syllabus reference

3.2.13 Classification of programming languages

Know that machine code and assembly language are considered to be low-level languages and explain the differences between them.

Additional information

Students should understand these points:

- Processors execute machine code and each type of processor has its own specific machine code instruction set.
- Machine code is expressed in binary and is specific to a processor or family of processors.
- Assembly language is often used to develop software for embedded systems and for controlling specific hardware components.
- Assembly language has a 1:1 correspondence with machine code.

6.2 Programming languages

Machine code and assembly language

Introduction

Software is held in the computer using a code called machine code. In this section you will learn how machine code instructions are created.

Machine code

Everything inside the computer is in digital form. All instructions are stored as binary number codes. The processor reads an instruction code from the memory. Then it carries out the instruction. We say the processor "executes" the instruction.

There is a binary number to match every action of the processor. The set of all these codes is called the instruction set. In general, each type of processor has a different instruction set. If two processors share the same instruction set they are said to be in the same "family" of processors. They are often made by the same manufacturer.

The general term for the number code that matches numbers to instructions is "machine code". A computer file made of machine code is called an executable file. That means it is a file of instructions that the processor can execute.

Writing software

If you want to develop a new software application, you must write the instructions. You could write new software by writing machine code.

It is difficult to write software in machine code. A long series of binary numbers is hard to read. It is easy to make a mistake as you type in the numbers. For these reasons, more advanced computer languages were invented. Programs written in computer languages are easier for a human programmer to write, read and understand than programs written in machine code.

Programmers write programs using a programming language such as Python.

The program commands are converted into machine code. The computer can process the machine code. It can execute the instructions.

Assembly language

Programmers use programming languages to write programs because machine code is difficult to use. The first type of computer language to be invented was called assembly language. Assembly language uses short text words instead of binary number codes. These words are generally three letters long.

Using words instead of numbers makes it easier for the human programmer to write the code. For example, in machine code the instruction to add two values will be a binary number. In assembly language, the instruction might be the word "ADD".

As well as three-letter words a line of assembly language might also include some numbers. The numbers represent data values and memory locations.

A piece of software called an assembler is used to convert the assembly language commands into machine code that the computer can understand:

- The input to the assembler is a program written in assembly language.
- The output of the assembler is an executable file.

The process of turning a program into machine code is called translation. Assembly language is quite similar to machine code. In general, one line of assembly language turns into one instruction of machine code.

How instructions are represented

The instructions inside the computer are held as electrical on/off signals. These instructions can be represented in many ways. Some are easier for a human reader to understand.

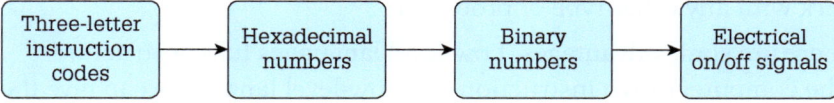

| Three-letter instruction codes | → | Hexadecimal numbers | → | Binary numbers | → | Electrical on/off signals |

Test yourself

1. What type of data would you find inside an executable file?

2. What is the job of an assembler? What goes into an assembler, and what comes out of it?

3. An assembly language program includes code words. What do the code words stand for?

4. Explain why assembly language is called a low-level language.

Learning activity

Make a poster of the diagram from this page. Include examples of all the representations of instructions.

Extension activity

There are short tutorials in assembly language online. If you have time learn a small number of assembly language instructions.

Syllabus reference

3.2.13 Classification of programming languages

Know that there are different levels of programming language: low-level language, high-level language.

Explain the main differences between low-level and high-level languages.

Understand that most computer programs are written in high-level language and explain why this is the case. Understand the advantages and disadvantages of low-level language programming compared with high-level language programming.

Low-level and high-level languages

Introduction

You have learned that the processor is controlled by machine code instructions. But a programmer does not write software using machine code. Instead a programmer writes instructions using a different programming language. The instructions are converted into machine code. Programming languages can be "high-level" or "low-level". Low-level languages include machine code and some other languages that are similar to machine code. High-level languages are much less similar to machine code.

Low-level languages

A language that is similar to machine code is called a low-level language. Assembly language is a low-level language. There is a close match between assembly language and machine code. The three-letter codes in assembly language turn into single machine code instructions.

It is quite difficult to write a program in a low-level language, so low-level languages are not used by most programmers. Low-level languages are based on the instruction set of one processor. A program written in that language may not work with any other type of processor.

However, there are some advantages. Low-level languages have a structure similar to the computer's own instruction set. Low-level languages can give the programmer better control over the way the computer operates. The programs are shorter and often quicker to execute than other programs.

Assembly language is sometimes used to write system software. Device drivers are instructions that let the processor communicate with input, output, storage or other devices. Assembly language is often used to create device drivers for new types of hardware. These programs are short and work quickly.

High-level language

Most programs are written in a high-level language. A program written in a high-level language is not very similar to machine code. Instead high-level languages are designed to make it easy to write the program. High-level languages have features which make it easier for programmers to create working programs. For instance high-level languages let the programmer define various types of loop. Most languages allow the programmer to declare and use data structures such as lists. High-level languages include procedures and functions. Programmers can use identifiers with helpful names, and add comments. These make the code easier to read.

High-level languages are not linked closely to a single instruction set, so they can be run on any computer once they have been translated into that computer's machine code. Some different languages are designed for different purposes. You would choose a language by considering what you want to do. Here are some examples:

- To build a program using visual building blocks you might use Scratch or App Inventor.
- To learn good programming methods you might use Python or Pascal.
- To work with logic you might use Lisp or Prolog.
- To make system software you might use C or C++.
- To create programs to run in a web page you might use JavaScript.

In this book, you have learned Python programming.

Advantages and disadvantages

Each type of programming language has advantages and disadvantages. These are summarised in this table.

	Advantages	Disadvantages
Low-level language The instruction set of a processor, or a language which is a very close match to that instruction set. **Example:** Machine code, Assembly language	Compared to a high-level language program which carries out the same task, a low-level language program is typically: • Shorter in length • Quicker in run time • Makes more efficient use of the available resources (processor and memory) • Allows the programmer to make use of every possible command which can be implemented by the instruction set	It is hard for a human programmer to read, write or modify these programs. Data is stored by identifying numbered memory locations instead of named variables. Commands are given as numbers, or short codes (typically 3 letters) which are hard to read and understand. The language does not provide simple support for a range of iterative or conditional structures. A program written in a low-level language may only work with the instruction set of one processor.
High-level language Code written in this language uses structures and terms familiar to human programmers. **Example:** Python, C++, Java, Perl and many others	Writing a program in a high-level language has many advantages for the programmer: • Code is more readable, for example due to layout, meaningful identifiers and comments • Code is more structured, including the use of subroutines and shared modules • All high level languages offer commands which make it easier to create iterative and conditional structures • Programmers can name and use variables and data structures, rather than building in references to locations in computer memory	The commands that the programmer has written need to be converted into machine code before they can be carried out. This makes the program longer. It takes longer to carry out. Because the programmer is not writing directly in machine code, some machine code instructions may be hard to use – this depends on the particular language in use. In some cases it takes a lot of code to implement a simple command.

More programs are written in high-level language than in low-level language. However, some very important pieces of software are written in low-level languages. Examples are: computer start-up commands and the software that controls much of the hardware we use every day.

Test yourself

1. What do we call a language that is closely matched to the instruction set of a processor?

2. Which type of language would you recommend for a person learning programming – high or low-level? Explain your answer.

3. Why is assembly language closely linked to a particular type of processor?

4. Why are there lots of different high-level languages? Wouldn't it be easier to just have one common language?

Learning activity

Make a poster for the classroom showing the table of advantages and disadvantages of the two types of language.

Extension activity

Find examples of program code written in many different programming languages.

Syllabus reference

3.2.13 Classification of programming languages

Understand that ultimately all programming code written in high-level or assembly languages must be translated into machine code.

Understand that there are three common types of program translator: interpreter, compiler and assembler. Explain the main differences between these three types of translator. Understand when it would be appropriate to use each type of translator.

Translators

Introduction

Every program must be translated into machine code before it can be executed. This section reviews the different ways of translating programs into machine code.

Programs written in assembly language, or a high-level programming language must be turned into machine code. Then the processor can execute the code. The program file is sometimes called source code. The file of machine code instructions is called the executable file.

Turning source code into machine code is called translating the program. There are three pieces of software that do this job:

- assembler
- interpreter
- compiler.

Assembler

An assembler turns an assembly language program into machine code. It saves the machine code instructions as a separate file. There is an exact match-up between the lines of the assembly language program and the instructions in the machine code file.

Here is an example of how this might work. It isn't real machine code.

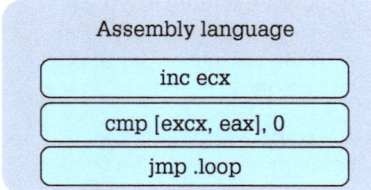

Assembly language	Machine code
inc ecx	3A B7
cmp [excx, eax], 0	09 5C 00
jmp .loop	72 01

After the assembler has translated the assembly code into machine code you have two files on your computer. The second file is an executable machine code file. This is the one that will control what the computer does.

Compiler

A compiler turns a high-level language program into machine code, and saves it as a file:

- The input to the compiler is a high-level language program.
- The output is an executable file.

The new executable file is placed in storage. The instructions in the file will not be executed until you decide to load and run the file. Languages translated by compilers are called compiled languages.

As with an assembly language program, the program and the executable file exist as two separate files in memory. If you make changes to the source code, you must translate it again.

You can pass on the executable file to another person to use on that person's computer.

Interpreter

An interpreter translates the program code and executes it as it translates. The interpreter reads enough of the code to work out the next action to take. Then it uses the instruction set to carry out this action. When the action is complete, the interpreter moves on to translate and execute the next part of the program code. Languages translated by interpreters are called interpreted languages. Python is an interpreted language.

The interpreter does not make an executable file. To run the program you must run the source code. To pass the program to another person you must give that person the source code. The person will have to translate it every time he or she wants to use the program. The person must have the translator on his or her computer.

Comparison of different translators

Type & use	Example language	Advantage	Disadvantage
Assembler (used to write a device driver)	Assembly language	If a program is written in assembly language, an assembler is the only way to turn it into machine code. It makes an executable file. The file can be used without further translation.	The file will only run on a particular processor.
Compiler (used to write computer games and other software for) commercial sale)	C++	It makes an executable file. The executable file can be given to another person or sold. The executable file can run on a computer without any additional software being needed.	If you make a change the program must be compiled again. The executable file is linked to a particular instructions set so it is not portable between computers of different types. Different versions can get mixed up. This is particularly a problem for inexperienced coders.
Interpreter (used for developing programs by learners, or source code to be shared with other programmers)	Python	It creates source code to share with others. If you change the source code you can test the effect immediately. The source code may be translated into the instruction set of any computer, so it is portable.	There is no executable file. The program can only run if you have the interpreter on your computer.

## Chapter 7

Syllabus reference

3.4.4 Systems architecture

Explain von Neumann architecture.

Explain the role and operation of the following major components of a CPU: arithmetic logic unit (ALU), control unit, buses.

7.1 The processor

Components of the CPU

Introduction

You have learned that the computer is an electronic device. Electronic circuits process data inside the computer. The part of the computer that carries out the processing is known as the central processing unit (CPU). In this section you will learn about the work and structure of the CPU.

The computer system

The processor is at the centre of the computer system. It is connected to input devices, output devices and storage devices.

The arrows in this diagram show the flow of data.

Input devices send data into the processor. Storage devices hold data that the processor can use. Output devices display data from the processor. Together, these devices are known as "peripherals".

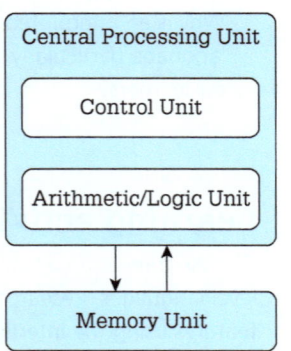

The processor

The processor – also called the central processing unit (CPU) – is divided into three main components:

- the arithmetic and logic unit (ALU)
- the control unit
- the system clock.

The processor is connected to the main memory of the computer.

Main memory

Main memory is also sometimes called main store, primary memory, primary store, or immediate access store (IAS). Main memory consists of a large number of memory locations. Each has an address: a number that identifies exactly that location. Each memory location can hold one item of data, in the form of a binary number.

The instructions that tell the processor how to process the data are themselves numbers. Like any other binary numbers, they can be stored in main memory. The CPU can only work with data that is stored in the main memory. The CPU can only follow instructions that are stored in the main memory.

Buses

The different components of the processor are connected by short connections called buses. A bus is a collection of wires that transmit electrical signals. There are three types:

- An address bus transmits addresses.
- A data bus transmits data.
- A control bus transmits control signals, telling the receiver to do something.

Signals travel through the buses to small memory areas called registers. The registers hold the signals ready to be processed within the CPU. Buses are also used to connect the processor to hardware items such as input and output devices.

The ALU

All processing happens in the ALU. In the ALU the binary electrical signals that represent data are passed through logic circuits. The logic circuits transform the data. The ALU carries out arithmetic processing and logical processing:

- Arithmetic processing means finding the numerical answer to mathematical problems.
- Logical processing means finding the true/false answer to logical deductions.

You have learned to write programs that carry out both types of processing.

The control unit

The control unit controls the other parts of the processor. Signals from the control unit tell the ALU to read data from main memory, process it then write the results back to main memory. The control unit also tells peripherals to transfer data to and from the main memory. The control unit sends control signals in the right order and gives each action time to finish before it sends the next signal.

John von Neumann

The basic structure of the computer shown in this section is called the von Neumann model or von Neumann architecture. It is named after the US scientist John von Neumann who first proposed this model. Von Neumann based his work on the ideas of the computer pioneer Alan Turing.

Von Neumann architecture

The key features of the Von Neumann architecture are:

- a CPU containing an Arithmetic Logic Unit and a Control Unit
- main memory that stores data and instructions in electronic form
- external storage which retains data and instructions in non-electronic form
- input and output devices connected to the processor.

Test yourself

1. What are the main components of the CPU?
2. What are the three types of peripheral?
3. What two types of work does the ALU carry out?
4. What happens to the new data that the ALU makes?

Learning activity

Use a graphics application to create a diagram of the components of a computer system, including the parts of the CPU.

Extension activity

The development of modern computers was done by a range of pioneers. Von Neumann was one of these. Carry out some research into the history of computers and the speed and power of the earliest computer systems.

Syllabus reference

3.4.4 Systems architecture

Understand and explain the fetch-execute cycle.

Additional information

The CPU continuously reads instructions stored in main memory and executes them as required:

- Fetch: the next instruction is fetched to the CPU from main memory.
- Decode: the instruction is decoded to work out what it is.
- Execute: the instruction is executed (carried out). This may include reading/writing from/to main memory.

The fetch-execute cycle

Introduction

You have learned that the processor is at the centre of the computer system. Processing is carried out in the CPU. Processing is done in a regular order called the fetch-execute cycle. In this section you will learn about this cycle.

The operation of the CPU

When the computer is switched on, the CPU repeats a set of actions called the fetch-execute cycle.

1. The control unit fetches an instruction from main memory. The instructions are coded as binary numbers.

2. The control unit decodes the instruction so it knows what action to carry out.

3. The ALU carries out the action. That is called executing the instruction.

The fetch-execute cycle is repeated millions of times a second.

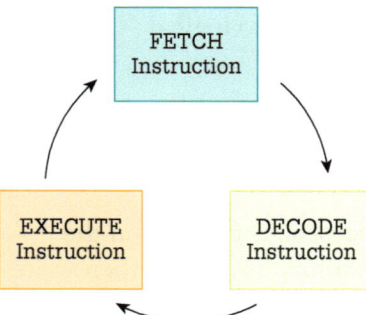

Fetch

Software consists of machine code instructions stored in a file. Before the software is run, all its instructions will be loaded from secondary storage into main memory. This is because it is much slower to read individual instructions from external storage than from main memory.

When the software has been loaded, the user can run the software. Each instruction in the executable file is carried out by the processor.

The first step of the fetch-execute cycle is fetching an instruction from main memory. The instruction is a binary number. The number is copied into a small storage space inside the CPU called the instruction register. The register can only hold one instruction at a time.

Decode

Every CPU has a specific set of instructions it is able to follow. This is called the CPU's instruction set. CPUs from different companies may have different instruction sets.

Each instruction in the set is represented by a different range of binary numbers. Decoding the number is the job of a logic circuit in the control unit. The logic circuit is called the "instruction decoder". The instruction decoder analyses the number in the instruction register. It works out what the instruction is. The control unit then selects one or more actions that will make that instruction happen.

Execute

"Execute" in this context means to carry out an instruction. The control unit has decoded the instruction. Next the control unit sends signals to the ALU to tell it what to do. The ALU carries out each action. The ALU might solve an arithmetic problem (a numerical calculation) or make a logical deduction (a true/false comparison). The process will result in new data, and this will be sent back to the Memory Unit to be stored.

Extension – stored program model

The early developers of the computer realised that both data and instructions could be stored as binary numbers in the computer's main memory. The control unit fetches instructions from memory and sends data to the ALU for processing. All computers follow this basic model. It is called the stored program model.

A slightly more complex computer model, called the Harvard model, sets aside different sections of memory for instructions and data. Instructions and data are accessed separately by the control unit. However, the basic idea of the fetch-execute cycle remains the same. Many modern processors use a modified structure that has aspects of both the von Neumann and Harvard models.

Test yourself

1. Draw a diagram of the fetch-execute cycle.

2. Explain how the instruction register is used in the fetch stage of the fetch-execute cycle.

3. How does the control unit decode the instruction in the decode stage of the fetch-execute cycle?

4. Where is the execute stage of the fetch-execute cycle carried out?

Learning activity

Carry out Internet research to find diagrams of the fetch-execute cycle. Find several examples. Some are more complex than others.

Extension activity

The fetch-execute cycle is carried out millions of times per second. You have learned that Hertz is a unit meaning the number of repetitions per second. Find out the typical speed in Hertz of a modern processor.

Syllabus reference

3.4.4 Systems architecture

Explain the role and operation of main memory.

Understand the differences between RAM and ROM.

Additional information

Students should be able to explain the terms "volatile" and "non-volatile". Secondary storage is considered to be any non-volatile storage mechanism that is not directly accessible by the CPU.

Understand the differences between main memory and secondary storage.

Understand why secondary storage is required.

Main memory

Introduction

You have learned that computers process data in digital form. Storage devices hold digital data when it is not in use by the processor. In this section you will learn about primary storage. This is storage that is attached directly to the CPU.

Registers

Inside the CPU, data is held as electric charges and passes down buses as electrical signals. The CPU changes those signals by processing them and returns them to memory. In this way, the computer changes data into information.

Inside the processor, data and instructions are held in small electronic circuits called registers. Registers are inside the CPU. That means the CPU can read and use the contents of registers with almost no delay. There is no need to wait for a signal to arrive from outside the CPU.

A register can hold only one item at a time. There is no room in the CPU for more than a small number of registers. The speed of a computer is limited by how quickly the computer can access data and put it into the registers.

The advantage of a register is that the CPU can access the data and instructions very fast. The disadvantage is that a register can only hold one item of data or one instruction.

Registers are used to store the data or instruction that is used in a single fetch-execute cycle.

Main memory

Main memory holds data and instructions as electrical charges. Main memory holds the instructions and data the CPU needs for its current work. Main memory contains two distinct forms of memory which work in different ways:

- RAM
- ROM

RAM

RAM is the active electronic memory of the computer. It holds all the data and instructions the CPU needs for whatever task it is currently doing. The CPU can access the data in RAM very quickly. A computer with more RAM can be a faster computer. If a computer does not have enough RAM, it will be slow.

RAM works by storing electrical charges. The charge (or lack of charge) at a single location represents a 1 (or 0) bit in a binary number. When the electricity is switched off, the charges dissipate, so all the data disappears. Memory that loses its contents when the electricity is turned off is called volatile memory.

The advantages of RAM are that it holds lots of data and instructions, and it is quick for the CPU to access. The disadvantage is that RAM is volatile: it loses all its data when the computer is switched off.

RAM is used to store all the software applications and systems software that the computer is running.

Read-only memory (ROM)

When you first turn on a computer, its RAM is empty. That means RAM cannot be used to store the start-up instructions for the computer.

ROM is a small area of non-volatile memory. Memory that does not lose its contents when the electricity is turned off is called non-volatile memory. As ROM is read-only, the computer can read data or instructions stored there, but cannot write to ROM. This means it cannot store completed work or new instructions. The contents of the ROM are set up in the factory when the computer is made.

The advantage of ROM is that its contents are not lost when the computer is switched off. The disadvantage is that its contents cannot be changed, so ROM cannot be used to store new data.

ROM is used to store the instructions that make the computer start up. These instructions are read by the CPU when you switch on the computer. In some small computer systems all the instructions are held in ROM. These are called embedded systems. You will learn more about embedded systems later in this book.

Secondary storage

Secondary storage, sometimes called permanent storage or permanent memory, is storage outside main memory. The data in secondary storage is not lost when the computer is switched off. The purpose of secondary storage is to retain data and instructions that are not currently in use by the processor. However, the CPU does not have a direct link to secondary storage. The processor cannot access the data directly. This means that access to secondary storage is much slower than access to primary storage. Most secondary storage uses magnetic or optical media, or semiconductor flash memory. You will learn more about these different types of secondary storage on pages 204–209.

Test yourself

1. What does "volatile" mean?

2. Why does a computer speed up when you install more RAM?

3. What does "read-only" mean?

4. Why is the RAM completely empty when you turn on a computer?

Learning activity

Complete the following table to set out the advantages and disadvantages of each type of memory, and the typical uses of each type.

Type of memory	Advantage	Disadvantage	Uses
Registers			
RAM			
ROM			

Extension activity

The instructions the computer uses to start up are called BIOS. These instructions are held in ROM. Research what BIOS means and why it is needed when the computer is switched on.

Syllabus reference

3.4.4 Systems architecture

Explain the role and operation of the following major component of a CPU: clock.

Explain the effect of the following on the performance of the CPU: clock speed, number of processor cores, cache size.

Performance factors

Introduction

Some computers work faster than others. Some features of the CPU are linked to better speed and more-powerful computers. You will learn about these features in this section.

Performance

As with any other device or machine, people are interested in measuring and comparing computers. People want to know whether a computer is good value for money. They want to know whether a computer can do a particular job. They want to know whether the computer has good or bad "performance".

The performance of a computer is generally measured in terms of its speed. For example, how many operations can the computer carry out in one second? Various factors can improve the performance of a computer including:

- clock speed
- number of processors
- cache size.

Clock

The CPU uses a timer called the system clock. The system clock is based on a crystal. It sends out regular pulses of electricity. The control unit uses these pulses to regulate its actions. The control unit will count one or more pulses before it sends the next signal to the other components of the computer. Waiting for the pulse makes sure that each component is given enough time to act on the signal before another one is sent.

Clock speed is measured in Hertz (Hz). 1 Hz means one cycle per second. The frequency of the system clock is the number of pulses that occur in one second. The CPU processes several instructions for every pulse of the system clock. A typical figure would be two billion instructions a second. This is written as 2GHz. GHz stands for 'giga Hertz' and means one billion cycles a second.

Clock speed

The CPU spends some time in every cycle waiting for the system clock to send a pulse. Increasing the speed of the system clock can make the computer work faster. The CPU will send out instructions more often.

There are two big disadvantages to increasing the speed of the system clock:

- Some of the components of the computer might not be able to work fast enough. That means that new signals might be sent by the CPU before the old signals have been fully carried out.
- Every action of the computer generates a small amount of heat. Increasing the clock speed means more actions and more heat. The computer can overheat.

Processor cores

A modern processor may contain more than one core. Each core can carry out one instruction at a time.

Modern computers often have a dual core (two cores) or a quad core (four cores).

Using multi-core processor has several advantages compared to using one large processor:

- More than one instruction can be carried out at the same time, so the speed increases a lot.
- Cores that are reliable and tested can be linked together to increase power without the risk of using a new design.

However, there are some disadvantages:

- Software must be written specially to take advantage of the double (or more) processing power.
- Not all software makes full use of the extra power of the system.

Cache size

You have learned that the CPU can get data more quickly from registers than from main memory. However, the registers can only hold one instruction at a time.

To avoid this problem, computers have a larger area of quick-access memory. It is called the cache. The cache stores instructions and items of data. They have been copied from main memory. The contents of the cache can be accessed quickly by the CPU. It is quicker to fetch instructions and data from the cache than from main memory.

In general, a larger cache means the computer does not have to go to main memory so often. This makes the computer go faster.

---

1. AMD A8-7670K

Ideal for laptop users

Processor Cores: 4 | **Thermal Design Power:** 95W | **Graphics Controller:** Radeon R7 Series | **Clock Speed:** 3.6GHz | **Processor Socket:** FM2+ | **L2 Cache:** 4MB

↑ Part of a review of a processor. What does this say about cache, number of cores and clock speed?

Test yourself

1. A student bought a computer. He increased the speed of the system clock to make it go faster. What might go wrong?
2. A processor can only carry out one instruction at a time. However, some computers can carry out more than one instruction at the same time. Why is that?
3. What is the function of cache memory in the CPU?
4. Explain how increasing the size of cache can improve the performance of a computer.

Learning activity

Read reviews of new processors. What do these reviews say about the performance of the computers? What are the values for clock speed, cache size and number of cores?

Extension activity

As well as performance, modern computers are evaluated in terms of their energy efficiency. Find out what factors improve the energy efficiency of a computer processor.

Syllabus reference

3.4.4 Systems architecture

Understand the term "embedded system" and explain how an embedded system differs from a non-embedded system.

Additional information

Students must be able to give examples of embedded and non-embedded systems.

Embedded systems

Introduction

We mainly think of a processor as the working core of a computer. However, processors are built into many other devices. These are known as embedded systems. In this section you will learn about embedded systems.

Embedded systems

Embedded systems are computers designed to do one specific task. Embedded systems are built into devices, machines and common household objects. Embedded systems regulate and control the devices.

The instructions for an embedded system are called firmware. Firmware is typically stored in read-only memory (ROM). The instructions stay the same the whole time the embedded system is in use. Apart from the firmware the embedded system may have little electronic memory, low processing power and no user interface.

How common are embedded systems?

Embedded processors are typically smaller and cheaper than non-embedded systems. For this reason, there are more of them. It has been estimated that 90 per cent of modern processors are in embedded systems.

The family car may have several embedded systems. There may be embedded systems in electrical devices such as washing machines, microwave ovens and burglar alarms.

Micro-controllers

A typical non-embedded computer uses a micro-processor. This has several components, joined together by buses.

A typical embedded system uses a different type of processor called a micro-controller. A micro-controller is a small computer with all its components in a single chip. It has a simpler design because it is only made to do one task.

The simple design of a micro-controller makes it smaller and cheaper than a micro-processor. This means it is economical to add computerised controllers to all kinds of devices. For example, there may be dozens of micro-controllers in a family home.

Features of embedded processors

An embedded system has different features from a non-embedded computer processor:

- The processor is only used for a limited range of actions; it is built to do only these.
- The controls and display are very limited – consisting of a small screen or a single button, for example.

- The processor is small and light, so it can be fitted into all types of equipment.
- Processing speed and power may be low.
- The processor must be very reliable – it may operate continually for years.
- The processor has low requirements for power – it may run from a small battery.

Examples of embedded systems

Embedded systems fall into several categories:

- Consumer electronics, such as MP3 players and cameras, include embedded processors.
- A household device or appliance, such as a fridge or a central heating system, may be regulated by an embedded processor.
- Cars and other large items of equipment, including industrial machinery, can be partially or fully controlled by an embedded processor.
- Micro-controllers can have medical uses such as regulating heart rate.

Modern embedded systems often include wireless Internet connectivity. A wireless connection can be used to control and monitor embedded systems.

Advantages and disadvantages

Embedded systems offer advantages:

- A processor in a device can regulate its action. It can make the device operate better, use less energy, and be more safe. The embedded processor works all the time to maintain the working of a device.
- An embedded system is smaller, cheaper and lighter than a non-embedded system. It only needs to do one task so it is designed to do that task very well.

These are the disadvantages of embedded systems:

- If an embedded system breaks, the whole device may need to be replaced. Embedded systems are difficult to adjust and upgrade.
- An embedded system can typically do one task only. They are less flexible and versatile than non-embedded systems.

Test yourself

1. Would we call a laptop an embedded computer system? Explain your answer.

2. What are the main differences between a micro-processor and a micro-controller?

3. What is firmware? Where is firmware usually held?

4. An embedded system must be small, reliable and low in energy requirements. Explain why.

Learning activity

Create a table showing the advantages and disadvantages of embedded and non-embedded systems.

Extension activity

Look for examples of embedded computer systems in your home, or your school or college. List the examples you find.

Syllabus reference

3.4.4 Systems architecture

Be aware of different types of secondary storage (solid state, optical and magnetic).

Explain the operation of magnetic storage.

Discuss the advantages and disadvantages of magnetic storage.

Magnetic storage

Introduction

You have learned that secondary storage is a non-volatile store for data accessed through a peripheral device. "Non-volatile" means the data is not lost when the computer is switched off. One way that data is held is using magnetic storage. In this section you will learn about the different types of magnetic storage.

Storage capacity

You have learned that data size is measured in bits and bytes. The "capacity" of storage means how many bytes of data it can hold. Modern storage is typically measured in megabytes, gigabytes and terabytes. Find out more about these measurements on page 133.

Magnetic storage

Some materials, such as iron oxide, are easy to magnetise by bringing a magnet near them. The magnetised spot of material is itself a magnet, with a north pole and a south pole. The direction the magnetised spot faces (N–S or S–N) can be used to represent one bit of binary data: one direction means 1 and the other means 0.

A magnetic storage device converts data from the computer into spots of magnetism. The device uses an electric current in a coil of wire. Current flowing in one direction writes a 1 and flowing in the other direction it writes a 0. The spot stays magnetised after the electric current is taken away. That means the data remains even after electricity is switched off. If you delete a file, the spots can be remagnetised, so they can be used for new files.

Hard disk drive (HDD)

The main type of secondary storage used by a non-embedded system is a hard disk drive (HDD). This is a stack of rigid discs spinning in a metal case. The discs are magnetised and used to store data.

The advantage of storage on the HDD is that, as it is wired directly to the processor, access to the HDD is quite fast. The disadvantage is that because an internal HDD is fixed inside a single computer, you cannot easily take it away to use on another computer.

⬆ An internal HDD

Off-line storage

Off-line storage is like secondary storage but it is outside the computer. The storage must be plugged into the computer through a port. Access to off-line storage is slower than access to secondary storage.

A portable (or removable) hard disk works in the same way as a normal HDD. The only difference is that it is outside the case of the computer. It is connected through a cable that plugs into the computer case. When using a portable hard disk access may be slower than when using an internal hard drive because the portable hard disk is outside the computer. However, you can unplug the portable drive and move it to another computer, so you can take the data with you.

Advantages and disadvantages

Magnetic storage is used quite widely in modern computer systems. It has many advantages over the alternatives. The magnetic spots can be changed, so magnetic storage is read/write storage. At present magnetic storage can be less expensive than other systems. It is tried and tested. Many computers are designed to use magnetic storage.

There are disadvantages. Magnetic storage can be wiped by strong magnetic or electrical fields. Magnetic storage can take up more space and weigh more than other types of storage. If it is jolted or shaken it can break.

⬆ A removable HDD can be moved between computers

Test yourself

1. What is the advantage of magnetic storage compared to electronic storage in RAM?

2. Why is it quicker for the computer to access data from an internal hard drive than from a portable hard drive?

3. What is the advantage of an external hard drive?

Learning activity

Look online for examples of magnetic storage devices, disks and tapes for sale. Compare the storage capacity and the price.

Extension activity

Ask your technician at school to show you an example of a hard disk that is no longer in use. If possible, take it to pieces. Make an accurate sketch of its construction.

Syllabus reference

3.4.4 Systems architecture

Be aware of different types of secondary storage (solid state, optical and magnetic).

Explain the operation of optical storage.

Discuss the advantages and disadvantages of optical storage.

Optical storage

Introduction

You have learned about digital storage. In this section you will learn about optical storage, which is storing digital data in a form that can be read by a laser beam.

Optical storage

All digital data is in the form of 1s and 0s. On an optical disc, the 1s and 0s are represented by microscopic pits or marks made in a spiral pattern on a thin reflective layer.

To read the data, an optical drive spins the disc and focuses a laser's light onto its surface. When the light hits a pit or mark, its reflection from the disc is dimmer than from the unmarked background. A light sensor on the drive detects this. The difference in light represents the 1s and 0s of digital data.

The laser that reads the pits can focus on a very small spot, so the pits can be made very small and close together. A CD pit is less than one micrometre across. A micrometre is one millionth of a metre. Millions of pits can fit on the disc surface, so it can hold a lot of data.

Storage media

Storage media means the material that is used to store data, for example magnetic tape or CD. Optical media can be used for any data, but the most typical use is to store sound and video:

- CD – a standard CD will hold about 80 minutes of music.

- DVD (digital versatile disc) – the pits on a DVD are read with a narrower laser spot than is used for a CD. The pits on DVD are smaller than those on a CD so a DVD can store more data. A DVD can hold several hours of video.

- Blu-ray – a Blu-ray disc has even smaller pits and can hold high-resolution video. Blu-ray systems use blue laser light to read the disc.

↑ A CD uses optical storage

Type of access

Data on a standard CD cannot be changed. The pits have been moulded into the surface so the data is fixed. Different types of optical media offer different types of access:

- You can buy a CD with music on it, or a film on DVD. This storage is "read only". Your computer or DVD player will be able to read the data, but you cannot make changes to it. It is manufactured by stamping the pattern of pits all at once into the molten plastic disc as it is moulded.

- You can also buy blank discs called CD-R and DVD–R. This storage is "write-once". A computer's DVD writer works by focusing a laser onto the disc's reflective layer to burn marks into it. Its less powerful reading laser can detect these marks the same way it detects the pits from a stamped CD or DVD. You can store extra files at the end of the disc, but once it is full you cannot clear it for new data.

- The data on a standard CD or DVD cannot be altered or deleted. A different type of disc is "rewritable". This has a special surface that can be melted, so its marks disappear. The data is erased and the disk can be used for new data. This type of disk is called CD-RW, DVD–RW or DVD+RW. (RW stands for "rewritable".)

Advantages and disadvantages

CDs and other optical media are generally inexpensive. However their storage capacity is small compared to other storage media. That means that the same amount of storage space (for example one megabyte) is more expensive if you use optical storage than it would be if you use magnetic or solid state storage. CDs are portable, light and don't take up much space. A disadvantage is that standard CDs cannot be erased to hold new data. CDs can be broken or scratched. Rewriteable CDs can lose data quality if they are written and rewritten many times.

Test yourself

1. What is the difference between a read-only, a write-once and a rewritable CD?
2. Explain why a DVD can hold more data than a CD.
3. What is the advantage of using a CD for storage compared to using an internal HDD?
4. What is the disadvantage of optical storage compared to magnetic storage?

Learning activity

Look for adverts for optical media online. Create a table showing the costs and storage capacity of a range of optical storage media.

Extension activity

Optical storage is not as widely used nowadays as it used to be. Look at adverts for modern computer systems and see what devices they include that can read from, or write to, optical storage media.

Syllabus reference

3.4.4 Systems architecture

Be aware of different types of secondary storage (solid state, optical and magnetic).

Explain the operation of solid state storage.

Discuss the advantages and disadvantages of solid state storage.

Solid state storage

Introduction

A recently-invented type of storage is called "solid state storage" or "flash memory". Use of this type of storage is widespread because it has many advantages. Learn about solid state storage in this section.

Solid state storage

All atoms are composed of electrons in motion around a nucleus. Electrons are very small particles. An electric current is a flow of electrons. A material that doesn't normally let electrons flow is called an insulator.

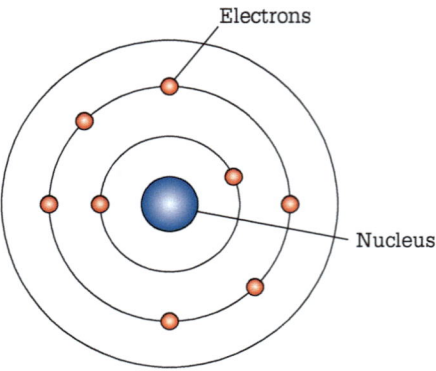

Electrons

Nucleus

↑ Electrons are one of the basic particles of matter

Flash memory works by trapping electrons. A "flash" of electricity forces electrons through an insulator. When the electricity is removed, the electrons are stuck there. The memory device can detect the stuck electrons, so they represent data: a location with stuck electrons represents a 0 bit, and if it has none, it represents a 1. Once the electrons have been put in place, they stay there even when the computer is switched off. A flash of electricity in the reverse direction will drain any trapped electrons and erase the data. This means flash memory is readable, writable and erasable storage.

This type of storage is called solid state because the storage happens inside the solid structure of matter. It is called flash because of the flash of electricity that sets the electrons in place.

Storage media

Flash memory is built into an integrated circuit (IC). It can be packaged in many different ways.

USB flash drive

USB stands for "universal serial bus". USB is a type of connector that allows many types of peripherals to be plugged into a computer. A USB flash drive is flash memory IC with a USB connector plug. It can be plugged into any modern computer. This is a very convenient type of storage. It holds a lot of data for its size. Using a USB drive for storage is very popular. There are several other names for a USB drive, such as a thumb drive, flash memory or data stick.

↑ A USB drive

Solid state drive (SSD)

Flash memory can be used in place of a computer's built-in hard disk drive (HDD), which you learned about on page 204. A solid state drive (SSD) uses the same case and connections as an HDD but contains a number of flash memory ICs. It is sometimes called a solid state disk, but it does not contain magnetic discs or any other moving parts. Compared to a magnetic hard drive, flash memory is reliable and has high storage for its size. The disadvantage is that it is more expensive, adding to the cost of the device.

⬆ A solid state drive

Mobile devices

Many mobile devices, such as smartphones and tablets, use solid state storage. This means they can hold a lot of data, and they are light and portable.

Advantages and concerns

Solid state storage has many important advantages compared to other types of storage. It is small, light, stores a lot of data, and is erasable and rewriteable. No moving parts are involved in reading from or writing to flash memory. This increases the robustness and reliability of the devices. For this reason, flash memory is a very popular choice, and has replaced other types of storage in everyday use. Flash memory is slightly more expensive than magnetic memory. However, its price is coming down.

Some people are concerned about the long-term reliability of flash memory. Flash memory is guaranteed for a certain number of read or write actions. This number is very high – hundreds of thousands of actions. However, when this number is exceeded the storage may start to lose data. Flash memory was invented fairly recently, so nobody can be certain whether it will retain data in the long term.

Test yourself

1. Explain what happens at the atomic level when solid state storage is used to read, write and erase data.
2. Why has the development of solid state storage been so important for the mobile phone industry?
3. What are the advantages and disadvantages of a solid-state drive compared to an HDD?
4. What are the advantages of a USB flash drive compared to a CD?

Learning activity

Draw a table showing the advantages and disadvantages of magnetic, solid state and optical storage.

Extension activity

Research the costs and capacity of different storage devices and media that use solid state (flash) memory.

Syllabus reference

3.4.4 Systems architecture

Explain the term "cloud storage".

Additional information

Students should understand that cloud storage uses magnetic and increasingly solid state storage at a remote location.

Explain the advantages and disadvantages of cloud storage when compared to local storage.

Understand why secondary storage is required.

Choosing the right storage

Introduction

You have looked at the different storage media that are available. Each has advantages and disadvantages. In this section you will look at how we choose the right storage solution, and consider whether cloud storage offers a reasonable alternative.

Cloud storage

The term "cloud storage" does not describe a storage medium. It describes how the storage is accessed.

When you store your data with cloud storage, the data is sent through an Internet connection to storage. It is not stored on a computer or storage medium that you own yourself. The data is stored by an Internet company on its computers. The Internet company could use any method of storage. Typically, the Internet company will use magnetic storage on huge arrays of hard disk drives. Nowadays these companies also make use of large amounts of flash memory. This is used increasingly as it comes down in price.

You may have to pay for cloud storage. Some companies offer free storage for users with limited personal storage requirements.

Use of cloud storage

Many people use cloud storage. Internet companies have large servers with large capacity magnetic or solid state drives. These drives store data for millions of users. Examples include Google Drive and Dropbox, but there are many others.

Advantages of cloud storage include the following:

- You don't need to buy your own storage devices and media.
- You can access your data from any device with an Internet connection.
- The company backs up the data so there is a low risk of being lost.
- Cloud storage doesn't take up any space on your own device, so it is very popular for use with smartphones and tablets.

There are possible disadvantages:

- There may be concerns about the privacy of your data, because it is held by someone else.
- You cannot access the data if your Internet connection fails.
- A cyber-attack or system failure affecting the Internet company can mean that millions of users lose their data.

Choice of storage

When choosing storage you must consider a range of factors:

- Capacity: How much data do you need to store?
- Portability: Do you need to move your data between computers?
- Costs: How do the options compare?

- Speed of access: Drives wired into the computer are the fastest.
- Reliability and durability: How likely is it that the data will be lost or corrupted?

Different storage choices suit different needs. Flash drives and cloud storage are good choices for small mobile devices. Devices with solid state drives tend to be more expensive than those that use magnetic storage.

Summary of storage methods

Storage method	Advantages	Disadvantages	Some key uses
Magnetic	Readable and writeable by most computer systems. The most inexpensive choice for the same size of storage.	Tends to be heavier and bulkier than other forms of storage.	Used very widely as built-in secondary storage for many desktop and some mobile computer systems.
Optical	Light to store and carry. Individual CDs have limited capacity but are cheap to buy.	Many forms of optical storage are read-only. The most expensive choice for the same capacity of storage.	Used to pass on data or software files, for example to customers. The add-on cost of an individual CD is not too great, and read-only memory is appropriate for this purpose.
Flash memory	The most compact and portable form of memory. Read/write devices do not have moving parts so less likely to break.	Somewhat more expensive than magnetic storage. Some concerns about long term memory failure.	Flash memory stick is a common form of portable personal storage. Used for built-in storage in many mobile computer devices such as tablets and smartphones.
Cloud storage	Can be accessed from any device that has an internet connection. There are a range of pricing options, with many companies offering some free storage for personal customers. Very large capacity storage is available. The reassurance of using computer systems maintained and backed up by a large company.	Cannot be accessed if Internet connection fails. Some concerns about privacy and vulnerability to hacking. You do not have a local copy of your own data on your own system.	Used instead of or as well as local storage in many computer systems. Useful for businesses with lots of data and users in different locations. Useful for people who work at many different computers or use mobile devices.

Making backups

It is important to make regular backups of stored data. A backup is a copy of all the data. If your storage media breaks or fails you could lose all your data, unless you have made a backup. A backup should be stored in a safe place. Normally it will not be used. However, if your main data is lost you can use the backup to restore your lost data. Storage media for backup should be reliable and inexpensive. It must have high capacity. Fast access to the data is not needed. Often magnetic tape is used.

Test yourself

1. Explain the advantages and disadvantages of making a weekly backup of your data.
2. Explain why magnetic tape is suitable for making a backup, but not for most other storage uses.
3. A business woman asks you if she should use cloud storage for her financial records. Explain what cloud storage is, and the advantages and disadvantages of this type of storage.
4. Evaluate flash memory in terms of capacity, portability, reliability, cost and speed.

Learning activity

You are going to set up an imaginary mail-order business selling storage solutions. Investigate what items you might sell in your business. Find real examples of items, such as USB drives.

Extension activity

Make a web page or a document that advertises the different types of storage you will offer for sale. For each type include an image, a description and a price guide. You can find out prices and specifications from online research. Include enough information for your customers to be able to choose which type of storage is right for them.

7.3 Boolean logic

Logic gates and circuits

> ### Introduction
> You have learned that data is stored in electrical form inside the computer. The computer does not only store the data. It also changes the data. This is called processing. In the next few sections you will learn about how the computer processes data.

Data processing

You have learned that a computer processes data to make information. The data is held inside the computer in the form of electronic signals. The data is processed by changing the electronic signals. This happens inside a part of the computer called the processor. The processor is at the centre of the computer system. The processor transforms data into information by changing the electronic signals in regular and organised ways. In this section you will learn how the processor works.

On/off switches

When we describe the operations of the processor, we need to talk about on/off switches, and their effect on an electric circuit. We can use the terms:

- "on and off", meaning the switch allows or does not allow current to flow in an electric circuit
- "high and low", meaning the switch connects a point in an electric circuit to a relatively high electrical potential (for example 3 volts) or low electrical potential (for example 0 volts)
- "1 and 0"
- "True and False".

These are all ways of describing the state of the on/off switches inside a computer. When a switch is on, a current can flow through it; when the switch is off, no current can flow.

Logic gates

On/off switches are combined to make electrical circuits. These circuits are called logic gates. Electrical signals pass into logic gates, and electrical signals pass out. Every logic gate has input and output:

- The input to a logic gate is the electrical signal that goes into the gate. Some logic gates have one input, some have two inputs. Each input can be either on or off. There are no other possible inputs.
- The output from a logic gate is the electrical signal that comes out of the gate. All logic gates have one output. The output can be on or off. There are no other possible outputs.

There are no other states for input or output. A logic gate's inputs and output are both binary values: each has only two possible states.

The logic gate transforms the inputs into new outputs. The different types of gate produce different outputs. There are different types of logic gate. Each type decides its switch setting in a different way. In this chapter you will learn about three types of logic gate:

- the NOT gate
- the AND gate
- the OR gate.

Logic circuits

Logic gates can be connected together into a logic circuit. The output of a gate can be connected to the input of other gates. Each gate transforms the signal in some useful way. Logic gates can be joined together in different ways to create many different circuits. Each circuit will transform its binary input signals in a different way. You will learn more about logic circuits in this section. A logic circuit can have more than two inputs.

This logic circuit has three inputs and one output.

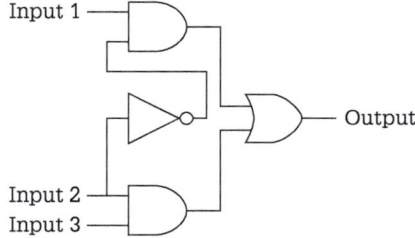

Boolean logic

George Boole was an English mathematician in the 19th century. He devised a way of writing down logical expressions, and the rules for transforming them.

These rules are known as Boolean logic. You will learn more about Boolean logic on page 215.

You will learn more about Boolean logic on page 215.

Test yourself

1. What determines the output of a logic gate?

2. What does a logic gate do to an electrical signal?

3. The output from a logic gate can be in two different states. What are these two states?

4. Explain the differences between a logic gate and a logic circuit.

Learning activity

Do an online image search for images of logic circuits. Copy one of the diagrams into a document and save it. Don't worry if you don't understand it yet. You will do more work with this image later.

Extension activity

Use suitable graphics software to draw your own version of the logic circuit you found.

NOT gate

Introduction

You have learned that logic gates are circuits that change a binary signal. In this section you will learn about a logic gate called the NOT gate.

The NOT gate

The NOT gate is a simple logic gate. It changes every binary signal into its opposite. If the signal is 1, it makes it 0. If the signal is 0, it makes it 1. In logical terms, it changes True into False. This gate works like the word "not" in everyday speech. If we put "not" into a sentence it changes the meaning to the opposite. For example, "I am not tired" means the opposite of "I am tired". The word "not" reverses the meaning of a sentence. The NOT gate inverts a binary signal.

Gate symbol

Each type of logic gate has a different symbol. This is the symbol for a NOT gate.

Input ——▷○—— Output

The line coming into the gate from the left is the input. The line coming out on the right is the output. A NOT gate has one input and one output.

Input and output

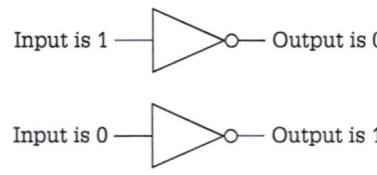

Logic gates are predictable and logical. If we know the input to a gate, we know what the output will be. Only one signal goes into a NOT gate. This signal can be 1 or 0:

- If the signal going in is 1, then the signal coming out is 0.
- If the signal going in is 0, then the signal coming out is 1.

Truth table

A truth table is a way of showing all the possible states of a logic gate. Each state is shown on a different row of the table. The truth table for the NOT gate is very simple. It only has two rows.

Input	Output
0	1
1	0

The first row shows input 0, output 1. The second row shows input 1, output 0. Those are the only possibilities.

Logical expressions

Logical expressions are statements that can be true or false. They have a definite "truth value". In real life, there are many statements of this kind. For example:

- Paris is the capital of Sweden.
- It is my birthday today.
- Python is a programming language.

Which of these statements are true and which are false? All these statements have a truth value.

We can work out that if:

"It is my birthday today" is true

then:

"It is NOT my birthday today" is false.

This is called a logical deduction.

In Boolean algebra letters are used to stand for logical expressions. That means we can concentrate on the logic without worrying about the details of statements. The laws of logic are true whether we are talking about birthdays, or capital cities or any other statement.

Boolean algebra

In Boolean algebra we use the letter A to stand for a statement.

A

We use the letter A with a line over it to stand for NOT A.

$\overline{A}$

Remember: whatever expression "A" stands for:

- If A is true then $\overline{A}$ is false.
- If A is false then $\overline{A}$ is true.

Logic gates match logical expressions

It is not a coincidence that the logic gates inside a computer match up with logic expressions and Boolean algebra. Computers are designed to match the way that logic works in the real world. That is why we can use computers to help find the solutions to real problems.

Test yourself

1. If the input to a NOT gate is 1, what is the output?

2. The NOT gate can be in two states. Describe the two states in words. Include a description of both input and output.

3. Explain how the NOT gate has a similar effect to the word "not" in common everyday speech.

4. Why is it correct to say that the output of a NOT gate is "predicable and logical"?

AND gate

Introduction

You have learned that logic gates transform binary signals. In this section you will learn about the AND gate. This gate transforms two inputs into a single output.

The AND gate

The AND gate is a circuit that takes two binary signals and turns them into one signal. The inputs can be 1 or 0:

- If both inputs are 1, the output is 1.
- In all other cases, the output is 0.

We can express this using True and False:

- If both inputs are True, the output is True.
- In all other cases, the output is False.

The AND gate is like the word "and" in a sentence. We use "and" to say that two things are both true. For example, "I like sport AND books", or "I am tired AND hungry". The sentence is only true if both parts are true. The AND gate works like this. The output is only True if both inputs are True.

Gate symbol

The symbol for the AND gate looks like this.

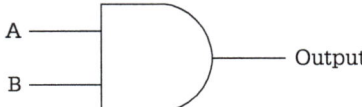

There are two inputs to the AND gate. We can label the two inputs as A and B. A and B are independent of each other; they don't affect each other. They only affect the output of the gate.

Possible states

You learned that the NOT gate can be in two possible states (input 1 or 0). The AND gate is more complicated because it has two inputs, and each input can be 1 or 0. That gives four possible input states altogether:

- A is 0, B is 0
- A is 0, B is 1
- A is 1, B is 0
- A is 1, B is 1.

The AND gate will only output 1 if both the inputs are 1.

Truth table

We use truth tables to set out all possible states for a logic gate. The four possible states are shown like this:

0 0

0 1

1 0

1 1

Did you spot that this list is the same as the first four binary numbers? If you need a reminder, go back to page 130. We can put those four inputs into a truth table. Each input is shown on a different row of the table.

A	B	Output
0	0	
0	1	
1	0	
1	1	

Now the output is filled in for each case.

A	B	Output
0	0	0
0	1	0
1	0	0
1	1	1

The output is always 0, except on the bottom row of the table. When both A and B are 1, the output is 1.

Boolean algebra

In Boolean algebra A and B are shown as letters. The expression "A AND B" is shown as the letters with a dot in between them: A.B

If A is true and B is True then A.B is True.

Test yourself

1. What are the four possible states of the inputs to an AND gate? Describe them in words.

2. A and B are independent of each other. What does that mean?

3. Draw the symbol of the AND gate. Label the inputs A and B, and label the output.

4. If A is True and B is False, what is the value of A.B?

Learning activity

Create a page about the AND gate on the computer or in your notebook. Include a description of the gate, its symbol, its Boolean expression and its truth table.

Extension activity

Look at your copy of diagram of a logic circuit from page 213. Identify any AND gates in this logic circuit. Mark them on your copy with the word "AND".

OR gate

Introduction

You have learned about the AND gate and the NOT gate. In this section you will learn about another logic gate: the OR gate.

The OR gate

The OR gate takes two binary input signals and turns them into one output signal. Each input can be 1 or 0, True or False. The OR gate will output 1 if at least one of the inputs is 1. It works like this:

- If both inputs are 1, the output is 1.

- If one input is 1, and one is 0, the output is 1.

- If both inputs are 0, the output is 0.

The OR gate works like the word "or" in a sentence. We use "or" to say that at least one thing is true, for example "I will eat some cake or bread". The sentence is true if either part is true, or if both parts are true. The OR gate works in the same way. The output is on if at least one of the inputs is on.

Gate symbol

The symbol for the OR gate looks like this.

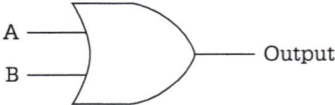

There are two inputs to the OR gate. In this diagram we have labelled the inputs A and B. Like the AND gates, these inputs are independent of each other.

Truth table

The truth table for the OR gate shows the four possible states of the OR gate. It shows the output in each state. Columns A and B are the same as the truth table for the AND gate. The final column, which shows the output, is different. This is because the OR gate has a different effect.

The output of the OR gate is 1 in every row except the first row.

A	B	Output
0	0	0
0	1	1
1	0	1
1	1	1

Boolean algebra

The symbol for A OR B is:

A+B

Some students find this confusing because the symbol + looks like the plus sign. They think it means "add" or "and", but in Boolean algebra A+B means A OR B. If A is False and B is True, then A+B is True. What other conditions make A+B True?

Boolean expressions

You have learned about three Boolean operators: AND, OR, NOT. We can use these operators to make Boolean expressions. Every Boolean expression has a truth value. Here is an example:

Q = A.B

Q is a new value. It is defined as A AND B. That means Q is True, if A is True AND B is True. In all other cases Q is false.

Order of precedence

A more complex Boolean expression may have more than one operator. Over the next few pages you will look at how we work with complex expressions. A key issue is order of precedence. If the expression uses more than one operator, which part of the expression do we work out first?

A complex expression may include brackets:

Q = A.(B+C)

If an expression has brackets in it, then the first step is to work out the truth value of the part that is in brackets. In this case we would work out the value of (B+C) first.

Sometimes a complex expression does not have brackets:

Q = A.B+C

In this case we work out the answers in this order:

1. Apply any **NOT** operators

2. Apply any **AND** operators

3. Apply any **OR** operators

So in this case we would work out the value of A.B (A AND B) first.

On the next few pages you will look at more examples of complex Boolean expressions.

Learning activity

Create two pages on the computer or in your notebook where you will record information about the OR gate. Describe the OR gate then draw its symbol and the truth table. Give the Boolean expression for A OR B.

Test yourself

These four Boolean expressions define a value called Q. Q can be True or False. Look at each expression. If A is True and B is False, give the value of Q (is Q True or False) in each case.

1. $Q = \overline{A}$

2. $Q = \overline{B}$

3. $Q = A.B$

4. $Q = A+B$

Extension activity

Look at your copy of the diagram of a logic circuit from page 213. Identify any OR gates in this logic circuit. Mark them on your copy with the appropriate word.

Logic circuits

Introduction

You have learned about logic gates. Logic gates can be wired together to make a logic circuit. In this section you will learn about simple logic circuits.

What is a logic circuit?

Logic gates take in binary signals and transform them. You can fit logic gates together. In real life that can mean wiring together electronic logic gates. Each gate's output flows as an electrical signal to the input of any gates wired to it. A set of logic gates, wired together so that a logical signal can flow through, is called a logic circuit.

Drawing logic circuits

You can make a drawing of a logic circuit that is made of electronic logic gates wired together. You have learned the symbols for three different logic gates. You can draw a logic circuit using the symbols for the logic gates. You draw the symbols next to each other. Then draw a line to show the wire that takes the signal from one gate to another.

Here is an example. Which gates are used in this example?

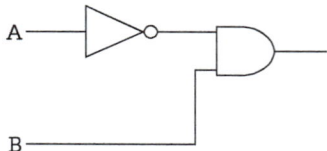

You can use special software to make neat diagrams of logic circuits. However, you should practise drawing them by hand, so that you can always draw a logic circuit if you are asked to.

Making circuits to match logic statements

You have seen that logic gates match with logical expressions and Boolean algebra. A short logical expression will match a single logic gate. A longer expression might need several logic gates joined together. In other words, it will match a logic circuit.

Example

Here is an example logical expression, in words:

(A AND B) OR C

Here is the same statement shown in Boolean algebra:

(A.B)+C

Now we will see how to make a logic circuit that matches this logical expression.

A logic circuit

The statement consists of two parts. If you are making or drawing a logic circuit to match a statement, remember the order of precedence. Expressions in brackets are evaluated first. If there are no brackets evaluate in this order

NOT

AND

OR

In this example there are brackets so this is what we evaluate first.

The section in brackets says A.B. This means A AND B. Therefore, we begin the logic circuit by drawing the AND gate. A and B are the two inputs.

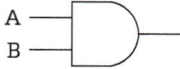

C is just a simple input. It does not have a logic gate. It is just shown as a line.

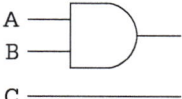

Now we can complete the logic circuit. These two parts are joined together by OR. We take the two outputs and join them with an OR gate. It looks like this.

This is the complete logic circuit that matches this expression:

(A.B)+C

Modify a logic circuit

We can change this logic circuit to show the result of this expression:

(A.B).C

The second logic gate has changed from OR to AND. The logic circuit looks like this.

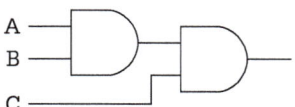

Test yourself

Draw a logic circuit to match these statements:

(A.B)+C

A+(B+C)

(A.B)+$\overline{C}$

$\overline{A}$+B.C

Learning activity

Draw neat versions of the logic circuits shown on this page.

Extension activity

Use graphics packages to make electronic images of these logic circuits.

Syllabus reference

3.4.2 Boolean logic

Be able to draw a logic circuit that implements a Boolean expression.

Construct truth tables for simple logic circuits.

Interpret the results of simple truth tables.

Interpret logic circuits

Introduction

In the previous section you learned to make logic circuits to match written logic statements. In this section you will learn to draw truth tables to match the circuits.

Making a truth table from a logic circuit

To make a truth table from a logic circuit you follow these steps.

1. Label all inputs and outputs.
2. Draw a truth table with a column for every input and output.
3. Fill in the inputs.
4. Fill in the outputs.

Example with two inputs

Below is a picture of a simple logic circuit. It matches this Boolean expression:

$\overline{A}.B$

The circuit includes two logic gates that are wired together. In this section you will make a truth table to match this logic circuit. Remember the order of precedence. NOT comes before AND. We add NOT A first. Then combine this with B using the AND gate.

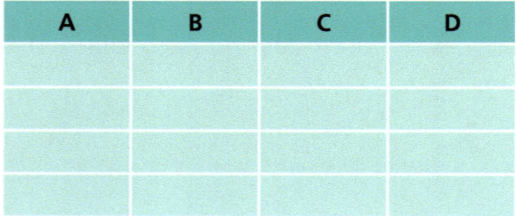

Label all inputs and outputs

The truth table shown in this image has two logic gates. The first step is to label the input and output of each gate. Here is how the circuit is labelled:

- The two inputs to the circuit are labelled A and B.
- The output of the NOT gate is labelled C.
- The output of the AND gate is labelled D.

D is the final output of the whole circuit.

Draw a truth table

Now we can make the truth table. There should be a column for every input and output in the circuit.

A	B	C	D

Show the inputs

First we fill in the initial inputs. You know how to count up in binary. Columns A and B are filled in using the first four binary numbers.

A	B	C	D
0	0		
0	1		
1	0		
1	1		

Work out the outputs

Now we fill in the outputs. These are labelled C and D in the circuit.

C is the output of a NOT gate. A is the input to the NOT gate. This means C is the inverse of A.

A	B	C	D
0	0	1	
0	1	1	
1	0	0	
1	1	0	

Next we fill in the value of D. That is the output of the AND gate. B and C are the inputs to the AND gate. The output of an AND gate is 0 unless both inputs have the value 1. Now we can fill in the final column.

A	B	C	D
0	0	1	0
0	1	1	1
1	0	0	0
1	1	0	0

The truth table is now complete. We can use the truth table to find out the answer to a logical question. In this example the logical question is "what values of A and B produce a True output".

A	B	C	D
0	0	1	0
0	1	1	1
1	0	0	0
1	1	0	0

If A is 0 and B is 1, the output of the circuit is 1. In all other cases the output is 0.

Test yourself

Draw a truth table to match the logic circuits you created in the previous lesson.

Learning activity

Draw a logic circuit and a truth table to match this Boolean expression.

$\overline{A}+B$

When is the output of this circuit False?

Extension activity

Draw a diagram of a simple logic circuit. Challenge another student in your class to produce a truth table to match this circuit.

Syllabus reference

3.4.2 Boolean logic

Be able to write a Boolean expression to represent a logic circuit and to draw a logic circuit that implements a Boolean expression.

Additional information

Students should be able to construct truth tables which contain up to three inputs.

Logic circuits and Boolean expressions

Introduction

In the previous section you learned to draw a truth table to match a logic circuit. In this section you will look at a more complex example.

Example with three inputs

This example circuit has three inputs.

We can use the methods we learned in the previous section to create a truth table.

1. Label inputs and outputs and draw the truth table.
2. Show the inputs.
3. Calculate the outputs.

Label inputs and outputs and draw the truth table

The first step is to label all inputs and outputs. Then draw a truth table with a column for every input and output.

Show the inputs

We fill in all the initial inputs. There are three inputs. To fill in all the possible inputs, use the first eight binary numbers.

A	B	C	D	E
0	0	0		
0	0	1		
0	1	0		
0	1	1		
1	0	0		
1	0	1		
1	1	0		
1	1	1		

Calculate outputs

Now we will calculate the outputs. First fill in the values for D. D is the output of the AND gate. A and B are the inputs to this gate. That means D is 1 if A and B are 1. In all other cases D has the value 0.

A	B	C	D	E
0	0	0	0	
0	0	1	0	
0	1	0	0	
0	1	1	0	
1	0	0	0	
1	0	1	0	
1	1	0	1	
1	1	1	1	

E is the final output of the circuit. It is the output of an OR gate. C and D are the inputs to the OR gate. E is 1 if either C or D is 1.

A	B	C	D	E
0	0	0	0	0
0	0	1	0	1
0	1	0	0	0
0	1	1	0	1
1	0	0	0	0
1	0	1	0	1
1	1	0	1	1
1	1	1	1	1

Interpret the truth table

Using this truth table we can see what inputs produce an output of 1.

There are five combinations of input that produce the output 1.

Test yourself

On this page you used a truth table to analyse a logic circuit. List all the values of A, B and C that produce an output of 1.

Extension activity

Write a logic statement. Challenge another student in your class to draw a logic circuit and a truth table to match the statement you have written.

Learning activity

Use this logic statement to answer the questions that follow:

$(A+B).\overline{(C)}$

1. Draw a logic circuit to match this statement.

2. Create a truth table that matches this logic circuit.

3. By looking at the truth table, say what inputs will produce a True output from the logic circuit.

## Chapter 8

Syllabus reference

3.5 Fundamentals of computer networks

Define what a computer network is. Discuss the benefits and risks of computer networks. Describe the main types of computer network including: local area network (LAN), wide area network (WAN).

8.1 Networks

What is a network?

Introduction

In this chapter you will learn how computer systems can be joined together to make computer networks. In this section you will learn what networks are and what advantages they offer to us.

A network is a system that connects computers together. The connections between computers are called communications links.

A computer that is not connected to a network is called a stand-alone computer. Nowadays most computers are connected to a network.

What do you need for a network?

To create a network you need a range of items as well as the computers themselves. The items are:

- a network interface card (NIC) inside each computer, which converts the information inside the computer into a signal
- a driver (software) that allows the computer to use the NIC
- a transmission medium, which carries the signal between the computers
- specialist network hardware such as a switch or a router.

Benefits of a network

Joining computers into a network has many benefits:

- The computers can share information.
- Software can be installed onto computers from the central server and upgraded in the same way.
- The computers can share expensive items of hardware such as printers.
- The computers can share services such as security and backup.
- The human users of the computers can send messages and communicate with each other.

Risks and costs of networks

Most individuals and businesses consider that the benefits of networking are greater than the risks. However, there are some risks and costs when you link computers to a network:

- There is the expense of buying the hardware and software and connectivity.
- There may be extra work: many businesses need to employ staff to set up and maintain the network.
- Security risks arise. There is a risk to any data stored on a networked

computer. Data can be read, altered or deleted without permission. Viruses can get onto the system.

LANs and WANs

There are two main types of network:

- local area network (LAN): where all the computers in one building, or on one site, are joined together

- wide area network (WAN): where communications links join computers that are far apart, even in different countries.

If the computers in your school or college are joined together that is a LAN. If the computers in your home are joined together by a network that is a LAN. These are the key features of a LAN:

- The computers are quite near to each other – on the same site.

- The connections that join the computers together are privately owned, and only used for that network.

Typically, a school or home LAN is joined to a larger WAN. These are the key features of a WAN:

- The computers are far apart from each other – in different cities or countries.

- The connections between computers are in public or shared ownership. Typically, these connections are used by many different networks.

Some WANs are set up by large companies for their private business. The WAN of a large company joins its different offices together. This type of WAN makes use of the public phone or broadband system by paying a fee.

The Internet is a WAN that is not run by any single company. It uses many different types of connection. Any computer that can connect to the Internet can share information with any other Internet computer.

Typically, every LAN has a connection to the Internet. A piece of equipment called a router is used to connect a LAN to a WAN.

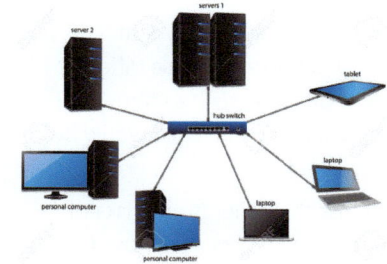

⬆ Local area network

⬆ The Internet, a WAN, spans the globe

Syllabus reference

3.5 Fundamentals of computer networks

Understand that networks can be wired or wireless.

Additional information

Students should know that wired networks can use different types of cable, such as fibre and copper, and when each would be appropriate.

Discuss the benefits and risks of wireless networks as opposed to wired networks.

Types of network

Introduction

You have seen that networks can be classified as LANs and WANs. Networks can also be classified according to the transmission medium they use. It can be wired or wireless. In this section you will learn about the differences between wired and wireless networks.

Transmission medium

The transmission medium of a network is what allows binary signals from one computer to get to another computer. A good transmission medium will transmit the signal accurately. The signal will arrive without any loss or changes to the data.

Cabling

There are two types of cable in common use to connect wired networks:

- twisted pair
- fibre-optic.

Twisted pair cabling consists of pairs of copper wires twisted together. The signal is sent as electrical pulses down the wire. Twisted pair cabling is inexpensive and flexible, but it can only be used over short distances of up to 90 metres.

Fibre optic cable is made of transparent plastic rods. The signal is sent down the plastic as pulses of light. The fibre optic signal is not affected by electrical interference. Fibre optic cable is good for all types of network link. It can be used for long-distance connections.

Most networks use a mix of copper twisted pair and fibre optic cables. Fibre optic is used for high-speed long-distance communication. Copper is used for slower, short distance communication. Modern networks will also include some wireless networking.

Wireless

Some networks use cable to connect computers. An alternative is to transmit the signal wirelessly. This is done using radio signals. The wireless signal is transmitted from a device called a wireless hub to the computers in the area.

Every computer in a wireless network uses a wireless card to allow it to send and receive radio signals.

Extension – wireless broadband

On page 166 you learned that sound waves have a frequency. Radio signals are transmitted by radio waves. Radio waves also have frequency. The frequency of a signal means how wide or narrow the waves are. Different radio signals use different frequencies. We can tune a radio to an identified frequency and then we can pick up a signal and listen to a radio station.

Wireless networks use set frequencies. That stops their signal getting mixed up with others in the area. A narrow network signal uses a narrow range of frequencies. A broad network signal uses a wide range of frequencies.

The term "broadband" means a wireless connection that covers a larger range of frequencies. A broadband signal can carry a lot of information. It can carry several signals at once. It will allow a lot of data to be transmitted.

If you have a broadband network connection it will work fast. More computers can use the network. You can transmit large files such as high-quality video and music.

Advantages and disadvantages

Wireless connections are very convenient. There is no need to put cables into the building. A device with a wireless connection (for example a tablet or a smartphone) can be carried around.

A disadvantage is that wireless connections can be interrupted or hard to pick up. The wireless signal only covers a limited area. Sometimes a thick wall or a ceiling can block the signal.

There are also security concerns. Someone outside the network can stand nearby and pick up the wireless signal. If they can guess the password then they can read the messages or even change the data on the network.

	Advantages	Disadvantages
Wired	Wired connections are secure and controlled. Some forms of cable are well protected against interference (for example fibre-optic cable). Fibre optic cable transmits signals as light, and therefore the signal travels very fast.	Wired connections are less flexible. All devices have to be kept plugged in to cable when they are in use. A wired connection can be slower. Metal wiring transmits signals at about one tenth the speed of light.
Wireless	Wireless devices can be carried around. A wireless connection saves the expense of laying cabling. It is easy to extend the network to new parts of the building. Wireless signals are transmitted as radio waves, which travel at the speed of light.	There are security concerns. It is hard to control who connects. The signal only covers a limited area and can be blocked by thick walls.

Learning activity

A family friend has set up a small business. She asks you for advice on what type of network to set up in her business. Write an email setting out the different network options and the advantages of disadvantages of each choice.

Test yourself

1. Which is the cheapest form of network cabling? What are the disadvantages of using this form of cabling to connect a network?

2. More and more people are using handheld devices. What type of networking is best with this type of computer hardware?

3. What are the main disadvantages and risks of wireless networking?

4. How could you overcome the disadvantages and risks that might affect wireless networking?

Extension activity

Research the prices of the different items of equipment and cabling that might be needed to set up a network. Find the price of the equipment you would need to set up a new wired or wireless network in your family home. How many people would be connected?

Network topologies

Syllabus

3.5 Fundamentals of computer networks

Explain the following physical network topologies: star, bus.

Introduction
You have learned about LANs and WANs. You have learned that networks can be connected by wires, or by wireless connections. In this section you will learn about the different shapes that networks can have. We call these network topologies.

Network topology

Networks are made by connecting computers together. The connections are made using a transmission medium. That can be wired or wireless. The network of connections can make different shapes. The different shapes are called network topologies.

Bus topology

A bus topology has a single main cable that transmits all the signals. This main cable is called the bus. Every computer is connected to the bus by a short connecting wire. The signals pass up and down the wire. At each end of the wire is a terminator. The terminator turns the signal around and sends it back up the wire.

The big advantage of the bus topology is that it is simple and inexpensive to set up. There is only one cable. Any computer on the network can connect through that single cable. If any computer breaks down the network will keep running.

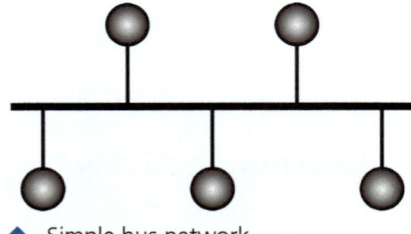

↑ Simple bus network

One disadvantage of the bus topology is that the cable can be overloaded with signals. If the network gets large or busy the signal becomes slow and unreliable. Signals can interfere with each other. This is called a collision.

Other disadvantages also arise from the reliance on a single cable. The whole network will fail if that cable fails. And there may be security concerns, as every user shares the same transmission medium.

Star topology

A star topology provides a different connection for every computer on the network. Here is a general diagram of the star topology.

One advantage in this system is that each computer has its own cable, so the network does not become overloaded. A fault in one part of the network, or one stretch of cabling, is easier to find and fix. It will not usually affect the rest of the network.

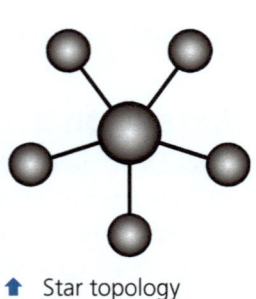

↑ Star topology

The star topology has some disadvantages. It uses more cabling than the bus topology, which is an additional expense. It contains a central 'switch' (see below) which is another additional expense. It is therefore more expensive to set up than a bus topology. Although cable failure will not disable the network, failure of the central switch stops the network from operating.

In a star network all communication passes through the centre of the star.

The equipment at the centre of the star is called a switch; this is a piece of equipment that receives signals from each computer in the network. The switch contains a processor that examines each signal and only sends the signal to one computer – the one that needs to receive it.

In many cases a star topology will include a server – this is a large computer that provides services and storage space to the other computers.

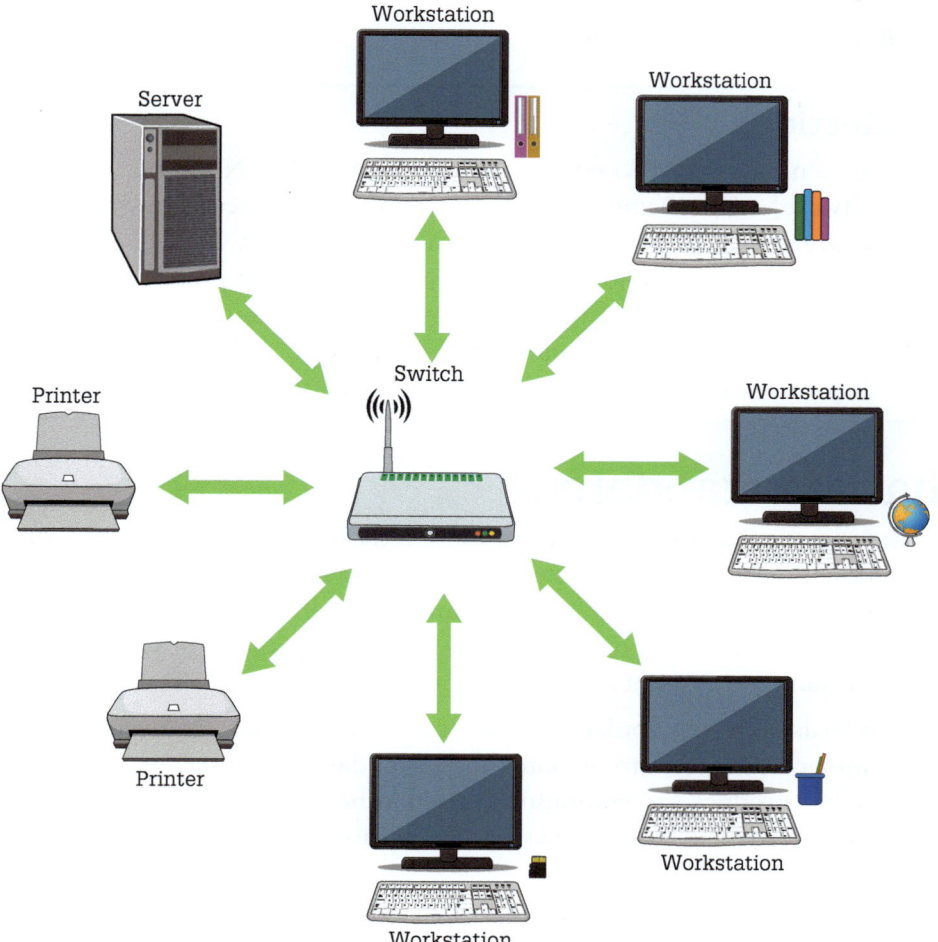

▲ Wireless star topology

In recent years, the cost of cabling has decreased. Wireless systems have become cheaper and more reliable. These changes mean that star topology is a good choice for modern networks. It is the most common topology for LAN networks nowadays.

Syllabus reference

3.5 Fundamentals of computer networks

Define the term "network protocol".

Explain the purpose and use of common network protocols including: Ethernet, Wi-Fi.

Network protocols

Introduction

You have seen how networks connect computers together. Networks need hardware, software and connectivity. Networks also need protocols. Protocols are standards for communication. In this section you will learn why protocols are important. Two important network protocols are Ethernet and Wi-Fi. There are many different protocols in use nowadays. Protocols are grouped together into families of protocols. One family of protocols is responsible for one part of the overall communication process.

What are standards?

Computer communications rely on common standards. Standards are common ways of doing things. If two computers use the same standards then they are able to send messages to each other. There are standards for the way hardware is designed, and for the way that equipment is linked together. ASCII and Unicode are standard ways of coding characters as binary numbers.

Some standards are very popular and widespread. Manufacturers decide to make equipment and software to match these standards. That means the computers they produce can communicate with other computers. It makes the manufacturers' products more attractive. It is in those companies' commercial interest to use standards.

Some standards are regulated by organisations. The organisations will test equipment or software to make sure it matches the standard. If it does conform to the standard then the manufacturer is allowed to state this in the product description. Manufacturers may be allowed to use the trademark or symbol. This makes their product more successful. For this reason, manufacturers work hard to meet the latest standards.

What are protocols?

Protocols are standards for the way signals are sent over networks. Protocols are rules about how signals are prepared, sent and received. There are many different communication protocols. We will learn about them in this section.

Ethernet

Ethernet is a system of protocols for preparing and transmitting data in a wired network. In the Ethernet system communications are broken up into small sections called packets. There are rules for the binary signals that mark the start and end of a packet. A packet is sent together with an address. The packet travels down the network until it finds the computer with the right address. It is then copied into that computer's memory.

Ethernet is supported by a non-profit making organisation called the Ethernet Alliance. This organisation checks equipment and promotes the Ethernet system.

ethernet alliance

Wi-Fi

Wi-Fi is a protocol used for wireless networking. Like Ethernet, it is a family rather than a single protocol. A wireless local area network is called a WLAN. Wi-Fi is a protocol used by WLANs.

Devices that are Wi-Fi enabled have been built to use the Wi-Fi protocol. These devices normally have a sticker on them to confirm they are Wi-Fi compatible. A device that can use the Wi-Fi protocol can connect to any Wi-Fi network. A place where a Wi-Fi network is in place is called a Wi-Fi hotspot.

You may recognise the Wi-Fi logo.

For example, if your tablet or phone is Wi-Fi certified, you will be able to pick up Wi-Fi connections. If you know the password to a Wi-Fi network, you will be able to log in to the network. Many businesses such as coffee shops offer a free Wi-Fi connection.

Wi-Fi is a trademark of a non-profit organisation called the Wi-Fi Alliance. This organisation tests devices to make sure they are compatible with the Wi-Fi protocol. Only product that pass the tests can call themselves Wi-Fi certified.

Test yourself

1. What is a WLAN? Which family of protocols is designed for a WLAN?
2. If a product has a sticker on it that says Wi-Fi certified. What does that mean?
3. What types of network use the Ethernet standard?
4. What is a Wi-Fi hotspot?

Learning activity

Find examples in places near you of networks using the Ethernet or Wi-Fi protocols. If your school or college has a network ask the network technician to tell you about the protocols it uses.

Are there Wi-Fi hotpots near to or inside your school or college? Consider a class project that involves mapping out networks in your area.

Extension activity

You have learned about the Wi-Fi and Ethernet protocols. Another protocol that is available is called Bluetooth. What is the Bluetooth protocol and what is it used for?

Introduction

You have learned that protocols are standards for communication. Shared protocols allow computers to communicate with each other. In this section and the next you will learn about the protocols that allow the modern Internet to function.

DARPA and the Internet

TCP/IP is a group of standards and protocols for high speed links over a wide area network (WAN). TCP/IP was developed in 1969 by a US government agency called DARPA. Since 1969 this system of links has grown into a worldwide network system known as the Internet.

There are a lot of protocols that control computer communications. These shared protocols are what make the Internet work. The protocols can be organised into a four-layer model. This is sometimes called the TCP/IP model or the DARPA model. The four layers are:

- application layer
- transport layer
- network layer
- link layer.

In this section you will learn about the application layer. On pages 236–237 you will learn about the other three layers.

Application layer

The application layer contains the protocols that make common Internet applications work. This includes the web browser software that you use to look at websites. It also includes applications that let you send and receive emails.

The most widely used application layer protocols include:

- hypertext transfer protocol (HTTP)
- hypertext transfer protocol – secure (HTTPS)
- file transfer protocol (FTP)
- simple mail transfer protocol (SMTP)
- Internet message access protocol (IMAP)

Hypertext transfer protocol (HTTP)

HTTP is the protocol used for transmitting web pages between a server and the web browser. HTTP is the protocol that defines "hypertext". Hyperlink means text in a website that makes a link to other web pages. Your web browser understands this protocol. When you click on a link your browser connects to a new web page. By clicking on links you can move around the Internet looking at different websites.

If you look at the name of a website in your browser you will see it begins:

http://

This shows that the web page uses the hypertext transfer protocol.

HTTP secure (HTTPS)

Another version of HTTP is called HTTPS. The "S" stands for secure. HTTPS is a safer way of connecting to a web page. Using HTTPS stops the people you don't want to read your messages from doing that. It can also stop people tricking you into giving them your personal details or money.

HTTPS includes extra security features such as encryption. Encryption means your messages to an HTTPS site are put into a code before they are sent over an Internet connection.

You can tell which websites you visit are protected by HTTPS. The name of the web page begins with the name of the protocol:

https://

File Transfer Protocol (FTP)

FTP stands for file transfer protocol. FTP is a way of getting data files from one computer to another. The computer that has the files is called the server. The computer that receives the files is called the client.

FTP is an older protocol that HTTP. FTP lacks many modern Internet features.

Simple mail transfer protocol (SMTP)

Simple mail transfer protocol (SMTP) has been used for many years. It is the protocol used to send email messages and attach files to emails. SMTP is a delivery protocol. That means SMTP delivers an email message to an address. It does not fetch your email messages for you. Originally, SMTP was text only but nowadays emails can include all types of images and file attachments.

Internet message access protocol (IMAP)

The Internet message access protocol (IMAP) is a protocol that gets your emails. Companies that offer email services store the emails on a large computer called a mail server. All emails sent to you will be stored in an inbox on the mail server. IMAP lets you look at the e-mail messages in your inbox, using an Internet connection. You can see the headings of the emails and open any of them to read the message.

Many email applications such as Gmail and Outlook use IMAP.

Learning activity

Investigate a range of Internet sites. Which sites use HTTP? Which use HTTPS? What type of site uses HTTPS? Write a report on what you have found.

Extension activity

Websites are read using software called a web browser. What are the most common web browsers in use today? See whether you can find out what percentage of web users use each type of browser.

Test yourself

1. How can you tell whether a website uses the HTTP protocol or the HTTPS protocol?

2. What extra features are included in the HTTPS protocol?

3. A web page contains hyperlinks. What are hyperlinks?

4. SMTP and IMAP work together to make email systems work. Explain how the work of sending and reading emails is divided between the two protocols.

Syllabus reference

3.5 Fundamentals of computer networks

Describe the four-layer TCP/IP model:

- application layer
- transport layer
- network layer
- link layer.

Explain the purpose and use of common network protocols, including:

- transmission control protocol (TCP)
- user datagram protocol (UDP)
- Internet protocol (IP).

Additional information

Students should know what each protocol is used for.

Introduction

You have learned about the protocols that make the application layer of the four-layer model. In this section you will learn about the other three layers of the model.

Transport layer

A web host is a company that operates a computer connected to the Internet. The transport layer holds protocols that allows web hosts to send messages and share data. It is sometimes called the host-to-host transport layer. A message between two web servers may go through many short connecting links. The transport layer does not deal with these smaller links. It controls the communication at the two ends. Transport layer protocols are responsible for establishing the connection between the two servers. The web services of the application layer can only work because the transport layer takes care of sending messages between two computers. The transport layer ensures the two computers are using the same settings, such as language and the size of the data packets they send and receive.

Two key protocols of the transport layer are transmission control protocol (TCP) and user datagram protocol (UDP):

- TCP allows the computers at the two ends of the communication link to recognise each other. Using TCP, each computer can read the messages sent by the other computer. TCP emphasises accurate transmission not speed.

- UDP is an alternative to TCP. It has reduced error-checking and works more quickly. It is only suitable when a message is short and the connection is very reliable.

Network layer

The transport layer protocols control the two ends of the transmission link. The network layer takes care of the detailed connections in between. A message must pass through many different connections on its route through the Internet. The network layer has protocols that control this journey. For this reason it is also sometimes called the Internet layer. We can imagine a packet of data being passed from point to point on a journey through the Internet. It may pass through many different smaller networks, servers and routers. But it will end up at the right destination. This process is controlled by network layer protocols.

The most important protocol in this layer is called the Internet protocol (IP). The IP makes sure that every message gets to the right Internet address.

Every web host has an IP address. Messages are split into packets and each packet is sent down an Internet route to the right IP address. Then the packets are put back together and the message is delivered.

Link layer

You have learned that TCP and IP work together to deliver messages over an Internet connection. The TCP/IP will deliver messages to any kind of computer or network that has an Internet connection. TCP/IP protocols are the same for all computer systems. That's why all different types of computer can use the Internet.

The final layer of the four-layer model is the link layer. The protocols in this layer convert the messages from the TCP/IP system into a form that the local network can use. Ethernet is a protocol at the link layer, which enables signals to go down local network connections. Device drivers convert signals from network hardware devices and transfer them to the processor. The network interface card converts binary signals from network devices into binary data inside each computer.

Summary

There are four protocol layers. All four layers are involved when a signal is sent through a network system such as the Internet.

Layer	Description	Protocols
Application layer	This allows software applications such as web browsers and email programs to work.	HTTP HTTPS FTP SMTP IMAP
Transport layer	This sends messages from one web host to another. It controls the two ends of the link.	TCP UDP
Network or Internet layer	This controls how a message travels through the Internet from one end of the link to another.	IP
Link layer	This turns messages from the Internet into a form that works on the local network or computer system.	Ethernet

These layers may be thought of as stacked on top of each other. A signal passes down through the stack. It starts at the application layer, then to the transport later. Next the network layer puts it on a route, and the link layer converts it into locally transmissible form. When it arrives, the signal passes back up through the layers. It ends up at the application layer in a new location.

Learning activity

Copy the summary table. Add an extra column to give a short description of each of the protocols in the table.

As a class project, turn this into a large poster for the computer room.

Test yourself

1. What are the main differences between TCP and UDP? What is the advantage and disadvantage of each protocol?
2. The IP controls packets and addressing. Explain what packets are and what IP addresses are.
3. Why does the Internet need both the transport layer and the network layer? Explain how the two layers work together to give a complete Internet service.
4. How does a network interface card help with the work of the link layer?

Extension activity

Find out more about the history of the Internet and the key figures involved in development of the protocols that enable the Internet to work. Write a magazine article for students.

## Chapter 9

Syllabus reference

3.6 Fundamentals of cyber security

Be able to define the term "cyber security" and be able to describe the main purposes of cyber security.

Additional information

Students should know that cyber security consists of the processes, practices and technologies designed to protect networks, computers, programs and data from attack, damage or unauthorised access.

9.1 Security threats

Importance of security

> ### Introduction
> Using computers brings great benefits to individuals, organisations and society. However, along with benefits come new risks and threats. In this chapter you will learn about the risks of computing and how we can overcome those risks so that we use computers safely and securely.

Computer security

Computer security means protecting the data stored on our computers. Data stored on computers is valuable for many reasons:

- Collecting and processing data takes time and money. We do not want the data we have collected to be corrupted or lost.
- Data is valuable and helpful to us. If we cannot rely on data to be accurate then it stops being useful.
- Our data can be private. We don't want people to see our personal details without our permission.

For these reasons, we must protect computers from data loss, corruption or unauthorised access.

Loss

Data loss means the data no longer exists in storage. For example, portable storage such as a USB flash drive could be mislaid, or a file could be deleted by mistake. Data loss can severely affect businesses. A business may have compiled a list of its customers' bank details. If this data is lost, the business will not be able to get money from its customers.

Corruption

Data corruption means the data has been damaged or changed. Changes mean the data is no longer accurate, or has the wrong format. For example, if customers' bank details were altered, money might be taken from the wrong bank account. Damage to storage media can corrupt data. For example, a CD-R can be scratched. If data corruption is severe, the data will no longer make sense and the computer will no longer be able to read it.

Unauthorised access

Some people have permission to see or alter data. Other people do not have permission. If they look at the data, copy it or make changes this is called unauthorised access. Key issues are data privacy and data integrity:

- **Privacy** means data is only seen or copied by people who have permission. Unauthorised access means someone who does not have permission has seen or copied the data.

- **Integrity** means the data is protected from unauthorised changes. Someone who does not have permission might make changes to the data. This is sometimes called hacking and it is a threat to data integrity.

Computer crime

Computer crime can cause a lot of damage and problems. Some examples are:

- taking a copy of music, games, movies, etc., without permission (sometimes called piracy)

- hacking (gaining unauthorised access to ICT systems) – hackers find out passwords or bypass security systems

- creating and distributing malware (computer viruses and other harmful software)

- identity theft, which is stealing someone else's personal details, and pretending to be that person

- deliberately damaging or stealing computer hardware and storage media.

Protecting data security

Many measures can be put in place to protect the safety and security of data, including the following:

- **Technology** – hardware and software methods can be used to protect computer systems. This includes encryption and installing anti-virus software and firewalls.

- **Practices and procedures** – we can take actions as individuals to protect our computer systems. In a large organisation, protective actions will be set down in official policies and procedures. New members of staff will be trained in secure use of the computer system.

Test yourself

1. Explain the difference between data privacy and data integrity.

2. Explain the difference between data loss and data corruption.

3. What makes the difference between authorised and unauthorised access to a computer system?

4. How can training help to protect the security of data?

Learning activity

A college decided to send an email to all students warning them of the importance of cyber security. Write a version of the text for this email.

Extension activity

A company decided to train all new employees in the importance of cyber security. Create a presentation that could be used to lead a training course for new employees.

Syllabus

3.6.1 Cyber security threats

Understand and be able to explain the following cyber security threats:

- weak and default passwords
- misconfigured access rights
- removable media
- unpatched and/or outdated software.

Threats to security

Introduction

You have learned that computer security is important. Good practice can help to protect your computer system. In this section you will see how poor practice can increase security risks.

Weak passwords

An authorised user is someone who has permission to use a computer system or website. To gain access to a computer system we use a password.

Criminals try to gain access to a system by guessing user passwords. Hackers have software that can try a million different passwords until they find one that works. Passwords are easier to guess if they have these features:

- They are short.
- They include common words or names.
- They are simple sequences of letters or numbers, for example 1234.
- They only have one type of character, for example lower-case letters.

A password that is easy to guess is referred to as weak. A password that is hard to guess is a strong password. Unfortunately, many people use weak passwords that are easy to guess.

Good password practice

You may have to choose a password when you use the network at your school or college. You may have a password to log in to your favourite web sites. Here are some rules about how to work with passwords:

- Use a strong password.
- Make sure you can remember the password.
- Do not use the same password on every website.
- Never tell anyone else your password.

Default password

Many computer systems have default settings. A default means the state of the system if you don't make any changes. Some computer systems give you a default password. Often it is the word "password".

You should never keep using the default password. You should always change it to a password made up of new series of characters that only you know. If you use the default password, it is like not having a password at all.

Access rights

Once you have established your identity, you have access to the computer system. Access means you can connect to the computer system. Different levels of access let you do different things:

- **No access** – you cannot connect to the system at all.
- **Read only access** – you can look at the data on the system but you cannot make changes.
- **Read/write access** – you can look at the data and you can also make changes to the data. Sometimes you have read/write access to parts of the data only.
- **Full access** or **admin access** – you can make changes to the data. You can also make changes to the system itself. For example, you can reset the passwords of other users, change settings and defaults or remove software.

If access rights are not set up correctly, then the wrong person might have the wrong type of access to the system. This puts all the data on the system at risk.

Removable media

Data can be copied from a computer system on to removable storage media. For example, you can copy data onto a flash memory stick or a removable hard disk. This is convenient but creates risk. A memory stick can fall into the wrong hands and so provide unauthorised access to valuable or private data. Another risk is that malware can be transmitted via a memory stick.

Some organisations do not allow the use of external or removable storage media. For example, the USB ports on those organisation's computers are disabled so memory sticks cannot be used.

Outdated software

The word "hacker" is used in different ways. Among people with good computer skills it is sometimes used to mean a person who likes to investigate and work with computer systems, to understand them better.

More generally – and more often in this book – "hacker" is used to mean a person who breaks into computer systems to steal data or make changes. This type of hacker is always looking for weaknesses in software. These weaknesses are also called vulnerabilities.

The older a software system is, the more likely it is to have vulnerabilities.

That means it is important to keep software up to date. A software update is a new version of the software. An update brings improvements and fixes problems. An update that fixes a security problem is called a security patch. A security patch will protect software again the latest threats.

> ### Learning activity
> This section contains is a list of four features of a weak password. What are the features of a strong password? Make a poster for the computer room, advising students about how to make their passwords stronger.

> ### Test yourself
> 1. Name four features that affect how strong or weak a password is.
> 2. As well as choosing strong passwords, what are the other features of good password practice?
> 3. A school computer system lets students look at their exam results online. What level of access is suitable for the students?
> 4. A school computer system lets technicians block students from the computer if they use it to play games. What level of access is suitable for the technician?

> ### Extension activity
> You have read about a number of practices that will make a computer system more or less secure. Write a policy for a small business that sets out good security practice for employees. Make sure you cover all the features mentioned in this section.

Syllabus reference

3.6.1 Cyber security threats

Understand and be able to explain the following cyber security threat: social engineering techniques.

Define the term "social engineering".

Describe what social engineering is and how it can be protected against.

Explain the following forms of social engineering:

- blagging (pretexting)
- phishing
- pharming
- shouldering (or shoulder surfing).

Social engineering

Introduction

You have learned that hackers will try to find out passwords. In this section you will learn about some of the tricks that hackers use to get passwords and other details.

Identity theft

Information such as your password and personal details should be confidential. Confidential means personal and secret. Confidential information should not be passed on to the wrong person. Hackers will try to get confidential information.

Identity theft happens when a criminal finds out your personal details. These might include your bank account, your passwords and your personal ID. The criminal can then use this information to pretend to be you.

Identity theft can enable criminals to steal money and personal property. For this reason there are lots of tricks that people use to get your personal details.

Social engineering

Hackers use software and technology to try to break password systems. Hackers also try to trick people into giving away their personal data and confidential information. In computing this is called social engineering.

Examples of social engineering are:

- blagging
- phishing
- pharming
- shouldering.

Blagging

A blagger often pretends to be someone who has the right to have information about you. They often use a phone call or an email to trick you into providing your personal data. Another word for blagging is "pretexting".

Phishing

Phishing means sending a fake email or another type of message. The email will look like an email from a company you recognise and trust, such as your bank. The email might ask you to confirm your password or send your bank details. However, this email is a trick.

Real companies should never ask you to send private details like this. Never reply to an email that asks for private details. If you are in doubt, telephone the company and check that someone who works there has contacted you. Do not use the phone number in the email though, because that might be a trick too. Find the phone number some other way.

Sometimes hackers send out thousands or even millions of fake emails. They hope that one or two people will be tricked into providing their details.

Pharming

Pharming is typically done by making a fake website. It looks like the website of a real company such as a well-known bank. You might look at the website and think it is the company's real site. You might log on, or enter your name and bank details. Now the criminals know your details and they can use them to get money in your name. Be extra careful that you have connected to the right website. Check for spelling mistakes and false URLs.

Pharming is often linked to phishing. The fake email will include the URL of the fake website.

Shouldering

Hackers often need to find out a password or PIN. PIN stands for personal identification number. A PIN is typically a four-digit code number. If someone steals your bank card they cannot withdraw money or pay for goods unless they know your PIN.

Shouldering is a way for hackers to find out a password or PIN. Shouldering means standing at someone's shoulder and watching the person enter his or her PIN or password.

When someone is entering a password or PIN it is good manners to stand a short distance away. Do not look at what the person is typing. If someone stands very near when you enter a PIN ask that person to give you more room. Sometimes you must enter your PIN in a crowded or public place. Stand so nobody can see what you type.

Test yourself

Without looking at your notes write a short definition of each of the main forms of social engineering:

1. blagging

2. phishing

3. pharming

4. shouldering.

Learning activity

Produce a leaflet for students that sets out the dangers of social engineering and how to avoid these tricks.

Extension activity

Write a script for a radio advert to alert young people to the dangers of blagging.

Syllabus reference

3.6.1 Cyber security threats

Understand and be able to explain the following cyber security threat: malicious code.

Define the term "malware".

Describe what malware is and how it can be protected against.

Describe the following forms of malware:

- computer virus
- trojan
- spyware
- adware.

Malware

Introduction

A major security threat in the modern world is caused by malware. Malware means malicious software. Malware is software that can get onto your computer without you realising. Then it can cause harm. In this section you will learn about malware and how to prevent it getting onto your computer.

Malware

Malware is short for **mal**icious soft**ware**. Malware is software that can harm your computer.

Why do people make malware?

Some people make malware as a joke or prank. Some people make malware to make a political protest, to cause trouble generally or specifically to harm their enemies. Others make malware to steal money. Malware can quickly spread around the world using Internet connections.

How does malware get onto your computer?

Malware might be hidden in a file you download from the Internet. Malware might be hidden in a file attached to an email. Malware might be on a storage drive that you use. You should always be careful when you open a file from an unknown source.

Computer virus

The most common type of malware is a computer virus. A virus is not a complete computer file. A virus is a set of computer commands. These commands get added to a file that is already on your computer. The commands might be in the form of machine code instructions. This machine code will be added to an executable file.

The virus copies itself into other files. If any of these are passed to another computer, that computer's files are infected with the virus too. The virus commands are attached to an existing file, so the virus is hidden and you may not know it is there. Most computer viruses cause significant problems. A virus can:

- delete files or wipe the entire storage
- alter your computer settings
- make your computer carry out actions such as sending emails.

Trojan

Trojan malware is hidden in a file that you will be pleased to receive. For example, it might be hidden in a free video game, or a free copy of a film you want to see. When you copy the game or film onto your computer, you copy some hidden malware too.

The name Trojan comes from a story in Ancient Greek myth. The story of the Trojan Horse reminds you how Trojan malware gets onto your computer. Remember the story if someone gives you a free gift for your computer.

Spyware

Spyware is a special kind of malware. Like a virus, spyware cannot be seen on the computer. Spyware records everything you do with your computer. The person who made the spyware can look at a record of your computer use. That might reveal every website you looked at, and what you typed on your computer. Spyware can be used by companies and governments to monitor people's behaviour. Spyware is used by criminals to find out people's passwords and personal details.

Adware

Adware is software that displays adverts on your computer. Some free software includes advertising. Some computer games and music services include adverts. That is not illegal. If you agree to seeing the adverts while you use the software, then that is not malware.

In other cases, you have not agreed to have the adverts displayed on your screen. The adware has entered your computer like malware. The adware shows adverts in pop-up windows on your screen. Sometimes you cannot close the window, so you have to look at the advert.

Avoid malware

It is important to keep malware off your computer. So how can you do that?

- Only download software and other content from legal, offical websites.
- Be careful of emails from people you do not know – don't open attachments or click on links in the email.
- Keep your software up to date – that includes application software and your operating system.

Anti-virus software

Remember that malware is hidden. It cannot be seen and removed with ordinary computer usage. Anti-virus software is made specially to stop malware. Anti-virus software will:

- check all new files and emails for malware
- scan your computer to find hidden malware
- remove malware from your computer
- warn you about possible dangers such as risky websites.

New viruses are being made all the time. Each new virus has special tricks to avoid anti-virus software. Anti-virus software must be updated regularly to keep up with these changes.

Syllabus reference

3.6.2 Methods to detect and prevent cyber security threats

Understand and be able to explain the following security measures:

- biometric measures (particularly for mobile devices)
- password systems
- CAPTCHA
- using email confirmations to confirm a user's identity
- automatic software updates.

9.2 | Ensuring security

Cyber-security protection

Introduction

You have learned that there are many threats to the security and integrity of data. Threats include social engineering and malware. Cyber security can be used to overcome security threats. In this section you will learn about cyber security.

Cyber security

"Cyber security" is a general term to describe the methods we use to protect computer systems from attacks. There are many types of attack, and so there are many different methods used to ensure cyber security. In this section you will learn about:

- passwords
- biometrics
- identity confirmation
- software updates.

Password systems

Weak passwords can help hackers to break into computer systems. Computer users can improve security by choosing strong passwords and by being aware of social engineering threats.

People who run networks and other secure systems can put measures in place to improve password systems. For example, they can require users to use strong passwords. They can make users change their passwords regularly.

Biometric measures

A biometric check is an alternative to a password. Biometric means a record of a physical characteristic. It is used to confirm identity.

Checking physical features needs special equipment and software. For example:

- a thumb or palm print reader
- an iris scanner
- facial recognition software.

A biometric check makes it difficult for criminals to pretend they are someone else. You can steal a mobile device and find out someone's password, but you cannot copy the person's physical features. For this reason, biometrics are often used nowadays to protect mobile devices such as smartphones and tablets. If a device like this is stolen, the criminal cannot use it.

⬆ A palm scan proves a person's identity

CAPTCHA

CAPTCHA is a system that checks whether a user is a real person. When you log on to a website you set up an identity and password. You may also need to complete a CAPTCHA check.

Automated systems find it difficult to read distorted text. CAPTCHA usually includes distorted text. You type in the text that you see. The idea is that only a human reader can read the text.

Email confirmation

Another way to confirm identity is by email. When you first log on to a system you set up an identity. You usually have to provide your email address. The site will send an email to that address. This is to check that your identity matches the address you have given.

Typically, you will receive an email at that address. It is sent by automated software. It usually comes quite quickly. The email will include a link. You must click on the link to confirm your identity.

Automatic software updates

Anti-malware software must be kept up to date. New viruses are being developed all the time. Anti-virus software must be updated with information about the new viruses that have been developed.

Cyber security depends on up-to-date software. Automatic updates are sent through your Internet connection. The updates come from the company that you bought the software from. An update will bring your software up to date, so that you have better cyber security.

Test yourself

1. I bought anti-virus software two years ago. Why do I need to update it?

2. What is CAPTCHA? How does the use of CAPTHA help to ensure the security of websites?

3. What are the advantages and disadvantages of biometric methods compared to the use of passwords for security?

4. A college technician wanted to make the password system as safe as possible for the students. What automatic rules might she put in place to ensure good password practice?

Learning activity

Write a report on biometric methods used with modern mobile devices. Look for examples on the Internet.

Extension activity

A school wanted to set up a security system at the entrance to the college. The three methods being considered were that visitors would have to:

- scan an ID card at the gate
- type a passcode on a keypad
- use a palm print reader.

Write a report to the college setting out the advantages and disadvantages of each of these methods.

Syllabus reference

3.5 Fundamentals of computer networks

Understand the need for, and importance of, network security. Explain the following methods of network security: authentication, firewall, MAC address filtering.

Network security

Introduction

Networks are very useful. They provide many benefits. In Chapter 8 you learned about computer communications and how networks operate. Many cyber security threats arise from networks and communications. In this section you will learn about ways that we can protect network security.

Secure protocols

You have learned that HTTP is the protocol that lets us connect to websites. An extended protocol is called HTTPS. This protocol offers extra security. If a web page's URL begins with https, you know it uses the more secure HTTPS protocol.

HTTPS includes two important security features:

- authentication
- encryption.

Authentication

Some websites are fake. They look as if they are run by a well-known company, such as a bank, but they are not. Many websites store content that is personal to you, for example payment details or a personal profile. Nobody else should be able to access that content.

"Authentic" means genuine. Authenticating a website means checking that it is genuine and not a fake site. HTTPS authenticates websites using a handshake system.

Handshake

A handshake protocol is a signal sent between the two devices at the start of communication. The handshake lets each device check that the other is genuine. A genuine website has a security certificate issued by a recognised certificate authority (CA). During the handshake the security certificate is checked. The handshake establishes a private link between the two devices.

Certification authority (CA)

Authentication uses a digital certificate. A digital certificate is like an electronic ID card that proves the computer's identity. Certificates are issued by a CA. An example of a CA is Verisign.

An organisation can request a certificate from a CA. The CA will check that the organisation is what it claims to be. It will check that the website is the real website of that organisation. Then it will issue a certificate. The CA will check each website certificate regularly. If the company has been involved in Internet fraud the certificate will be taken away.

Firewall

A firewall is a barrier between the Internet and the local network. The firewall traps every packet of data that passes in either direction. The firewall checks the data using programmed rules. The firewall will only pass on data that keeps to the rules. A firewall can prevent many Internet dangers:

- It will stop malware.
- It can prevent hackers getting onto the computer system.
- It can block unsuitable content.

Almost every Internet connection uses some kind of firewall. Business connections may concentrate on preventing access by hackers. Home connections may concentrate on filtering unsuitable content.

A firewall is made of hardware and software:

- Hardware – a firewall device is a piece of hardware. The wired or wireless link must pass its data through the firewall device to get in or out of the network.
- Software – the firewall software is a set of instructions. They tell the processor what to do with the signals that pass through the firewall device. The firewall software will have rules that help it tell the difference between safe data and dangerous malware.

MAC address filtering

You have learned that the Internet protocol (IP) makes sure that every message gets to the right Internet address. Every web host has an IP address. (For a reminder, refer back to page 236).

MAC stands for media access control. A MAC address is an identifying number, like an IP address. It identifies a single device such as a computer or printer. A device's IP address is used to route data across the Internet to a LAN. The MAC address is used to send the data across the LAN to the device itself.

The MAC address can also be used for security. Devices can be blocked from accessing a network. Other devices can be allowed. The MAC address is coded into the device, so it is a good method of securing access. MAC addresses are used in wireless networks. A secure network will have a list of devices which are allowed to connect to the network. The MAC address of each device will be listed. This is sometimes called a 'white list'.

Learning activity

Look at the website of Verisign or any other CA. Write a short report on the company.

Extension activity

You may work as a group. Interview your college technician about the security systems in place in your college. Ask about firewalls and MAC addresses. Write up the interview as a magazine article.

Test yourself

1. What is a handshake protocol?
2. Explain how a certification of authenticity is used in the handshake protocol.
3. What is the job of a certification authority?
4. What is the difference between an IP address and a MAC address?

3.5 Fundamentals of computer networks

Understand the need for, and importance of, network security. Explain the following method of network security: encryption.

Encryption

Introduction

You have learned that encryption is used to put messages into a secret code. This protects them from being read or changed as they go through Internet links. In this section you will learn how encryption works.

HTTPS

HTTPS is a communication protocol for secure websites. It includes authentication and encryption. You have learned about authentication. In this section you will learn about encryption.

WiFi

WiFi is a protocol for wireless networks. Security is very important for a wireless network. The modern WiFi protocol includes support for strong encryption and other security features. For example it dynamically generates a new 128-bit key for each packet of data.

Plain text and cypher text

Plain text is ordinary words and numbers. Plain text is not secure. Remember that an Internet message goes through lots of connections and devices on its way to its destination. The plain text could be read by anyone with access to those connections. Cypher text is text that has been scrambled or changed using a formula only certain people know. The process of turning a message into cypher text is called encryption.

For example, the computer could swap each letter for the letter two places further along in the alphabet. Here is a challenge: work out what this line says.

```
Ecp aqw tgcf vjku oguucig?
```

Encryption

Sometimes you will want a message you send to be private. For example, if you log in to an online bank service using a password, you don't want anyone else to know your password. When a message needs to be secure it can be sent as cypher text. The process of turning plain text into cypher text is called encryption. Encryption is done by the computer before the message is sent. The sender doesn't have to work out the cypher and doesn't see the scrambled text.

There are two stages to encryption:

- Encrypt: when plain text is turned into cypher text.
- Decrypt: when cypher text is turned back into plain text.

Two computers are involved in encryption:

- The sender encrypts the message (and sends it).
- The receiver decrypts the message (when it receives it).

Encryption key

Encryption uses a key. The key can be a string of text characters or a number. The key tells the computer how to encrypt plain text. It also lets the computer decrypt the cypher text. Encryption and decryption are done using a mathematical formula. As with passwords, a long and complex key gives stronger protection. Remember that as a computer user you do not have to know the key. For example, when you buy a product from Amazon your bank details are encrypted. You don't notice the encryption that is used. The computer encrypts and decrypts the messages before you see the details.

Extension – symmetric encryption

In symmetric encryption the key is kept secret from most people – only the sender and receiver know the key. The sender uses it to encrypt the message. The receiver uses the same key to decrypt it. The problem with the secret key is that it has to be sent over the Internet before encryption can begin. Anyone who finds out the secret key can decrypt the messages.

Extension – asymmetric encryption

In asymmetric encryption there are two keys: a public key and a private key. The two are mathematically linked. A message encrypted with one key can only be decrypted with the other key. These are features of the two keys:

- The public key is shared with any computer that needs to send a message. Any computer can download the public key: it is not a secret. Computers that want to send messages to you can use the public key to encrypt the messages before sending them.

- The private key is kept secret on your computer. Your computer can use it to decrypt the messages that are sent to you. The private key is never transmitted. This means that anyone can send you a secret message, but only you can decrypt those messages.

You never need to see the public and private keys. The computer generates them automatically, stores them securely, and takes care of encryption and decryption. The messages you see are all in plain text. Asymmetric encryption is safer than symmetric encryption, but slower.

Syllabus reference

3.6.1 Cyber security threats

Explain what penetration testing is and what it is used for.

Penetration testing

Introduction

You have learned about a range of methods used to ensure cyber security. It is important that cyber security measures are kept up to date. They must work perfectly. For this reason, cyber security measures are subject to regular testing. This is called penetration testing.

Internal and external threats

Threats to the security of a system can be internal or external threats:

- **External threats** are attacks on a computer system by hackers outside the organisation. The hackers do not have authentication or passwords. They will try to break the security system. Their attacks come from outside the firewall.

- **Internal threats** occur when people who have bad intentions can get inside an organisation's security system. They might get a job working for the company. They might become trusted. They may have their own password and read/write access.

Internal threats can be much more dangerous and harmful than external threats. Internal threats can be harder to spot. Good hiring practices will help to prevent the wrong people getting access to the system. Good supervision and management will help to prevent this type of attack. Cyber security must protect against internal and external threats.

What is penetration testing?

An attack on system security is an attempt to get access to the data stored on the system. Sometimes hackers want a copy of the data. Sometimes they want to delete or change data. Cyber-security methods try to prevent this.

Penetration testing is a way of testing cyber security. The people who are doing the testing try to break into the system. However, they are not hackers. They are computer experts who work for the organisation. They try to break into the system to see whether it is possible. If the testers can manage to break in, this shows there is a problem with cyber security. The testing has found the problem. Now the computer experts inside the organisation can fix the problem.

A penetration test is sometimes called a pen test for short. There are two main types of pen test. They are called black box and white box testing.

Black box and white box testing

- Black-box testing is testing for external threats. The testers work from outside the firewall. They do not use valid IDs or passwords. They break in using an external Internet connection.

- White-box testing is testing for internal threats. The testers have some inside knowledge – for example they might have a valid username and password. They might know the structure of the local network. They will try to cause damage to the computer system from inside the organisation. Of course, they do not do real damage.

Ordinary password testing will not be enough for white-box testing. An internal threat comes from a person who has a password and ID. Cyber-security methods against internal threats would include looking for suspicious patterns of behaviour. For example, an attempt to extend access rights.

Extension – black, white and grey hats

You have learned that the term "hackers" is generally used to describe people who try to break into computer systems. The term is sometimes used to mean a person who likes to investigate and work with computer systems to understand them better. To make things clearer people sometimes divide hackers into different categories:

- Black hat hackers are hackers who break into computer systems. If they find a problem with the security system they will exploit it. They are breaking the law.

- White hat hackers are people who have permission to work with computer systems. They are carrying out penetration testing. They will let the owners of the system know they are testing it. If they find a problem they will report it so it can be fixed.

- Grey hat hackers do not fit into the two previous categories. They may work without permission. However, they may not do any damage. They may let the owners know if they find a problem. Grey hat hackers are breaking the law. However, the main priority of the police will probably be stopping the hackers who cause damage.

Some hackers cause a lot of damage to computer systems. In extreme cases this can lead to financial loss or even harm to people. Although it is not publicised, it may be that some governments use hackers to spy on other governments' computer systems.

Test yourself

1. How does penetration testing help to improve the security systems of an organisation?

2. Which type of testing will include trying to get past the firewall?

3. What methods might you use to detect a cyber-security threat from inside an organisation?

4. Someone tried to hack into a computer network, but she wasn't breaking the law. Explain how this could be the case.

Learning activity

Imagine you were given the job of testing the security of your school or college system. What methods might you use to test the security? Write a short plan of action.

Extension activity

Write a Python program that checks a password to see whether it is weak or strong. For greater challenge, display a password report that analyses the password using several criteria.

10.1 Database design

Introducing databases

> ### Introduction
>
> In this chapter you will learn about database software. This is software used to store and organise data in the computer. First you will learn the basic structure of a typical data table.

Storing data

Computer systems often need to store data. Here are some examples:

- A college database might store all the data needed to organise subjects and classes, so that every student and teacher can go to the right class at the right time.
- A holiday booking database might store all the data needed to organise holidays, collect payments and send the right tickets.

Databases can be very complex and store many different facts and figures. It is important that the facts are stored in a structured and organised way.

Tables

Computers store data in a structured way. One database can contain data about many different items such as people, events and objects. We call these items "entities".

A large database may store data about many different entities. For example, a college database might store information about students, teachers, classes and subjects.

Facts about entities are stored in tables. Each database table holds the data about one type of entity. For example, a college database may include one table with data about teachers and one table with data about students.

Records

Data about one entity is called a record. If a holiday database stores data about 40 different destinations, then the destination table will have 40 different records in it. Each record will hold the data about one destination.

Fields

A record stores all the data about a single entity. A record holds many different facts about that entity.

Each fact is stored in a separate field. A record is made of several fields. Every record in a table has the same fields in the same order. For example, a table with data about teachers might include the following fields:

- surname
- first_name

- subject_taught
- email_address

The same four facts are stored about each teacher. Every record in the table has four fields.

Drawing a database table

When we draw a database table we typically draw it using a grid of columns and rows. Here is a table with information about animals in a safari park.

animal_code	Name	Species	date_of_birth	living_area
L233	Simba	Lion	10-08-2019	Paddock 5
L234	Lucy	Lion	10-08-2019	Paddock 5
L235	Beauty	Giraffe	14-08-2019	High enclosure
L235	Ginger	Gecko	01-09-2019	Small animal centre

The table is divided into rows and columns.

Each row holds all the information about one animal. One row is one record.

Each column of the table stores one fact. The table stores five facts about each animal. One column is one field.

Of course, inside the computer memory there isn't a grid shape like this. The data is stored as binary numbers in memory locations. However, a grid helps us to think about the structure of the database we made.

Test yourself

1. A car hire firm keeps records of the cars it owns. It has 200 cars. There are 12 facts about each car. How many records and how many fields are there in the data table?

2. Suggest one other data table there might be in a database used by the car hire firm.

3. Suggest three tables that might be included in a database used by an online shop such as Amazon.

4. A holiday firm uses a table to store data about flights. What fields would you include in this table?

Learning activity

In this section there is a description of one table from a college database. It is a table with records about teachers. There are four fields in the table: Surname, First name, Subject taught, Email address. Create a grid to show this table of data. Enter records for at least five different teachers from your college or school.

Extension activity

Imagine that you are designing a database for your school or college. Create a data table to store information about students. Decide what fields the data table should have. Show records with information about five different students. You can include yourself.

Syllabus reference

3.7.1 Relational databases

Choose appropriate data types
and (where appropriate) lengths
for fields in a table.

Table design

Introduction

You have learned that data tables are made of records and fields. Every field must have a data type. In this section you will learn how to choose the right data type for each field in a data table.

Define a data table

When you make a data table you decide what fields you need. Each field stores one fact. For each field you must choose:

- the name of the field
- the data type
- the length of the field.

Choosing names for fields is a similar task to choosing the names of variables. Choose a name for each field that reminds you what data is stored in that field.

Data type

The main data types to choose from are text, character, Boolean, integer and real. When you make a database table you must choose a data type for each field. The data type tells the computer how the data is to be stored. These data types have different uses.

Data type	Can be used for	Cannot be used for
Text	Can store any text data including letters, symbols and numbers.	Cannot be used in numerical calculations.
Character	Can store a single text character.	Cannot store more than one character. Cannot be used in numerical calculations.
Boolean	Can store Yes/No (or True/False) data.	Cannot store characters or number values. Cannot be used in calculations.
Integer	Can store whole numbers. Can be used in arithmetic calculations.	Cannot store decimal values or non-numeric characters.
Real or float	Can store any numerical value including decimals. Can be used in arithmetic calculations.	Cannot store non-numeric characters.
Date	Stores date as a sequence of three values (day, month and year, not necessarily in that order)	Restricted to date information only.
Time	Stores time as number of hours, minutes and seconds, and may include fractions of a second.	Restricted to time information only

Some database systems use a general data type ("numeric"), which covers integers and real numbers.

Choose the right data type

You may need to decide the right data type to use for a field:

- Look at the data you want to store in that field. Is it numerical or does it have other characters in it?
- Think about what you want to do with the data – will it be used in calculations?

Sometimes data can be made of digits, but you would not use a numerical field. For example, phone numbers are made of digits, but you would store them as text data. This is because you cannot use phone numbers in numerical calculations. It wouldn't make sense to do that. If a phone number such as 0702 555 5555 was stored as a number value, the zero at the start would be lost. The phone number would be wrong.

Field length

In some databases you must choose a field length. That tells the computer how much space to set aside for each item of data. The field length must be large enough to store the largest data you will ever need to store in that field.

In some databases the field length is flexible – the computer just uses however much storage it needs for each item of data.

Example

Here is a data table that stores information about bestselling albums.

ALBUMS TABLE			
Code	Artist	Title	Sales
MUSIC001	Taylor Swift	1989	6.0
MUSIC002	One Direction	Four	3.2
MUSIC003	Ed Sheeran	X	4.4
MUSIC004	Coldplay	Ghost Stories	3.7
MUSIC005	AC/DC	Rock or Bust	2.7
MUSIC006	Michael Jackson	Xscape	1.7
MUSIC007	Pink Floyd	The Endless River	2.5
MUSIC008	Sam Smith	The Lonely Hour	3.5
MUSIC009	Katy Perry	Prism	1.2
MUSIC010	Beyoncé	Beyoncé	1.4

There are four fields in the Albums table. We can use the text data type for Code, Artist and Title fields. These fields do not store numerical data. We can use the real (or float) data type for the Sales field. We would not use the integer data type because it includes a decimal point.

Test yourself

Answer these questions, referring to the Albums table.

1. A programmer wanted to extend the database. He wanted a new field to show the cost of each album. Pick a name and data type for this field.
2. Explain in your own words why sales are shown as a numeric data type.
3. Explain in your own words why Taylor Swift's album called 1989 is text data not numeric data.
4. Think of a date field you could add to this table.

Learning activity

Pick a subject you are interested in, and create a data table made of records and fields. Here are some suggestions:

- football teams in a league such as the Premier League
- tracks on your MP3 player.

Show your design as a grid with records as rows. Include at least ten records in your table.

Extension activity

Give the data type and width of each field in the table. Expand your table to include at least one field of each of the main data types.

Syllabus reference

3.7.1 Relational databases

Understand the following important database concept: primary key.

Select a suitable primary key for a table.

Introduction

You have learned that a data table is made of records and fields. Every field has a data type. One of the fields in the data table is used for identification. This is the primary key. In this section, you will learn to choose a primary key for a table.

Design a data table

When you design a data table, you must decide what the entities are. The entities may be objects, people, places, events, etc. In a library table the entities might be books. In a travel agent, they might be holidays. Each entity has a single record in the data table. A record makes one row of the table.

Next you must decide what the fields are. The fields are the facts that you will store about each entity. Every fact must have its own field. The fields are the columns of the data table. The Albums table on page 257 has these fields.

Field	Data type	Field length
Code	Text	8
Artist	Text	20
Title	Text	25
Sales (millions)	Real/numerical	4

When you choose a data type and field length think about every record in the data table. You must choose a type and size that suits every record. The Ed Sheeran album has a name that is one character. We don't use the character data type or a field length of 1 because that wouldn't work for all the other album titles in the table.

Also think about new data you might need to add. The largest album title has 17 characters, but we have chosen a field length of 25. That is in case we need to add an album with a longer name.

Write out the table design

To write out the table design, write the names of the fields like this.

```
Tablename(field1, field2, field3, ….)
```

In this case we would write the table design as:

```
Albums(code, artist, title, sales)
```

The rules of good design

When you are creating a database, you must follow these rules:

- Every record in the table has the same fields.
- Every field stores only one item of data.
- Every item of data is stored in only one field (there is no duplication).

If your database does not follow these rules the data can get mixed up and there is more chance of errors.

Primary key

Each record in a table must have something unique about it. That is how you can tell that record apart from every other record in the table. This unique data is called the primary key. The data in the primary key field is unique for every record in the data table.

Imagine a college database with records of students. Surname of student cannot be the primary key because you could have two students with the same surname. Date of birth is not a primary key, because two students could have the same birthday. There is a danger that students' records could get mixed up. For this reason the college database might identify every student using a code number. The code number given to each student would be unique to that student. The records would never get mixed up.

Having a primary key is even more important in a big data table. For example, a bank might have millions of customers. It is very likely that some customers will have the same name or the same birthday. It is important not to get their records mixed up, so every bank customer has a unique customer code.

Select a primary key

You have learned that the primary key is whatever field is used to uniquely identify each record in the database. Every data table must have a primary key. The primary key is usually a single field. It is usually a code. The primary key is usually the first field in the table. The code field is filled in when a new record is added to the data table. The code is different for every record in the table.

The code might be made of letters or other text characters. Or the code can be just numbers. Some database software will give each record a primary key automatically. When you add a record to the data table, the computer will make a unique code number for the new record.

When we write the database design we underline the primary key.

```
Albums(code, artist, title, sales)
```

Test yourself

1. In an Albums table why do we choose code instead of artist as the primary key?

2. Do you have a student code number? Do you know what it is?

3. A data table of bank customers gives each customer a unique code. What data type would you use for the code? Explain your answer.

4. Look for examples of code numbers in everyday life. You may find them on tickets, bookings, ID cards, the college network, etc. Make a record of all the code numbers you notice in one day. You do not have to include the code numbers themselves, just the place that you found them.

Learning activity

In the previous activity, you made a data table on a subject of your choice. If your table does not have a primary key add that as the first field in the table.

Extension activity

Write a Python program that lets you input a list of code numbers. Each code must be unique. If you try to enter a code that has already been used, the program will loop until you enter a unique code.

Write a Python program that automatically generates a series of unique code numbers. You can choose any code format you like.

Syllabus reference

3.7.1 Relational databases

Understand the following important database concept: foreign key.

Explain the concept of a relational database.

Understand that the use of a relational database facilitates the elimination of data inconsistency and data redundancy.

Relational databases

Introduction

You have learned how to design a data table. A typical database includes more than one data table. In this section you will learn how to combine many tables together to make a relational database.

Duplication

In a database each field stores only one fact. Each fact is stored in only one field. If a fact is stored in more than one field in the database this is called duplication. Duplication can cause problems, including the following:

- You must type in the same data more than once, so this causes extra work.
- Typing the same data twice might cause errors.
- The data might not match exactly between the fields.
- If you need to update the fact, you must change all the relevant fields.

We can sum these problems up under two headings:

- Redundancy – that means unnecessary work. Entering the same data more than once is redundant. It is not needed and can be a waste of storage space.
- Inconsistency – that means the data does not match. Entering the same data twice brings the chance of inconsistency.

For these reasons, we always avoid duplicating data. We never make a copy of any of the facts in the data table. Each fact is stored in one place only.

Links between tables

Instead of duplicating data we make links between tables. A database with links between tables is called a relational database.

If we need information from one of the data tables in another table, we don't copy the data. We only copy the primary key. We don't need to copy any of the other details. The computer can look up the details it needs, using the primary key.

Example

An online retailer has a data table that stores facts about products for sale.

product_code	product_name	Supplier	Description	Cost
HD001	Canvio Basics 1TB hard drive	Toshiba	Portable External Hard Drive 2.5 Inch USB 3.0 - Black	47.98
HD002	Maxtor M3 1 TB hard drive	Seagate	USB 3.0 Slimline Portable Hard Drive - Black	49.23
HD003	M3 Slimline 2 TB hard drive	Samsung	USB 3.0 Portable Hard Drive - Black	207.00

The retailer will also have a data table with facts about customers.

customer_code	Surname	first_name	Country	City
CUST0010	Limbu	Subid	Nepal	Kathmandu
CUST0011	Gurung	Deepak	Nepal	Kathmandu

Of course, in real life these tables would have more fields, and millions of records.

A third table stores details of customers' orders. Every time a customer orders a product a new record is added to this table. Here is an example of a single order record.

order_code	Date	customer_code	product_code	Quantity
ORD00903	17-10-18	CUST0010	HD003	1

Subid Limbu has ordered the Samsung 2TB hard drive. The table does not store any details about the person or the product. Instead the table stores the customer code and the product code.

The person who prepares the order will need to know what name and address to put on the parcel. The person will need to know what product to put into the parcel. This is how the computer can get this data:

- The computer uses the customer code to find Subid Limbu's details in the customer table.

- The computer uses the product code to find the product details in the product table.

In this way the computer can provide all the information that is needed without any duplication of data.

Foreign key

The Order table has a primary key. It is called the order code. This code uniquely identifies each order.

The Order table also holds primary keys from the other tables. It holds the customer code and the product code. These codes are used to link the orders to details of customers and products. These codes are the primary keys from other tables. When a primary key is copied into another table it is called a foreign key. Foreign keys are used to link tables. That's how we make the relations between tables in a relational database.

We use foreign keys instead of copying data from one table to another. Foreign keys are the only fields that should be duplicated in a relational database.

Learning activity

The example database described in this section includes three data tables. Write the table design for the three tables. Remember to underline the primary key of each table.

Extension activity

On pages 256–257 you learned to create classes and records in Python. Create a Python program that creates a product class, a customer class and an order class. Create new variables that are instances of these three classes. You can use the data on this page.

Test yourself

1. A relational database must avoid duplication. What does duplication mean?

2. Duplication can cause redundancy and inconsistency. Explain the meaning of these two terms and why they should be avoided in database design.

3. In the example on this page an order record is shown. List all the details you can find about the customer and the product. How did you find this data?

4. Explain what a foreign key is and how it is used in a relational database.

Syllabus reference

3.7.2 Database design

Produce a design for a relational database from a description of a scenario.

Introduction

In this section you will use the skills you have learned to create a relational database design.

Example

In this example you will create a database to record details of a football league. Here is a description of the requirements for this database:

- There are ten teams in the football league. Each team has 15–20 players. Each match is between two teams.
- We will store the name and email address of every player so we can send the player a reminder of when there is a match.
- We will store the date and time of each match. We will store the score of each match.
- Each team earns points from matches. We will store the number of points for each team.

Now you will make a design for this database.

What are the entities?

Each table in a database stores information about one type of entity.

The entities in this example are:

- players
- teams
- matches.

Links between entities

There are links between entities. Each player belongs to a team. Each match involves two teams. Remember that we use foreign keys to make links between tables in a relational database.

There are two ways to record links between players and teams:

- We could put the code for one team into each player's record.
- Or we could put the codes of all the players into the team record.

It is much better to use the first method. That way we only need to use one foreign key. Each player is in one team.

We need to make a link between two teams and a match. Is it better to:

- put the code for every match into the team record
- put the codes of the two teams into the match record?

Which is simpler and requires putting in fewer codes?

What data do we need to store?

We need to store the name and contact detail for each player. We will store the surname and first name in separate fields. This means we can use either field on its own if we need to. We will also store the code for the team that the player belongs to.

```
Player(playercode, firstname, surname, email,
teamcode)
```

Here is the table design for the team.

```
Team(teamcode, teamname, points)
```

Finally, here is the match record. It has links to the two teams and shows the score for each team.

```
Match(matchcode, date, time, teamcode1, teamcode2,
score1, score2)
```

In this database design, each field name is a single word with no spaces.

What are the primary keys?

Each table has a primary key. It is easy to identify a primary key. Every table should include a code field. In the following example, the code field is the name of the table, plus the word 'code'. This is the primary key. The primary key is underlined in the table design.

```
Player(playercode, firstname, surname, email,
teamcode)

Team(teamcode, teamname, points)

Match(matchcode, date, time, teamcode1, teamcode2,
score1, score2)
```

Links between tables

Use of foreign keys makes links between records in the different tables. For example, the player's record includes the team code. If we want to find the details of every player in a team, the computer could look through the list of players to find all the players with that team code.

Each match record is linked to two teams. The codes for both teams are added to the match record. If we need to know the names of the teams in a match, the computer can find that data using the teams' codes.

10.2 Structured query language (SQL)

Add data with SQL

> ### Introduction
>
> SQL is a computer language used to work with databases. You have learned how to design a relational database to meet a requirement. In this section you will learn to specify the structure and content of a database using SQL.

SQL stands for structured query language. SQL is a computer language. It is used to work with databases. SQL commands can be used to:

- create database tables
- add data to tables
- edit and delete data
- find and display data to answer a query.

In this section you will learn to add data to a table using SQL commands.

Table design and data types

Before you can add data to a table you need to know the design of the table. Remember the table design will be shown in the following form. This is the example showing the design of a table that stores data about football teams:

```
Team(teamcode, teamname, points)
```

In the example of the Team record we should choose the following data types:

- Teamcode: Text
- Teamname: Text
- Points: Integer

When you add records to your table you must provide data in the same order as the table design. You must make sure you add data of the right type.

Insert values

To add data to a SQL table you must give two commands:

- `INSERT INTO` then the name of the table
- `VALUES` then the values you want to add to the table.

For example, here is the command to add a new record to the Team table:

```
INSERT INTO Team
VALUES ("T0001", "Juventus", 24)
```

If a field is the text data type, then give the data inside quote marks. If a field is the Boolean or integer or real data type then there are no quote marks.

The command shown above gives the values for a single record. If we looked at the data table we would see this record in the table. This new record has been added by the `INSERT... VALUES` command.

Teamcode	Teamname	Points
T0001	Juventus	24

You can add several records one after the other using the `VALUES` command. When you want to move on to a different data table then give the `INSERT INTO` command again. Give the name of the new table. Then you can add records to that table.

Example

The following series of **SQL** commands adds records to the football database you looked at in the previous section.

```
INSERT INTO Player
VALUES("P0001", "Dani", "Alves", "alves@juventus.
com", "T0001")
VALUES("P0002", "Alex", "Sandro", "sandro@juventus.
com", "T0001")
INSERT INTO Team
VALUES("T0001", "Juventus", 24)
VALUES("T0002", "Real Madrid", 18)
INSERT INTO Match
VALUES("M0030", "11-19-18", "15:00", "T0001",
"T0002", 1, 0)
```

Test yourself

Here is an example of SQL. The programmer wants to add football team details to the Team table. There are several mistakes.

```
INSERT
VALUES(T0004 Aston Vila 12)
VALUES(Manchester City, "T0005", 20)
VALUES("Dortmund")
```

Write these commands without the mistakes.

Learning activity

On this page there are examples of `INSERT` commands used with the football database. On paper show the three tables of the football database after these commands have been carried out.

Don't forget the commands in the "Test yourself" section, that you corrected.

Extension activity

On pages 260–261 you saw an example of a database with three tables. The database stored data about products, customers and orders.

Create a program in SQL that will add at least three records to each of these data tables. You can choose the details of the products, the customers and the orders.

Syllabus reference

3.7.3 Structured query language (SQL)

Use the SQL commands UPDATE and DELETE FROM to edit and delete data in a database.

Edit data with SQL

Introduction

You have learned to add data to a SQL table using the INSERT command. In this section you will learn to delete records from a table. You will learn to make changes to the values in a table. These actions can be carried out with SQL commands.

The DELETE FROM command

You can delete all the records from a data table. Then you will be left with nothing but an empty table. For example, at the start of a new football season, the match records from the previous season might be deleted.

The command to delete all records is DELETE FROM. Complete the command by giving the name of the table:

        DELETE FROM Match

        DELETE FROM Player

The WHERE command

SQL has a command that lets us pick out one or more records from the table. It is the WHERE command. This command is always followed by a logical test. The computer will pick the records where the result of the logical test is True.

Here is a general example:

        WHERE field = value

Look at the table below. It contains data about replacement hard drives for computers.

Product Code	Product Name	Supplier	Description	Cost
HD001	Canvio Basics 1TB hard drive	Toshiba	Portable External Hard Drive 2.5 Inch USB 3.0 - Black	47.98
HD002	Maxtor M3 1 TB hard drive	Seagate	USB 3.0 Slimline Portable Hard Drive - Black	49.23
HD003	M3 Slimline 2 TB hard drive	Samsung	USB 3.0 Portable Hard Drive - Black	207.00

Here is an example of a WHERE command:

        WHERE Supplier = "Seagate"

This tells the computer to find records WHERE the supplier is Seagate. We must put the value "Seagate" in quote marks because it is a text field.

The computer finds this record.

Product Code	Product Name	Supplier	Description	Cost
HD002	Maxtor M3 1 TB hard drive	Seagate	USB 3.0 Slimline Portable Hard Drive - Black	49.23

The equals sign is used as a relational operator. We can use the other relational operators to pick out records. Here is an example of a `WHERE` command. It uses the relational operator > (more than).

```
WHERE Cost > 200
```

This command will select records `WHERE` the value in the cost field is greater than 200. Which record would be selected?

Using `DELETE... WHERE`

We can combine the `DELETE` and the `WHERE` commands to delete one record from the data table:

```
DELETE FROM Product

WHERE Supplier = "Seagate"
```

This command will delete only the selected record from the data table. What would the data table look like after this command?

The `UPDATE` command

As well as deleting records we can update records in a data table. The `UPDATE` command means make changes to the values stored in a record. The command to update a table looks like this:

```
UPDATE Table
SET Field = Value
```

Using `UPDATE... WHERE...`

We often combine the `UPDATE` command with the `WHERE` command. Here is an example:

```
UPDATE Product

SET Cost = 20.00

WHERE Supplier = "Seagate"
```

This command will find all the records `WHERE` the supplier is Seagate. It will `SET` the cost for these records to 20.00.

Learning activity

In this section you looked at a table called Products.

1. Write out the commands to add three new records to the Products table. You can choose the product details.

2. Give a command that will delete one record.

3. Give a command that will update one record.

4. Draw the product table as it would appear after your commands have been carried out.

Test yourself

1. Give the command to delete all the records from a table called Customers.

2. A database has a table called FaultLog. Give the command to delete all the records in FaultLog where the Year field has the value "2016".

3. A database has a table called Team. Give the command to change the Points field of all teams to the value 0.

4. A database has a table called Team. Give the command to change the Points field to 10 where the Team name is "Anderlecht".

Extension activity

Write a guide to the use of SQL commands to insert, delete and update records from a data table.

Syllabus reference

3.7.3 Structured query language (SQL)

Use SQL to retrieve data from a relational database, using the commands: SELECT, FROM and WHERE.

Select data with SQL

Introduction

You have learned the SQL commands to add, delete and edit the data in a database. In this section you will learn to use the SQL command SELECT. This command will display the data stored in a database. It will select the items of data you want to see.

Display data

You have learned how to store data. You have learned the commands to insert and change the data in a data table. A relational database is made of several data tables.

We also need to use the data stored in a relational database. That is the reason for storing the data. For example, you saw how an online retailer would store details of products, customers and orders. The retailer does this so it can manage its business. Staff can keep track of the items they sell, and send the right goods to customers.

This means we have to be able to tell the computer to show data from the tables. The command that does this is SELECT.

Select from a table

The SELECT command will tell the computer to display data from the database. The simplest form of this command is:

```
SELECT * FROM Table
```

The asterisk * stands for the word "everything", so this command will print out all the data stored in a table.

Select columns

It is rare that we want to see all the data in a table. We can make changes to the SELECT command. We can choose one or more fields.

```
SELECT field FROM Table
```

We can tell the computer to display only some fields from the table. For example, from the table of products we could ask to see only the product code and the cost of the product. Look at this example.

```
SELECT Supplier, Cost FROM Product
```

This command will display all the records. However, it will show only the Supplier and Cost fields.

Using SELECT... WHERE

On pages 266–267 you learned to use the WHERE command. The WHERE command lets you pick out one or more records from a table. Remember that the WHERE command is always followed by a logical test. The computer will find all records where the result of the logical test is True.

```
WHERE field = value
```

We can use this command to display some of the records in a table.

Combine these features to answer a question

Look at the table of bestselling albums you saw on page 257. The table is called Albums.

Suppose we wanted to see the title of any album selling more than 3 million copies. The command would be:

```
SELECT Title FROM Albums
WHERE Sales > 3
```

The output from this command would be.

```
1989
Four
X
Ghost Stories
The Lonely Hour
```

Select data from two tables

Introduction

In the previous section you learned how to select data from a table. You could choose what fields and records to select. In this section you will learn to extend the command to select data from more than one table.

Fields from two tables

Here is the design of the football database.

```
Player(playercode, firstname, surname, email,
teamcode)

Team(teamcode, teamname, points)

Match(matchcode, date, time, teamcode1, teamcode2,
score1, score2)
```

Let's imagine we want to show the first name and surname of all players, and the name of the team they play for. Those fields are from different tables. Here is the command we give:

```
SELECT Player.firstname, Player.surname, Team.teamname

FROM Player, Team
```

We can select fields from more than one table. We must give the name of the table before the name of the field.

This command is not finished yet.

Search for match

The field called teamcode is used to link the Player table and the Team table:

- Teamcode is the **primary key** of the Team table. Each record in that table has a different teamcode.

- Teamcode is a **foreign key** in the Player table. It links the Player table to the Team table. Teamcode shows the team each player belongs to.

We can tell the database to use this field to match player records with team records.

```
SELECT Player.firstname, Player.surname, Team.teamname

FROM Player, Team

WHERE Player.teamcode = Team.teamcode
```

This command will go through the Player table. It will display the first name and surname field of each record. It will find the matching team record. It will print the name of the team.

Boolean operators

On page 38 you learned about Boolean operators. The main operators are AND, OR and NOT. The Boolean operators can be used to combine logical tests:

- AND links two tests to make one test. The overall test result is True if both test results are True.

- OR links two tests to make one test. The overall test result is True if at least one test result is True.

- NOT combines with a single test. The overall test result is True if the original test result is False.

Here is the same command that you just looked at. However, it includes two logical tests. The tests are combined using the AND operator. The test result will only be True if both test results are True.

```
SELECT Player.firstname, Player.surname, Team.teamname
FROM Player, Team
WHERE Player.teamcode = Team.teamcode
AND Team.teamname = "Juventus"
```

The new command is Team.teamname = "Juventus". This will pick out that team record from the Team table. Records that are linked to a different team will not be shown.

This overall command will show the first name and surname field for each player, plus the matching team name. It will only show the details of players linked to the team Juventus.

Test yourself

1. What does this command do? Explain in your own words.

```
SELECT Team.teamname, Match.date, Match.time
FROM Team, Match
WHERE Team.teamcode = Match.team1code
OR Team.teamcode = Match.team2code
```

2. Write the command to print out the score of every match played by Juventus.

Learning activity

In the previous activity you worked in a group to write a data table and queries to extract data from the table.

Continue to work in the same group. Extend this project to include a second data table. Use a foreign key to link the two tables.

Repeat the activity, but this time write SELECT commands that take data from both tables. Pass each command to a partner as a challenge.

Extension activity

Expand your guide to SQL so that it includes everything you have learned. Share the completed guide with a partner and check your partner's understanding.

## Chapter 11

Syllabus reference

3.8 Web page design (3.8.1 Key concepts)

Know that web pages can be constructed using HTML.

Be aware of the key differences between HTML5 and earlier versions of HTML.

11.1 How web pages are made

What is Hypertext Mark-up Language (HTML)?

> ### Introduction
>
> In previous sections you have learned how application programs and apps for mobile devices are built using high-level programming languages. In this section you will learn about how web pages are built using HTML.

The Internet and the World Wide Web (WWW)

We often use the terms "Internet" and "WWW" interchangeably, as if they mean the same thing. In fact, the Internet and WWW are not the same.

The **Internet** is the all the cabling, network equipment and protocols that allow messages to be sent between computers anywhere in the world. You learned about network equipment and protocols in chapter eight.

The **WWW** is all the information on all the web pages across the world. Pages on the WWW are connected into a huge web of information by hyperlinks.

The birth of the WWW

The WWW was invented in 1989 by Tim Berners-Lee, a British scientist working at CERN, the European centre for nuclear research. His idea was to create a service to allow scientists around the world to share ideas. To achieve this, he developed:

- a simple computer language called HTML for creating web pages
- a piece of software called a browser to read an HTML document and display it on a computer screen.

What is HTML?

HTML is a mark-up language. HTML uses instructions called **tags** to control how a web page is laid out on screen. The word "tags" in the previous sentence is in bold text. To display a word in bold in HTML we use tags:

```
<strong>tags</strong>
```

- Tags in HTML are always enclosed in angle brackets : <>.
- Tags are instruction codes : <strong> is the instruction for bold text.
- Each tag usually has start and an end tag : </strong>.

Everything between a start and end tag is called an element in HTML.

Here is a sample of HTML code with the page it creates shown to the right:

```
<!DOCTYPE html>
<html>
<body>

<h1>HTML</h1>
<h2>Hypertext Markup Language</h2>

<p>Hypertext Markup Language
(<strong>HTML</strong>) is used to
create web page layouts. HTML controls
how a page looks on screen. It is also
used to create <em>hyperlinks</em>
between web pages.</p>

</body>
</html>
```

HTML

Hypertext Markup Language

Hypertext Markup Language (**HTML**) is used to create web page layouts. HTML controls how a page looks on screen. It is also used to create *hyperlinks* between web pages.

⬆ HTML example

HTML5

The latest version of HTML was introduced in October 2014 and is known as HTML5. The examples in this book use HTML5. These are improvements introduced in HTML5:

- The ways in which you add graphics and multimedia have been improved. New tags such as <audio> and <video> have been added.
- New elements have been introduced to make defining the various sections of a web page easier, for example <header> and <footer> tags.
- Some facilities that previously needed add-ins have now been built into HTML.
- There is improved support for developing complex web applications including how HTML "talks" to other applications through application program interfaces (API).

Test yourself

1. What does HTML stand for?

2. What are tags used for in HTML?

3. What is needed to complete this HTML code?

```
<h1>Section1 : Computer systems.
```

4. List three ways in which HTML5 has improved web development.

Learning activity

CERN have created a simulation of the original WWW site created by Tim Berners-Lee. You can find it here: info.cern.ch. Compare it with a modern website such as the BBC news site: bbc.co.uk. How are the two sites different and what are the similarities?

Extension activity

Research free sites that allow you to create web pages.

Syllabus reference

3.8 Web page design (3.8.1 Key concepts)

Know that web pages can be designed using CSS.

Know that HTML is used to create the structure of a web page and that CSS can be used to change the style of the page.

Designing web pages with cascading style sheets (CSS)

Introduction

You have learned that HTML is used to create web pages. In this section, you will learn that cascading style sheets (CSS) are used to control and change the look of a web page.

What are CSS?

You have learned that HTML is used to create web pages. HTML is used to organise content into pages, sections and paragraphs. A page created in HTML alone does not look very interesting. The professional looking design features that are common on all modern websites are created using CSS.

CSS were introduced in 1996. CSS form a set of rules that determine what a web page looks like on screen.

How CSS are used

The HTML instruction <h1>Design with CSS</h1> creates a level 1 heading that looks like this:

Design with CSS

This is the default <h1> style. Default means what the heading looks like unless other instructions are given. The default look can be changed. Here is an example of a CSS definition.

```
<style>
h1 {
    color: white;
    background-color: blue;
    font-family: Arial, Helvetica, sans-serif;
    font-size: 28pt;
}
</style>
```

If the CSS definition above is applied to a web page then all level 1 headings in the page will change.

- The colour of the text is set to white.
- The background of the heading is set to blue.
- The font is set to Arial 28 point.

A <h1> heading will look like this:

Design with CSS

Linking CSS to an HTML file

CSS are usually written in their own file and saved separately from the HTML file. An instruction is written in the HTML file that creates a link to the CSS file.

The same CSS file can be linked to all the pages in a website by adding a link to each HTML page. This means that any changes to the design only have to be made once in the CSS file and not on every HTML page.

This method of working explains what is meant by CSS. 'Cascade' is another word for waterfall. A change made in the CSS automatically cascades through all the pages that are linked to it, like a waterfall.

Advantages of CSS

These are the advantages of using CSS:

- **Using CSS saves time and reduces errors.** Storing the style information separately in each web page would mean that every page would have to be edited when a change was made. Entering so many changes could take a long time and lead to mistakes being made.

- **A design is consistent on every page of a website.** Using a single CSS file linked to every page in a website guarantees that the same design is used on every page.

- **Design and content teams can work independently.** Once the style of a website is agreed specialist designers can work on the CSS file without needing to wait for all the content to be completed.

Test yourself

1. What are CSS used for?

2. State two advantages of using CSS when creating a web design.

3. Why are CSS described as cascading?

4. Explain how using a CSS file can save time when updating a website design.

Extension activity

Open a browser and go to the site CSS Zen Garden: http://www.csszengarden.com/

CSS Zen Garden is a site where web designers from around the world applied their own CSS to the same HTML file.

1. Select the "View all designs" button in the top right of the home page. There are over 200 designs that show how powerful CSS can be as a design tool. Pick an example you like.

2. Compare your example with the home page.

3. Make a list of four or five ways that the designer of your example has changed the page design.

Learning activity

Write a CSS statement that will define a level 3 heading as: arial 14 point text in blue on a grey background.

When you have completed the definition research 'CSS font-style property' on the Internet. Add a line to your CSS definition that will change the text in your heading to italic.

3.8 Web page design (3.8.1 Key concepts)

Understand that server-side scripting languages can be used on a web server for dynamic generation of web pages.

Understand that client-side scripting languages can be used to add additional functionality to web pages.

Client-side and server-side scripting

Introduction

The WWW supports dynamic news, e-commerce, entertainment and social media sites. In this chapter you will learn that programs called scripts are used to make websites dynamic and interactive.

Creating dynamic web pages

In the early days of the WWW the information on a web page did not change. A web page was similar to a word-processed page. Once saved, the content on the page would stay the same until the page was opened, edited and resaved. A web page that does not change automatically is described as a static page.

Modern websites use dynamic web pages. Dynamic web pages are updated automatically without having to be edited and resaved. Websites that use dynamic pages are able to provide a wide range of services to their users. News pages provide minute-by-minute updates as stories unfold. Social media sites allow users to take part in online debates with message boards and chat windows updating automatically.

Client-side and server side-scripts

Dynamic web pages use short programs called scripts. Scripts have changed the way we use the WWW and increased the services it offers. There are two types of script.

A **client-side script** is a small program that is embedded into a web page. A client-side script is downloaded from a server along with the HTML page it is embedded in. The script runs on a user's computer, which is called the client. Client-side scripts are usually written in a language called JavaScript. Almost every web page you use will include JavaScript.

A **server-side script** is a program that runs on a web server. The script is not downloaded to the client computer. The client sends a request to the server to start the script. Let's take the example of when you send a search string to the Google search engine. The search engine runs server-side scripts and sends a list of relevant websites back to you. Many programming languages are used for server-side scripts, including Java and Python.

Uses for scripts

Client-side scripts are used to make web pages more interactive. These are some common uses:

- Navigation tools, such as drop-down menus are used.
- There may be personalisation of a web page – some sites allow you to move parts of a web page around to suit your needs.

- There may be validation of information when a user fills in a form. A script can be used to check information is complete and in the correct format before it is sent to the server.

The advantage of running client-side scripts is that they run quickly as there is no need to send instructions and data over the Internet. The disadvantage of client-side scripts is that they are insecure. They are never used when databases have to be accessed or when sensitive data needs to be transmitted across the Internet.

Server-side scripts are used for secure applications, particularly when databases need to be accessed. These are some common uses:

- E-commerce – a user sends a request to purchase an item to the server where scripts process the payment and complete the order.

- Online news – news events are stored in a database and the latest updates are sent automatically to update a news page.

- Social media sites – a user sends a message to a social media site where scripts add the message to a thread, update statistics and notify other users who might be interested in the post.

Test yourself

1. What is the difference between server-side and client-side scripts?
2. Give an example of a computer language used for client-side scripts.
3. Explain why client-side scripts are not used for e-banking applications.
4. List two uses for server-side scripts.

Learning activity

1. Open the BBC website (bbc.co.uk). Browse the site for a few minutes.
2. Make a list of two or three dynamic features you can find on the site. You will need to look for anything that appears to update automatically or any part of a page you can interact with.

Extension activity

1. Open the Oxford University Press website page in your browser (oup.com).
2. Right click on the page and select 'View page source' to display the HTML code for the page. In many browsers, pressing Control-U is another way to display the HTML code.
3. Explore the HTML and make a note of any evidence you can find that shows JavaScript or CSS are used on the page.

Creating web content

Building a basic web page

> ### Introduction
>
> In this section you will learn how to create a basic web page using HTML. You will create your web page using a text editor. You can use Microsoft Notepad, which will be available on your computer if you are using Microsoft Windows. If you are using another operating system your teacher will advise you on a suitable text editor.

The structure of a web page

There are three parts to an HTML page.

1. The **document type declaration** comes right at the start of your document.

   ```
   <!doctype html>
   ```

   Everything after the declaration is enclosed in <html> </html> tags

2. The **head** contains important information such as any styles and scripts to be used on the page.

3. The **body** contains the content that the user sees on screen. Tags are used to define blocks of text such as headings and paragraphs. Tags also define special effects such as bold.

Your first HTML page

Now you will create your first HTML page. Study the HTML code below. Identify the three sections of HTML code listed above:

```
<!DOCTYPE html>
<html>
<head>
<title>My first web page</title>
</head>
<body>
<h1>This is my first HTML page</h1>
<p>This is a paragraph. An HTML paragraph is a
block of text with a space above and below
it</p>
<p>Here is a second paragraph</p>
</body>
</html>
```

The top level, largest heading <h1> is used, but if you need different levels of heading you can use <h2>, <h3> and so on.

Creating your page

Open your text editor program and enter the HTML code example in the image above. Be careful to enter the text exactly as it appears. You will not be able to use colour as the example code does. The colour is not important. It is there to make the code easier for you to read.

Once you have entered the code, save it using the file name myfirstwebpage.html. Create a new folder for your file. Remember that you should always save your HTML files with the file extension .html.

Viewing your page

Once you have typed in the page you can view it in a browser. Open the folder containing the file you have created. You will see the file you have just saved. Double click on the file. It will open in a web browser window. Your file should look like the image below. If it doesn't look like this, open your file again in the text editor and make any corrections that are needed.

Test yourself

1. What does the body of an HTML page contain?
2. What is the difference between content in the head section of an HTML document and content in the body section?
3. What is the <title> tag used for?
4. There is an error in the HTML code below. Can you correct it?

```
<!DOCTYPE html>
<head>
<title>Page Title</title>
</head>
<body>
<h1>This is a web page</h1>
</body>
```

Learning activity

1. Create a basic home page for a website about yourself. Your page should contain:
   a a title that will appear in a browser tab when you page is viewed
   b a main heading that contains your name (for example "Jaswant Kaur – her home page")
   c a short paragraph that says who you are
   d three level-2 headings: "My hobbies", "My friends" and "My favourite things".
2. Save the page in a new folder using the filename myhomepage.html.
3. Test your page by opening it in a browser and correct any errors.

Extension activity

Carry out Internet research and find an online HTML reference guide. You should look for a reference guide that is aimed at schools and provides plenty of examples of how HTML is used. Try a search string such as "HTML guide for schools". When you have found a reference you like bookmark it. It will be useful later in this chapter.

Syllabus reference

3.8 Web page design (3.8.2 Hypertext Mark-up Language – HTML)

Be able to create the structure of a web page using HTML.

Using inline and block-level tags to improve web page layout

Introduction

You have learned how to create a basic web page. In this section you will learn how to use HTML to improve the look and structure of your page. You will learn how to change the colour of text and add effects such as bold and italic. You will also learn how to create lists using HTML.

Inline and block-level tags in HTML

There are two important groups of tag in HTML:

- **Inline tags** are used to affect the look or action of a group of words in a line of text. For example, you might want to add a bold effect to a single word.
- **Block-level tags** are used to apply effects to an entire section of a web page. Block-level tags can be used to set the font, text colour and background colour for a paragraph or to create a list.

Using inline tags

Here are some useful inline tags you can include in your HTML:

- <strong> is used to create bold text.
- <em> is used to emphasise a word in italic text.
- <span> is used to apply special effects such as colour to one or more words.
-
 is used to create a line break.
 is one of very few tags that does not need an end tag.

Here is an HTML example with inline tags applied. Study the code and make sure you understand what each tag does.

```
<p>My name is <strong>David Brown</strong> and I
live in Birmingham, England. My favourite color
is <span style="color:blue">blue</span>. I have
many friends.My <em>very best</em> friend is
Abdul Rahim.</p>
```

This is what the code looks like displayed in a browser:

My name is **David Brown** and I live in Birmingham, England. My favourite color is blue. I have many friends.My *very best* friend is Abdul Rahim.

Tags and attributes

In the example the <span> tag is used in a different way to other tags such as <strong> and <em>. The <span> tag contains the extra information, style

="colour:blue". This information is called an attribute. Attributes are used to change the effect of a tag. In this case an attribute called "style" is used to change text colour to blue.

Sometimes we use more than one attribute when defining a tag. This example creates a level-1 heading that is green and centred on the web page:

```
<h1 style="text-align:center;color:green">My web
page</h1>
```

Using block-level tags

These are some useful block-level tags you can include in your HTML:

- **<p>** creates a paragraph element.
- **<hx>** creates a heading element. A number replaces the x to define different levels of heading. <h1>, <h2>, <h3> and so on.
- **<ol>**, **<ul>** and **<li>** are tags used to create lists.

Making lists in HTML

The tags <ol>, <ul> and <li> are used together to create lists. There are two types of list in HTML:

- <ol> creates an ordered list where the items in the list are numbered.
- <ul> creates an unordered list where the items are bullet points.

In both cases the tag <li> is used to indicate each list item. Here is an example:

```
<h2>My favourite subjects</h2>
<ol>
  <li>Physics</li>
  <li>Art</li>
  <li>Maths</li>
</ol>
```

My favourite subjects

1. Physics
2. Art
3. Maths

Test yourself

1. How will a word that is enclosed in <strong> tags appear in a browser?

2. What is the difference between a list created with the <ol> tag and one created with the <ul> tag?

3. Explain the difference between in-line tags and block-level tags.

4. What is an attribute in HTML?

Learning activity

In the previous activity you created a basic web page about yourself.

1. Use inline tags (<em>, <strong>, <span>) to format important words in the paragraph about yourself.

2. Under the "My hobbies" heading create an ordered list of your hobbies.

3. Under the "My friends" heading add an unordered list of your best friends.

Extension activity

Reformat your main page title by adding attributes to the <h1> tag. Use the example in the text as a guide.

Sections, images and links

Introduction

In this section you will learn how the design of a web page can be managed if the page is divided into sections. You will also learn how to create links to other web pages and other resources such as images.

Using div to create a section on your web page

The <div> tag is a block-level tag that can be used to create a section on an HTML page. Any attributes applied to the <div> tag will change the look of anything held inside it. Here is an example:

```
<div style="color:white;background-
color:grey;text-align:center">
<h1>My home page</h1>
<p> This page is about me, my friends, my
interests and my favourite things.
Welcome to my world!<p><br/>
</div>
<h2>My links</h2>
<ul>
<li>My friends</li>
<li>My interests</li>
<li><a href="myfavthings.html">My
favourite things</a></li>
</ul>
</body>
</html>
```

The <div> tag in this example creates a section that includes the main page heading and a paragraph of text. The style attribute applied to the <div> tag does 3 things: changes text colour to white, the background to grey and centres the text. The three attributes apply to everything in the section.

There are other tags in HTML that can be used to define sections in a page. Examples are <header>, <footer> and <nav> . Header and footer are used to create sections at the top and bottom of a page. Nav creates an area for a menu. Web developers use sections like these as building blocks to create a site.

Adding images to a web page

In HTML <audio>, <video> and <img> tags are used to add media files to a web page.

To insert an image on your webpage you use the <img> tag:

```
<img src="lion.jpg" alt="snarling lion">
```

This example uses two attributes:

- **src** is the source of the file you want to insert into your page. Just using a filename works if the image file is in the same folder as the web page containing the link.

- **alt** is alternative text to be used if the image is not available. This is important to someone with a visual impairment. The <alt> text can be read out loud by a screen reader.

Note: the <img> tag does not need an end tag.

Adding links to a web page

Links are very important in web design. Hyperlinks, as they are called, create the network of information we call the WWW. The anchor tag, <a>, is used to create links in a web page. Here is an example:

```
<a href="http://www.bbc.co.uk/">BBC News</a>
```

The <a> tag in this example has one attribute called href. The href attribute is used to define the destination of the link, in this case the BBC website.

The text between the <a> tag and the </a> tag ("BBC News") becomes the link. Clicking on that text takes the user to the BBC site.

Two more examples

In this example the <a> tag links to another page in the same website. The page is stored in the same folder as the page that contains the link:

```
<a href="myfavourites.html">My favourite things</a>
```

It is also possible to make an image into a link.

```
<a href="lionfacts.html"> <img src="lion.
jpg" alt="lion"> </a>
```

Test yourself

1. What is the <div> tag used for in HTML?

2. What is the <a> tag called and what is it used for?

3. Why should you always use the alt attribute when putting an image on a web page?

4. What is the href attribute used for in an <a> tag?

Learning activity

In the previous two activities you created then expanded a web page about yourself.

1. Create a new web page and save it to the same folder as your first page using the name myfavthings.html. Your new page should have a <h1> heading "My favourite things". Add two <h2> headings to your new page: "My favourite animal" and "My favourite website".

2. Open your home page. Add an <a> tag to the "My favourite things" heading that creates a link to your new page, myfavthings.html.

Extension activity

1. Open myfavthings.html. Add a picture of your favourite animal under the "My favourite animal" heading.

2. Type a brief description of your favourite website under the "My favourite website" heading.

3. Use an <a> tag to create a link to your favourite website.

Syllabus reference

Be able to use basic CSS to control the layout of a web page.

Designing a web page using CSS

Introduction

In this section you will learn how CSS can be used to change the design of your web page.

A CSS file is a set of rules

A CSS file is a set of rules and, as in all computer languages, those rules have syntax. A CSS rule has three parts:

- **Selector** is the element in your HTML page that the rule applies to, for example a header.
- **Property** is the aspect of the selected element that you want to define, for example colour.
- **Value** is the specific change you want to make, for example change to blue.

A CSS rule will look like this:

```
Selector {property:value}
```

Here is an example:

```
h2 {background-color:grey}
```

If you want to define more than one property for a selector you separate each property with a semi-colon. Here is an example:

```
h2 {
    background-color:grey;
    color:white;
    text-align:center
    }
```

Where CSS is placed in a web page

The CSS rules for an HTML document are placed inside a <style> tag in the <head> section. In the example shown below, style rules for the h2 heading and paragraph have been declared. These declarations will apply every time a <h2> or <p> tag is used in the body of the document. Any change you make to the declarations in the CSS will automatically cascade through the page changing all <h2> and <p> elements.

```
<head>
<style>
h2 {
    background-color:grey;
    color:white;
    text-align:center
    }

p {
    color:blue;
    text-align:center;
    }
</style>
</head>
```

The type selector in CSS

So far you have learned that CSS can be used to define text colour, the background colour and the alignment of text. You can also use CSS to define the position and size of an element, background images, the space around an element and much more. One important set of definitions control the fonts used in a web page.

Some of the important font properties you can set are:

- **font-family:**   p {font-family: Arial;}
- **font-size:**   p {font-size: small;}
- **font-weight:**   p {font-weight: bold;}
- **font-style:**   p {font-style: italic;}

The CSS instructions used to define the style properties of HTML elements such as <p> are called type selectors. The HTML element will display the properties in the CSS type statement every time it is used in an HTML page. This means you do not have to keep defining a style over and over again in a page.

The class selector in CSS

Suppose you are creating a page that will include some very important paragraphs. Those paragraphs will look like every other paragraph but to draw attention to them you want them to appear in red text. You can do this using the class attribute.

To define a class attribute in CSS, choose a name for a style selector and put a full stop in front of it:

```
.important {color:red; font-weight:bold}
```

This CSS declaration says "if something in the class is important it will be red and bold". The class important can then be included as an attribute in an HTML tag:

```
<h3 class="important">Important heading</h3>

<p class="important">Important paragraph.</p>
```

This is a way of applying special rules to your HTML documents.

``` <head> <style> .important {color:red; font-weight:bold} </style> </head> <body> <h3> A normal heading </h3> <p> A normal paragraph.</p> <h3 class="important">Important heading </h3> <p class="important">Important paragraph.</p> <p>Another normal paragraph.</p> </body> ```	**A normal heading** A normal paragraph. **Important heading** **Important paragraph.** Another normal paragraph.

Learning activity

Create a CSS file for your homepage. Create rules that define your headings, paragraphs and lists. If you have time create a class selector that you can use to highlight important information on your page.

Extension activity

Search the Internet for a reference guide to CSS. Use a search string such as "CSS reference for schools". Find information about CSS Properties. Can you identify and use two properties that are not included in the text? You might try borders and background image.

Test yourself

1. Identify the value, the selector and the property in this CSS rule
   ```
   h1{color:grey}
   ```
2. What are the errors in this CSS rule?
   ```
   <p>{background-colour:blue;text-align:centre
   ```

1 Foundations of programming

1.1 Begin programming

Introduction to Python

1. IDE stands for integrated development environment. IDE software allows you to save your program.

2. An IDE lets you type up your program and save it, runs your code, gives you guidance about errors in your code and uses colour to show the different features of the code.

3. IDLE has two windows called Python Shell and Program Editor.

4. The results will be shown in the Shell window.

Output

1. A string is a series of characters inside quote marks.

2. The computer passes over comments added to a program without turning them into machine code.

3. The syntax of a print command begins with the word "print" in lower case. Then there are brackets. The content that is to be displayed goes inside the brackets.

4. When you run a Python program, the lines of the program are converted into machine code one by one, and immediately executed.

Variables

1. A variable

2. `TicketCost = 19.99`

3. `print (TicketCost)`

4. **a** `Character Name` is bad as it includes a space

   b `firstName` is good as it is clear what the value is showing

   c `5Star` is bad as it needs to start with a letter

   d `myvariable` is ok but it is not clear what the value is showing from the name

   e `Star*Rating` is bad as the * symbol is included

Input

1. A prompt tells the user what to type in.

2. If you enter an input command without a variable, the user input won't be stored, so the content will be lost.

3. If you enter an input command with a variable, the user input will be stored in an area of memory given the name of the variable.

4. `print("User Name")`: this command will print the words User Name in that exact form.

   `print(UserName)`: this command will print whatever value has been stored in the variable called `UserName`.

Flowcharts

1. An algorithm describes a set of steps to solve a problem. An algorithm can also describe the logical structure of a program so it sets out all the actions that the program will carry out. The reason programmers create algorithms is so they can have a clear idea of the steps required to solve the problem in a general sense before they try to work out the actual code.

2. The input box should say input and the variable and the output box should say output and the details of what the output is.

3.

This rounded rectangle shows the start and stop/end of the flowchart.	This parallelogram shows the inputs and outputs.	This rectangle shows the value of a variable.

4. The arrows show the sequence of the flowchart.

Pseudocode

1. The variable is `Month`. The expression is January and it is a string literal.

2. `EmailAddress ← USERINPUT`

3. `OUTPUT Game Over`

4. `Height ← 99`

1.2 Calculation

Numerical expressions

1. The four main arithmetic operators are + (add), – (subtract), × (multiply), and / (divide).

2. 4.5, –9, –56, 17.5

3. `–4 * –5`

4. `Result = 81/7`

Data types

1. 36 is an integer; 36.0 is a real number; 36 * 10 is an integer as both values are integers; 36 + 1.0 is a real number as 1.0 is a real number; 36/6 is a float/real number.

2. `Age = "Over 21"` is a string; `Age = 22` is an integer; `Age = 22.0` is a real number; `Age = input("Enter your age")` is a string.

3. Earnings would be a float/real number.

4. `Age = 33.0`

Convert data type

1. input and print

2. `HourlyRate` is a float.

   Hours will be a string but this is an error (next questions), it should be an integer.

   Pay will be a float once the program is fixed (next questions).

3. The user input was not converted into a numeric type, and it is not possible to multiply a string by a float.

4.
```
HourlyRate = 12.00
Hours = input("Enter how many hours you worked")
Hours = int(Hours)
Pay = Hours * HourlyRate
print(Pay)
```

Integer division

1. **a** Dividend is the number before the division operator.

   b Divisor is the number after the division operator.

   c Quotient is the number of times the dividend goes into the divisor with no remainder.

   d Modulus is the remainder after the quotient when doing integer division.

2. `Hours` has the value 3; `Minutes` has the value 40

3.
```
Days = 40
Weeks = Days // 7
RemainingDays = Days % 7
```

Constants

1. Because user input can always change depending on what the user types

2. The size of the bill is not a constant because different bills will be different amounts.

3. `g = 9.8`

4. It will make the code easier to read when they use the tax rate, and if the tax rate ever changes, they will only have to change it in one place.

Processing values

1. Pi is a constant; the value of Pi will not change over the course of the program, so it is a constant.

2. `Radius ← USERINPUT`

3. `Circumference ← 2 * Pi * Radius`

   The circumference of the circle is calculated using 2 times pi times the radius

4. `OUTPUT Circumference`

   The value of Circumference is output (the exact value depends on the user input)

1.3 String handling

Strings

1. `Password = input(sEnter the password: ")`

2. `PasswordLength = len(Password)`

3. `print("Your password has", PasswordLength, "characters.")`

4. `Password = input("Please enter a password.")`
   `PasswordLength = len(Password)`
   `print("Password:", "*" * PasswordLength)`

Substrings

a X

b AX

c TAX40

d 40078

e TAX40078

1.4 Selection

Logical decision

1. In an algorithm with two paths, the computer uses a logical test to choose which path to take. If the result of the test is "Yes" it takes one path. If the result is "No" it takes the other path.

2. These are the four most common relational operators, with the meaning of each one:

   = equal to

   <> not equal to

   < smaller than or less than

   > bigger than, more than or greater than

3. A relational operator compares two values. The result of the comparison will be True or False.

4. This is the flowchart symbol used to represent a decision:

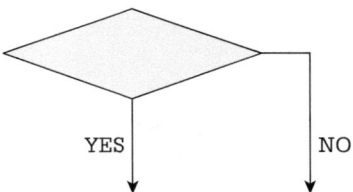

Selection

1. : (colon)

2. The indented lines of code belong inside the `if` statement.

3. It appears after the word if and before the colon.

4. The input function always returns a string, so if we do not convert `Age` into a numerical type, the comparison Age < 15 will not work as expected.

if…else…

1. The variables `Num1` and `Num2` are converted to integer data type because input variables are always string. A calculation can only be carried out using a numerical data type such as integer.

2. The computer adds the two numbers together and stores the result in the variable answer.

3. The computer subtracts one number from the other and stores the result in the variable answer.

4. The program will crash because Python is trying to convert a string with a decimal point into an integer that doesn't have a decimal point.

5. To allow decimal numbers change the lines

```
int(Num1)
int(Num2)
```

to

```
float(Num1)
float(Num2)
```

Nested `if`

1.
```
WaterPH = input("Please enter pH value: ")
WaterPH = int(WaterPH)
```

2. `if WaterPH == 7:`

3.
```
if WaterPH == 7:
    Microbes = input("Please enter number of
    microbes: num
    Microbes = int(Microbes)
```

4.
```
WaterPH = input("Please enter pH value: ")
WaterPH = int(WaterPH)
if WaterPH == 7:
    Microbes = input("Please enter number of
    microbes: ")
    Microbes = int(Microbes)
    if Microbes == 0:
        print("Water purity verified")
```

Boolean operators

1. Arithmetic and relational

2. To join two logical tests together to make one big test

3. When you join two tests with the and operator the result is only true if the first AND the second test are both true.

4. The programmer used *and* instead of *or* in the if statement:
```
print("You must be aged 16 to 18 ")
age = input("enter your age")
age = int(age)
if age<16 or age>18:
    print ("you are the wrong age")
```

Selection in pseudocode

1. The IF statement in pseudocode and the if statement in Python both begin with the word "if" and a logical test. The differences between the IF statement in pseudocode and the if statement in Python are as follows. In pseudocode:

- IF is in upper case.
- The word THEN comes after the test, instead of a colon.
- The whole structure ends with the word ENDIF.

2.
```
Age ← USERINPUT
IF Age<15 THEN
    OUTPUT "sorry come back when you are
    older"
```
```
ELSE
    OUTPUT "have you signed the agreement
    form?"
    Agree ← USERINPUT
    IF Agree = "yes"
        OUTPUT "you can buy a ticket at your
        own risk"
    ENDIF
ENDIF
```

Loops

1. An exit condition is what makes the loop stop repeating.

2. "Increment" means to increase by 1.

3. Definite iteration: The exit condition is the number of repetitions.

Indefinite iteration: The exit condition is a logical test.

4. In a program to process the results of exactly 100 student tests, the teacher needs a definite iteration.

5. The loop kept repeating without stopping on its own.

Counter loops

1. 10

2. The commands to repeat will be indented.

3. This is converting the input from a string (which is given by the input function) into an integer. It is necessary because for loops require integer start and stop values.

Condition loops

1. 5

2. The contents of the while loop would not be run even once, and so the user would immediately get the win messages.

3. The lower case "w" is not equal to the upper case "W", so the contents of the loop would be run, and the user would get the messages about being surrounded by hedges and would be asked for another direction input.

4. Change the line
```
while Direction != "W"
```
to
```
while Direction == "W"
```

Nested loops

1. 4 times

2. 8 times

3. The numbers 1 to 8 will be printed

Loops in pseudocode

1. `FOR i ← 1 to 10`

2. `WHILE choice ≠ "Y"`

3. You can look for the statement which ends the loop, e.g. ENDFOR or ENDWHILE.

4. If the conditional statement is not true at the start of the loop, then the contents of the loop are skipped entirely.

End-conditional

1. To make a loop with the test at the top of the loop, use a WHILE loop.
2. To make a loop that stops when the test result is True, use a REPEAT. . . UNTIL loop.
3. To make a loop that repeats 100 times, use a FOR loop.
4. A WHILE loop has a test at the top. The loop iterates if the test result is True. A REPEAT loop has the test at the bottom. The loop iterates if the test result is False.

   The REPEAT loop always runs at least once, whereas the WHILE loop might not run at all.

2 Further programming

2.1 Data structure

Lists

1. Start: [and end:]
2. With a comma.
3. 0
4. `Rainbow = ["red", "orange", "yellow", "green", "blue", "indigo", "violet"]`
5. `print(Rainbow[1])`
6. `print(Rainbow)`

Output a list

1. `print(Rainbow)`
2. This is better code, because if the number of elements in the list changes later then the loop will still work, but using multiple lines of code would not.
3. Because the index 0 gives the first element of the list in Python.
4. He used the `len` function which counts the number of items in the list, e.g. `len(ExampleList)`

Add elements to a list

1. The command to make an empty list called Months is:

   `Months = [ ]`
2. The command to append the value January to the list Months is:

   `Months.append("January")`
3. The first line of a definite iteration that will add 12 elements to the list is:

   `for i in range (0,12):`
4. Two lines that will (a) take user input (b) append that value to the list are:

   `NewValue = input("enter the next element of the list")`

   `Months.append(NewValue)`

Arrays in pseudocode

1. Any type
2. 0
3. 9
4. `Marks[10] ← 44`

2-D arrays and lists

1. The length of grid is 3 (it is a list that holds 3 lists)
2. `print(grid[0])`
3. `print(grid[0][0])`
4. `grid[2][2] = 0`

Records

1. It is a field.
2. `E78.species = "Elephant"`
3. `print(E78.species)`
4. `E78.name = "Nelly"`

Make a list of records

1. A string
2. The data type is Animal.
3. The user can add as many records to the list as they like. The loop will keep going until they do not enter "Y" when asked. Since we do not know how many items they will add, we must use a `while` loop. But when we go to print the list, we know how many items the user has entered (using `len(animal_list)`), so we can use a `for` loop.

2.2 File handling

Write to a file

1. testresult.txt
2. string
3. Results of spelling test

   Total marks = 10

Read from a file

1. `with open("password.txt") as myfile:`

   `    mypass = myfile.read()`
2. string
3. It is not plain text, it will contain other information such as formatting and layout.
4. You could create it with another Python program that you have written.

   You could create it using software that only works with plain text like Microsoft Notepad.

   You could create it using word processing software, but you would have to be careful to change the saving file type to be plain text.

Files in pseudocode

1. `Username ← USERINPUT`

   `WRITELINE(details.txt, 1, Username)`

2.
```
FOR i ← 1 TO 4
    Name ← USERINPUT
    WRITELINE(names.txt, i, Name)
ENDFOR
```
3.
```
Password = READLINE(Password.txt, 1)
OUTPUT Password
```
4.
```
WRITELINE(password.txt, 3, "Station99")
```

2.3 Subroutines

Introduction to subroutines

1. Because you can write a block of code once and then call it multiple times in the same program.

2. The programmer only has to write the code once rather than in multiple places, and if they decide to change the code later they only have to update it in one place.

3. Subroutines have names. A line of code that calls a well-named subroutine is often easier to understand than the block of code inside the subroutine.

4. Once a problem was split into subroutines, each member of a team can be assigned a different one to write, meaning the full program gets finished faster.

Random numbers

1. An integer

2. Yes

3. `import random`

4.
```
import random
Minimum = input("Please insert a minimum
value: ")
Maximum = input("Please insert a maximum
value: ")
Number = random.randint(Minimum,Maximum)
```

Define and call procedures

1. Because they do not create new values

2. The subroutine calls should include brackets, i.e. login() and welcome()

3. The subroutine should be named to tell the reader what the subroutine does.

4. Defining a procedure is where you write the code, it is just saved for later, not run.

   Calling a procedure is when you just write the name of the procedure after it has been defined, this is where the code is actually run.

Parameters

1. vertical

2. text

3. letter

4. vertical("HOTEL")

Multiple parameters

`box("*",10)` – The width parameter should be an integer, this will try to multiply two strings giving an error

`box(9)` – The box procedure requires exactly two parameters, only one is given here

`box(3.3,8.2)` – The parameters should be integers, these are floats

`box(10,10,10)` – The box procedure requires exactly two parameters, here three are given

Functions and returned values

1. battle

2. 4

3. score

4. You can tell a value is being returned because it is being captured in the variable score, and this makes it a function.

2.4 Structured programming

The structured approach to programming

1. procedure

2. `gofaster()`

3.
```
def gofaster(speed):
    return speed+10
```

4. `speed = gofaster(40)`

Advantages of the structured approach

1. Decomposition, because it is used to break down a problem into smaller parts, before composition is used to build the solution from subroutines.

2. They must write subroutines for each of the small tasks.

3. Subroutines are smaller and so easier to write and test, so mistakes are less likely and easier to find when they happen.

4. As a parameter.

Structured algorithms

1. `return count`

2.
```
FUNCTION login():
    password assw
    WHILE password ≠ "tt5566"
        password asswordsswo
    ENDWHILE
ENDFUNCTION
```

3. Because we do not know how many times to ask the user for their password, they might get it right first time or it might take multiple attempts.

4.
```
FUNCTION login():
    REPEAT
        password ← USERINPUT
    UNTIL password = "tt5566"
ENDFUNCTION
```

2.5 Robust programming

Data validation

1. Balance is a float; Money is a float
2. Money must be greater than 0, less than Balance, and less than 250.
3. "You cannot be less than 0"
4. Range checks – the number must be within a valid range

   Length checks – making sure the input has the right number of characters

   Type checks – the input must be of the correct type e.g. string, int

Secure programming

1. It is a string of length zero, i.e. it has no characters
2. For a string named example, you can do

   `if len(example) == 0`
3. Because if the first logical test is false, the nested if statement will not be run.
4. The advantage is that the code will keep asking the user to try again if they get the password wrong, so the user does not have to run the code again. This might also be a disadvantage if the user does not know the password, as they could be stuck in the program, or they might be given enough chances that they can guess the password and access data they should not be able to.

Testing

1. Test data is input.
2. Because they want to make sure the software does what it is supposed to without errors, otherwise the client will be upset.
3. This is an example of erroneous data.
4. This is also erroneous data, we expect this value to be rejected, however it makes sure the program uses a range check and not just a type check.
5. This tells the programmer that the software has passed this test.
6. The test has failed so the programmer must fix the software.

3 Representing algorithms

3.1 Interpret algorithms

Algorithms and programs

1. The most common arithmetic operators are + (add), – (subtract), × (multiply), and / (divide). We also sometimes use DIV (integer division) and MOD (remainder).
2. The most common Boolean operators are AND, OR, and NOT.
3. Definite iteration (for loop) and indefinite iteration (while or repeat loop)

4. An algorithm is a set of steps that solves a problem. A computer program is an implementation of an algorithm – this is code that can actually be run to solve the problem, but it is less general and may require making some specific choices, e.g. which programming language to use.

Abstraction

1. It depends on the exact problem, but generally the necessary details are ones which, if left out, could change the solution. A website might sell many goods which have different sizes and prices. For an online shopping program the sizes might be unnecessary detail. But for a program which works out how to organise the warehouse the sizes are necessary but the prices are not.
2. Many problems have the same basic structure. Once a programmer understands the basic algorithm, they can apply it to many situations.
3. She would include details about the number of apples, the weight of individual apples, and perhaps the number of trees and how many apples they produce. She could leave out details such as the location of the orchard, the owner of the orchard, and the other fruits that are produced.
4. Flow charts and pseudocode.

Purpose of an algorithm

1. Each variable will have a name, which helps you understand its purpose, making the logic behind the algorithm easier to follow
2. ←
3. The for loop will be followed by a range of values, e.g. FOR i ← 1 TO 5. The exit condition of the loop is when the variable has a value that is outside of the range. In this example the exit condition is when i is 6.
4. They are used in if statements to make conditional code, and they are used in while and repeat loops to make code which repeats.

Trace tables

1. The trace table has a column for each variable in the algorithm.
2. The values held by each variable at each line of the algorithm should be entered into each row of a trace table.
3. Data can be input to a variable. A calculation could be performed and the result assigned by a program command.
4. You can leave out lines where no variable changes values. This makes the trace table shorter and easier to read.

Trace tables with loops

1. By entering any letter other than Y after they have inputted a value.
2. If the test is True, then the contents of the if statement will run on line 6. This will cause the value that the user input to be stored in the variable A.

3. This algorithm takes values from the user until they wish to stop, and then it will output the largest value they entered.

4. A – MaximumValue
   B – ShouldContinue
   C – InputValue

3.2 Search algorithms

Linear search

1. When the value is contained in the list.
2. When the search item has been found.
3. Yes, if the search item is not in the list.
4. What position of the list the item is in.

Search function

1. Boolean
2. result
3. biglist and myvalue
4. biglist is a list, and myvalue can be any type depending on what is in the list
5. False

Search a sorted list

1. Before
2. First element is 0, last element is 19
3. The midpoint is either element 10 or 11
4. 5

Implement the binary search algorithm

1. `binsearch(biglist, 7)`
2. When the search item is before the current midpoint.
3. If the search item is the first element of the list.
4. If the search item is the item at the current midpoint.

Compare search algorithms

1. If the list is not sorted it is not possible to use binary search, so it might be quicker to use linear search than it is to sort the list and use binary search
2. It is much faster than linear search, particularly on longer lists
3. 20
4. No. Using search as an example, if a programmer only knew binary search they would struggle with unsorted lists, but if they only knew linear search their code would be unnecessarily slow on sorted lists. A good programmer knows multiple algorithms that solve the same problem, and the advantages of each.

3.3 Sort algorithms

Sorting a list

1. First swap: position 0 and 1, values 16 and 10
   (New list: 10, 16, 4, 7, 1)

Second swap: position 1 and 2, values 16 and 4

2. 10, 4, 7, 1, 16
3. 1, 4, 7, 10, 16

Bubble sort

1. If the value at position i in the list is bigger than the value that follows it
2. It will swap the two values at positions i and i+1
3. Because it is testing the item against the one that follows it, and the last element in the list does not have a 'next' item
4. When the number of swaps is zero at the end of a pass

Merge sort

1. Because merge requires the two input lists to already be sorted
2. Merge sort
3. They are length one, just a single item each
4. Because the merge method requires sorted lists, and a list with just one item is guaranteed to be sorted

Compare sort algorithms

1. Merge sort
2. It will work and it will not be too slow since 50 is not a very large number, but merge sort will still be faster
3. The size of the list being sorted
4. How close it is already to being sorted – bubble sort will stop as soon as the list is in order

Graphing time efficiency

1. The worst place would be the last position in the list.
2. The time will be proportional to n^2 ($n \times n$).
3. The binary search is quicker, $\log(n) < n$ for all values of n.
4. Bubble sort works through the list in passes, one pass is one iteration through the list, and may contain many swaps. Sorting a list usually requires multiple passes. If the algorithm completes a pass without swapping any numbers, then the list must be sorted, so it can stop. So, two lists of the same length can take different times to sort using bubble sort if one list is closer to being sorted at the start. For example, inputting an already sorted list into bubble sort will only take one pass, no matter how long the list is.

4 Number systems

4.1 Binary systems

Binary data

1. A computer's memory is often used to store numbers, so it's convenient to show a stored bit as the numeric value it represents. Even non-numeric data such as text is coded as numbers, so a numeric representation works for that too.
2. Computers work only with binary data, so data in any other form must be converted to binary before the computer can deal with it.

3. There are lots of good examples. Many pieces of equipment can be on or off. A door can be open or shut. Be careful not to choose an example that can be in more than two states. For example, water can be solid, liquid or gas (steam).

4. We can answer this question in many different ways. The key to the usefulness of computers is that they turn data into information. Information is data that has been processed and organised to make it more useful.

Bits and bytes

1. A bit is a single on/off signal. A byte is a collection of eight bits.

2. 250 × 8 = 2000 bits

3. Of course pictures vary a lot in size. However the example in the text says "A picture may be 3 megabytes". A gigabyte is 1000 megabytes.

   Use division: 1000 ÷ 3 = 333.3

   The answer is roughly 330. As the size of an image varies so greatly you could say "roughly 330".

4. 1TB is 1,000GB, which is 1,000,000MB, which is 1,000,000,000KB.

Binary and decimal

1. There are ten possible symbols for each position (0 to 9), and so the base values of the digits go up in powers of ten.

2. The value of a digit in a denary number depends on its position in the number. For example, the digit 9 can stand for 9, 90 or 900 in different positions.

3. There are four bits.

4. In the binary number 0010, the 1 stands for the number 2.

Convert between binary and decimal

1. 25, 80, 147, 255

2. 31 is 00011111, 55 is 00110111, 70 is 01000110, 101 is 01100101

What is hexadecimal?

1. 180

2. 64

3. F (which is decimal value 15)

4. FF (which has decimal value 255)

Hexadecimal and binary

1.

A	B	C	D
1010	1011	1100	1101

ABCD = 1010 1011 1100 1101

2.

A	F	A	0
1010	1111	1010	0000

1010 1111 1010 0000 = AFA0

3. (The answer depends on your age.) If you are 15 years old, that is F in hexadecimal and 1111 in binary.

4. It is more convenient to use hexadecimal than decimal for people who need to work with binary values because there is an exact match-up between hexadecimal and binary. One hexadecimal digit always converts to exactly four bits. Unlike decimal conversion, you don't have to worry about remainders or extra bits.

How hexadecimal is used

1. Each colour is represented by a byte of data. One byte is eight bits. Three bytes are 8 × 3 bits.

2. Programmers use hexadecimal instead of denary to represent binary codes because it is easier to convert between binary and hexadecimal than binary and denary.

3. There are many right answers to this question, including text, video and sound.

4. An error message tells you that an error has occurred. Debugging means finding and removing errors. This is made easier by referring to error messages because they help you to find an error and give you some information about what the error is.

4.3 Binary arithmetic

Binary addition

1. 10001001
2. 11010100
3. 11101010
4. 10110000

Binary multiplication

1. 00101000
   In decimal: 20 × 2 = 40 (00101000 in binary)
2. 01111000
   In decimal: 15 × 8 = 120 (01111000 in binary)
3. 101010100
   In decimal: 85 × 4 = 340 (101010100 in binary)
4. 10010000
   In decimal: 9 × 16 = 144 (10010000 in binary)

Binary division

1. 00001010
   In decimal: 20 ÷ 2 = 10 (00001010 in binary)
2. 00011110
   In decimal: 240 ÷ 8 = 30 (00011110 in binary)
3. 00010110
   In decimal: 88 ÷ 4 = 22 (00010110 in binary)
4. 00001011
   In decimal: 176 ÷ 16 = 11 (00001011 in binary)

5 Digital data

5.1 Character encoding

Character codes

1. COMPUTER SCIENCE

2. KEYBOARD

3. COMPUTER SCIENCE: 43 4F 4D 50 55 54 45 52 20 53 43 49 45 4E 43 45
   KEYBOARD: 4B 45 59 42 4F 41 52 44

4. 3000 words × 5 characters per word = 15000 characters
   15000 characters × 7 bits per character = 105000 bits
   105000 bits / 8 = 13125 bytes or just over 13 kilobytes

Unicode

1. 97 – Unicode matches all ASCII values

2. It can represent a much wider range of characters, including those from non-European writing systems and non-text characters such as emoji.

3. ASCII text only uses 7 bits per character, but Unicode uses more than this, between one and four bytes per character. This is necessary to encode the additional characters.

4. The growth of the Internet has meant that people from around the world are able to communicate in a way that was never possible before. This highlights the importance for technology to be universal. Just as ASCII can only represent European (Latin) characters, there are old systems for writing other languages such as Japanese or Russian, and these are typically not compatible. If a website using ASCII asks for your name, you should be able to enter it in your own alphabet. Unicode tries to unify the technology to allow this, so that everyone gets a consistent experience, even if they cannot read the content.

Converting text to characters

1. `ord('%')`

2. `chr(40)`

3. `character[0]` takes the first element of the variable called character, which in this case is a string, so it is the first character of the string (which is called character). This value is then assigned to the variable character, replacing the original string.
   For example:
   ```
   character = "hello"
   character = character[0]
   print(character) # prints 'h'
   ```

4. ```
   UserInput = input("Enter a string: ")
   for i in range(0, len(UserInput)):
       print("The ASCII value of", UserInput[i],
       "is", ord(UserInput[i]))
   ```

5.2 Images

Bitmaps and pixels

1. 630,000 pixels (might also be called approximately 0.6 megapixels)

2. 256 colours is 8 bits per pixel (one byte), therefore the file would use 630,000 bytes or 630 kilobytes

3. 24 bits per pixel is 3 bytes per pixel, so the total would be 630,000 × 3 = 1,890,000 bytes, 1,890 kilobytes or just under 2 megabytes

4. A high colour depth means more shades of colour are possible. This means that colours can be more accurate, and it is possible to smoothly transition between colours, which will avoid visible 'bands' of colour or edges between colours.

Image quality and file size

1. High resolution means that the pixels that make up the image are small. The advantage is that the image is clearer with well-defined details, but the disadvantage is that the file size is bigger because they need more pixels to create the same size image.

2. White

3. The advantage of a high colour depth is that the image looks more realistic since the colours can be more accurate and transition smoothly. However, it means that each pixel requires more bits to store its value, and so this increases the overall file size.

4. Pixelation is where the pixels of an image are too big to the point where they are visible as squares – it is the opposite of high resolution. The image looks grainy and blurred.

Turn an image into binary

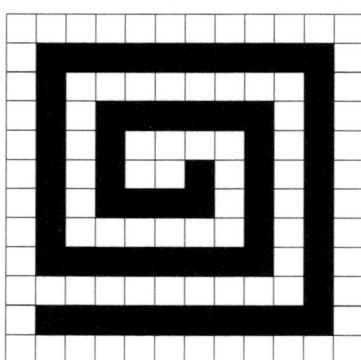

Creating coloured images

1. First tile design:
   ```
   11101110111011
   10010101010101
   11011110111001
   10011001011101
   11011110111001
   10010101011101
   11101110111001
   ```
   Second tile design:
   ```
   11000100110011
   00110011001100
   10000100100010
   00110011001100
   11000100110011
   00110011001100
   11000100110011
   ```
   ```

2.

5.3 Sound

Analogue sound

1. Analog
2. Digital
3. That the amplitude of the sound is high (loud) at this point
4. That the frequency (pitch) of the sound is high at this point
5. Because more details of the sound are captured, so it will sound closer to the original

Calculating file size

1. 5MB × 60 (minutes) = 300MB
2. 8 × 8,000 = 16,000 bits per second
3. 16,000 × 60 (seconds) = 960,000 bits, which is 120,000 bytes or 120kB
4. A wider range of amplitudes can be stored, so numbers have to be rounded less significantly, and will therefore be closer to the original sound.

5.4 Compression

Why compression is important

1. The main advantage of compression is that it reduces the file size. This also means that it is faster to transfer, such as over the Internet or to load from storage.

   The disadvantage is that the compressed file must be decompressed before it can be used normally, this might be slower than reading the original larger file. Also, some compression (lossy) can cause a loss of quality – details will be lost.
2. Lossless compression is where a file is made smaller, but the computer can decompress the small file and get an exact match for the original file – so no details have been lost. With lossy compression, the original file cannot be reproduced exactly, so some details are lost. However, this can come with some advantages, such as a much smaller compressed file, and in many cases the lost details are too small to be noticed by a human.
3. The advantage is the quality of the file. High resolution images can be cropped (zoomed in), they can be used on large posters and billboards, or on screens which have very high resolution displays, and they will retain their original clarity. The disadvantage is the increased file size, and if the image is being used in a place where it is very small then the extra quality will not be noticeable and is a wasted increase in size.

4. Could reduce the number of channels (e.g. going from surround sound to stereo, or from stereo to mono): this could decrease the feeling of immersion in the sound, and may mean that some special effects (e.g. panning) no longer produce the same effect.

   Could reduce the sample rate: this could decrease the sound quality. It would lose detail, and sound 'muddy', like you were listening to it through a closed door.

   Could reduce the resolution, i.e. use fewer bits per sample: this could also decrease the quality. The sound would get 'fuzzy', it will sound like your speakers are broken, like an analog radio that is slightly out of tune.

   Finally, could use lossless or lossy compression. Lossless compression would not affect the sound quality at all. Lossy compression might have some effects, but it would depend on the algorithm and they would be unlikely to be as noticeable as the other effects listed.

Run-length encoding

1. 9 0 2 1 3 0 12 1 10 0
2. 5 0 12 1 12 0 7 1
3. 7 0 5 1 9 0 2 1 9 0 4 1
4. 12 1 12 0 9 1 3 0

Huffman coding

1. 10
2. 111
3. 1100

Build a Huffman tree

1. 11
2. 100
3. C
4. B

Huffman compression

1. 13,400 × 7 = 93,800 bits or 11,725 bytes (just under 12 kB)
2. Count the number of bits for each Huffman code, and multiply by the frequency, then add these all together
   2000 * 3 + 900 * 4 + 3000 * 2 + 500 * 4 + 7000 * 1 = 6000 + 3600 + 6000 + 2000 + 7000 = 24,600 bits, or 3,075 bytes (just over 3kB)
3. The reduction in size is 69,200 bits or 8650 bytes, which is a reduction of about 70% of the original size

6 Software

6.1 Types of software

Hardware and software

1. The input is whenever a user touches the screen to direct the device, for example opening an app or typing

on the on-screen keyboard. The output is the display, just like a normal computer monitor, a touchscreen can display information for the user.

2. Loading software is when the code is copied from secondary storage into main memory (RAM). Running software is when the instructions are actually executed.

3. Microphone, buttons, touchscreen and camera would usually be included on a typical smartphone.

4. Typically this would be using speakers or headphones.

System and application software

1. An icon is a small image used to represent an application so that a user can identify it quickly

2. This will vary between schools but it is most likely to be some variant of Windows, perhaps Windows 10. You should be able to find out from the computer log in screen, or from a teacher or technician.

3. Of course, this answer will vary too. You might have used a word processing application, which allows you to write text-based documents such as essays or books. Or you might have used a social media application, which can be used for sharing text and images, and talking to your friends.

4. Because applications are written to be compatible with a specific operating system. This has to be specified when the application is made, so it is not usually possible to run an application made for Linux on a Windows machine for example.

Operating systems and utilities

1. The operating system finds free space in storage for each file. Files need to be stored in different locations, so that they don't overlap with each other. The operating system sometimes splits a file, storing it between several different storage areas.

2. Storage space and processor time.

3. Because the operating system came with a driver that supported the mouse already

4. There are types of utility software that do not come as standard with operating systems but might still be useful. For example, you might have a need for advanced security software, or you might have an unusual piece of hardware that requires a specific driver that did not come with your operating system.

6.2 Programming languages

Machine code and assembly language

1. An executable file just contains machine code

2. An assembler converts code written in assembly language into machine code. The input is assembly language code, and the output is an executable file.

3. The code words stand for instructions (usually for the processor)

4. It is called low level because there is a close match

between assembly code and machine code – the instructions that are sent to the processor.

Low-level and high-level languages

1. Low-level

2. Usually it is much easier to learn programming with a high-level language. The language itself is closer to normal language, and more tools are available so programming an application is much quicker.

3. Because assembly language is translated into machine code, and machine code is directly sent to the processor to be executed.

4. Some languages are better suited to some applications than others. For example the language C is very fast to run so it is good for time-crucial applications, whereas the language Java has several features that make the code easy to organise for large systems such as for organisations.

Translators

1. Compiler

2. You can send the executable file to someone else or even sell it, the person who receives it will not be able to view the code which might be good for commercial purposes.

3. Source code is the original code that the programmer wrote for an application. Executable code is the result of compiling the source code. Executable code can be run by a computer, and it can be shared as an executable file, but it cannot be read to understand what it does. Source code is just text, so it can be read by a programmer. It is not possible to run source code without the use of a compiler or an interpreter.

4. The main reason is you can very quickly run the code you have written to see the results. This means that if you change the code you can quickly test it to see the results. It is also often possible to run code 'line-by-line', which can aid understanding in the same way as tracing an algorithm can.

7 Hardware

7.1 The processor

Components of the CPU

1. The main components of the CPU are the arithmetic and logic unit (ALU) and the control unit.

2. The three types of peripheral are:
   - input devices
   - output devices
   - storage devices.

3. The ALU carries out calculations (arithmetic) and logical deductions.

4. The new data made by the ALU is sent to the main memory.

The fetch-execute cycle

1.

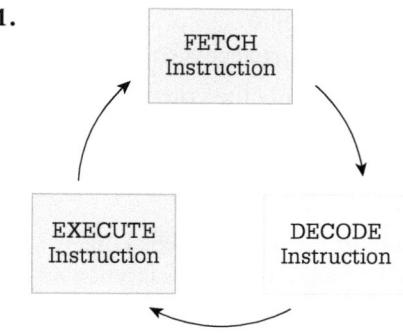

2. At the fetch stage of the cycle, the instruction is fetched from the main memory and copied into the instruction register.
3. The control unit uses a logic circuit to pick the right instruction from the instruction set, which has a code for every action that the computer can perform.
4. The execute stage of the fetch-execute cycle is carried out inside the ALU.

Main memory

1. Volatile memory loses its contents when the electricity is turned off.
2. Installing more RAM increases the amount of space available for applications that are currently in use. If there is too little RAM then the computer will be slow, so installing more can speed it up.
3. Read-only means that it is not possible to change the contents. For example, read-only memory (ROM) is used to store instructions that make the computer start up when you switch it on.
4. RAM is volatile, so when the computer is off it has no electricity and so loses its contents completely.

Performance factors

1. If the other components of the computer are not fast enough, then the benefit of the extra CPU speed will be lost, because it is just waiting for the other components. Also, increasing the clock speed can cause more heat and more wear on the CPU, which could damage the component.
2. Some computers have processors with multiple cores, and these cores are able to carry out instructions at the same time.
3. Cache memory is quick-access memory that can be used by the CPU to store instructions and data, it is significantly faster than if the CPU has to go to main memory.
4. The more cache available to a CPU, the more instructions and often-used data can be stored in this area of memory which is extremely fast to access. The CPU will not need to fetch from main memory as often, increasing the overall speed.

Embedded systems

1. No, a laptop is a general-purpose machine that can do multiple tasks and run code written for any purpose. An embedded system is designed for one specific purpose and cannot normally run new things.
2. A micro-processor is made of several components joined together by buses, this is found in a typical general purpose computer. A micro-controller is a simpler design with all components in a single chip, and these are used by embedded systems. Micro-controllers are cheaper and smaller than micro-processors, meaning it is more economical to add them to all sorts of household devices.
3. Firmware is the name for the instructions (i.e. the software) that runs on an embedded system. It is typically stored in read-only memory (ROM) so it remains fixed the whole time the system is in use.
4. Embedded systems are used in wide variety of devices from washing machines to heart rate monitors. Adding an embedded system can greatly increase the functionality of a device beyond what would be possible with simple circuitry. However, if the embedded system breaks then the whole device may need to be replaced, so they must be reliable. Furthermore, if they are too big, expensive, or use too much energy, then the device becomes less useful than before the embedded system was added.

7.2 Storage

Magnetic storage

1. The advantage of magnetic storage compared to electronic storage in RAM is that magnetic storage is not volatile. It retains data without an electrical connection.
2. It depends on the connection, but in many cases the connection is slower to an external hard drive. Changes in technology are improving that.
3. The advantage of an external hard drive is that you can move it between computers.

Optical storage

1. ● Read-only CD—the computer can take data from the CD but cannot use it to store new data.
   ● Write-once CD—the computer can store data on the CD but it cannot remove it, and once the CD is full it cannot store any more data.
   ● Rewriteable CD—this has a surface that can be melted to erase data so it can be re-used.
2. Data on an optical drive is stored as tiny pits burned into a reflective surface. The DVD uses smaller pits so more can be put into the same area of disk.
3. A CD is smaller, lighter and cheaper than an internal HDD. A CD can be used to transport data between computers.
4. Magnetic storage allows quick and easy writing, erasing and rewriting. A typical CD or DVD cannot be rewritten at all, and rewriteable optical storage is much slower to do so.

Solid state storage

1. Solid state storage uses electrons. Electrons are minute particles that are smaller than an atom.

   - Reading data—The computer can detect the position of the electrons; the position of the electrons represents the 1s and 0s of data.

   - Writing data—when data is sent to the solid state storage, a "flash" of electricity forces some of the electrons through an insulator. When the electricity stops the electrons are stuck in the new location.

   - Erasing data—a second flash of electricity returns the electrons to their original place and so erases the data.

2. Mobile phones can use flash memory as very compact storage with high capacity. This gives a small light mobile phone a lot of storage for photographs and other data.

3. Compared to an HDD, the advantages of a solid state drive are that solid state storage is much more compact and more robust (less likely to break). The main disadvantage is higher cost, though the difference is becoming less over time.

4. A USB flash drive is less likely to break than a CD. It will hold more data. It is erasable and rewriteable.

Choosing the right storage

1. Storage media can break or fail. An advantage of making a weekly backup of your data is that if you make a backup you will not lose your data when this happens.

   Disadvantages of making a weekly backup are that it takes time and requires the purchase of additional storage capacity.

   An extended answer would compare:

   - a weekly backup with a daily backup—a daily backup is more trouble but offers more protection

   - a weekly backup with a less frequent backup (such as monthly)—which is less trouble but carries greater risk.

2. Magnetic tape is suitable for backup because it is very inexpensive with high capacity. It is unsuitable for other uses because access is extremely slow compared to other forms of storage.

3. Cloud storage means the data is stored by an Internet company on its computers. The storage is accessed via an Internet connection.

   Advantages of cloud storage:

   - You don't need to buy storage devices and media.

   - You can access your data from any device with an Internet connection.

   - The company backs up the data so it is not at risk of being lost.

   - Cloud storage doesn't take up any space on your own device.

   Disadvantages:

   - There are privacy concerns.

   - You need an Internet connection.

   - If the connection fails you can't access your data.

4. Here is an evaluation of flash using the criteria given:

   - Capacity: flash memory has good capacity for its size.

   - Portability: flash memory is small and light and can be carried about easily.

   - Reliability: flash memory has a good record of reliability; however, its long-term results are not yet known.

   - Cost: flash memory is more expensive than other options, but its price is reducing.

   - Speed of access: access to flash memory is as fast as secondary storage can be. The limiting factor is the connection between the memory and the CPU.

7.3 Boolean logic

Logic gates and circuits

1. The type of logic gate that it is, and its inputs

2. A logic gate transforms electrical signals, either one or two of them, into another electrical signal (the output).

3. On and off, true and false, or 1 and 0

4. A logic circuit is when multiple logic gates are connected together to form a more complicated system, by joining the output of logic gates to the input of others. A logic circuit can have any number of inputs, but a logic gate can only have one or two.

The NOT gate

1. The NOT gate changes the signal to the opposite of what it was: 1 becomes 0; 0 becomes 1.

2. In one state, the input is 0 or False, and the output is 1 or True.

   In the other state, the input is 1 or True, and the output is 0 or False.

3. The word "not" in everyday speech reverses the meaning of a sentence: adding "not" to a sentence changes the meaning of something to its opposite. The NOT gate changes the logical signal to its opposite.

4. The output of a NOT gate is logical because it represents the logical values True and False, or 1 and 0. It is predictable because the output is determined solely by the input value. If you know the input, you can work out the output.

The AND gate

1. Four possible states of the inputs to an AND gate:

   - Input A is 0, input B is 0, output is 0

   - Input A is 0, input B is 1, output is 0

   - Input A is 1, input B is 0, output is 0

   - Input A is 1, input B is 1, output is 1.

2. The state of input A does not affect the state of input B, or vice versa. They change without any influence on each other.

3.

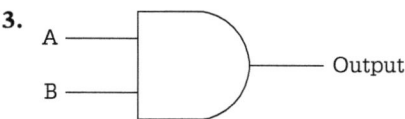

4. The dot represents AND, so A.B is False.

The OR gate

1. False

2. True

3. False

4. True

Logic circuits

(A.B) + C

A
B
C

A + (B + C)

B
C
A

(A.B) + $\overline{C}$

A
B
C

$\overline{A}$ + B.C

A
B
C

Interpret logic circuits

Labelled logic circuit:

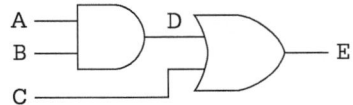

A
B
C
D
E

Truth table:

A	B	C	D	E
0	0	0	0	0
0	0	1	0	1
0	1	0	0	0
0	1	1	0	1
1	0	0	0	0
1	0	1	0	1
1	1	0	1	1
1	1	1	1	1

Labelled logic circuit:

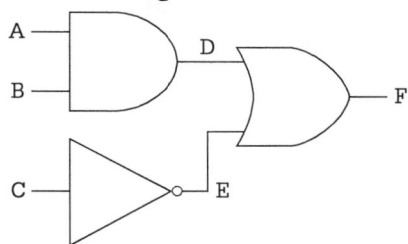

A
B
D
C
E
F

Truth table:

A	B	C	D	E	F
0	0	0	0	1	1
0	0	1	0	0	0
0	1	0	0	1	1
0	1	1	0	0	0
1	0	0	0	1	1
1	0	1	0	0	0
1	1	0	1	1	1
1	1	1	1	0	1

Logic circuits and Boolean expressions

There are five combinations that produce a value of 1:

A = 0, B = 0, C = 1

A = 0, B = 1, C = 1

A = 1, B = 0, C = 1

A = 1, B = 1, C = 0

A = 1, B = 1, C = 1

8 Communications

8.1 Networks

What is a network?

1. There are financial costs involved in buying network hardware and software, and possibility also the need to hire extra staff to set up or maintain the network. There is also a security risk involved with networking computers; data may be stolen or viruses might infect the system.

2. It is possible to set up items like printers to operate over the network, so they can be shared and used by multiple users, therefore meaning the company can buy fewer of them.

3. This is a LAN (local area network)

4. The main risk is security. If the proper precautions are not taken, then it is possible that data will be read, altered or deleted without permission, or viruses might get onto the system.

Types of network

1. Twisted pair cabling is the cheapest. The disadvantage is that it can only be used over short distances of up to 90 metres.

2. Wireless networks are best for this type of hardware because there is no need to be physically attached to any other device with a cable.

3. It is possible that the signal will be weak or interrupted, particularly at longer distance or behind thick walls. There are also security risks. It is harder to prevent unauthorised users, and once they are on the network they might have access to sensitive information.

4. To make a more reliable wireless signal, you can buy special hardware that will boost the signal quality and help it reach new areas. To keep the network secure, you should use a wireless security method with a strong password.

Network topologies

1. The bus topology

2. The star topology, because on a bus topology busy networks will lead to lots of collisions between signals which will cause the network to become slow and unreliable.

3. Wireless networks use a star topology, since there is no downside of extra physical cables

4. A hub sends incoming signals to all connected devices, whereas a switch only sends them to their intended destination.

8.2 Protocols

Network protocols

1. WLAN stands for wireless local area network. The Wi-Fi family of protocols is designed for WLANs.

2. It means they are compatible with the Wi-Fi protocols, they can connect to any Wi-Fi network.

3. LANs (local area connections) use Ethernet, it is designed for wired networks.

4. It is a place where a Wi-Fi network is available.

The four-layer model

1. The URL of the website will contain the name of the protocol. Specifically, if it is using https it will start with: https://. In some browsers this is not shown, but an HTTPS protocol should be signified with a padlock or other symbol showing it is secure.

2. It uses encryption to hide the information being sent so that only the receiver can read it. Someone connected to your computer reading your network traffic would not be able to understand the encoded data. This makes it safer to send personal information.

3. Hyperlinks are blocks of text or images that link to other websites – when you click on them the browser connects to a new page.

4. SMTP is used to deliver messages; IMAP is used to receive messages.

The four-layer model (continued)

1. UDP has reduced error-checking compared to TCP. This means that it is faster, but it is only suitable when the message is short and the connection is very reliable.

2. Before sending a message it is split into packets. These are smaller chunks that are sent through the network separately and are put together at the destination. Every web host has an IP address, which is the address which is used to specify where the packets should be sent.

3. A message across the Internet may go through many short connecting links, in fact it is possible that different parts of the message may take different routes to its destination. The Internet needs both layers because they handle the message at two different levels. The transport layer controls the two ends of the transmission link. The network layer manages the individual connections in-between.

4. The network interface card converts the binary signals from network devices into binary data inside a computer.

9 Security

9.1 Security threats

Importance of security

1. Retaining data privacy means the data is only seen or copied by people who have permission. Retaining data integrity means it is safe from unauthorised modifications.

2. Data loss means the data no longer exists in storage, for example a hard drive failing with no backups. Data corruption means the data has been damaged or changed, the data might be wrong and this might go unnoticed, which could have serious consequences. Or it might be so corrupted that the computer can no longer read it, which is very similar to data loss in effect.

3. The difference is whether the person has permission to access the system. Unauthorised access may be breaking the law. The issue of permission might be complicated; it is not always permission or no permission. For example, an employee may have permission to access their own work, but not have permission to delete the work of others.

4. Staff can be taught detailed rules and procedures which make it clear what they have permission to do with the system, and also good practices such as using strong passwords, which will prevent unauthorised access from others.

Threats to security

1. Length – the longer, the stronger
   Use of dictionary or other common words – these are easier to guess so make weak passwords
   Use of simple sequences of characters – these are also easy to guess so make weak passwords
   How many types of character are used, e.g. letters, numbers, special characters – the more types the stronger the password
2. Make sure you can easily remember it, use different passwords on different websites, and do not tell other people your passwords.
3. Read-only access
4. Admin access (or full access)

Social engineering

Blagging: pretending to be someone who should have access to your data

Phishing: sending a message that looks like it is from a legitimate source (such as your bank) asking for your information, often "to confirm" who you are, but they are really trying to steal the information.

Pharming: a fake source (such as website) that looks real in order to capture personal information

Shouldering: when someone looks over your shoulder to try to steal your password or PIN

Malware

1. Viruses can bypass normal operations, so you might think you have deleted it, but it is really still there. The anti-virus software knows how to delete the virus for good.
2. The file might contain a virus or other malware.
3. Spyware is a type of malware that hides on a computer and records what the user does, including the keys that they press on the keyboard. In this case the spyware recorded what the user was typing when they logged in, and so it captured their password.
4. There are many possible answers. They may include: damaging or deleting files, changing settings, carrying out unwanted actions such as sending email, capturing private information like passwords, displaying adverts that the user has not agreed to, redirecting Internet traffic to other sources against the user's wishes.

9.2 Ensuring security

Cyber-security protection

1. Viruses are always changing, and new viruses are being created that can avoid detection. Anti-virus software from two years ago may not be able to detect these new threats, and so the computer will be at risk unless it is updated.
2. A CAPTCHA is a system that attempts to check whether a user is a real human, rather than a bot or computer script. A common form of CAPTCHA is distorted text, which should be easy for a human to read but difficult for a computer.
3. Passwords are not linked to their user, so it is possible to forget a password, or to write it down and lose it. It is possible to have your password stolen, for example by phishing or shouldering. These are not risks for biometric methods – the biometric data is physically linked to the user, so this is significant advantage. The disadvantage of a biometric system is that it is more expensive and difficult to set up, passwords can easily be used on any computer with a keyboard, but biometric systems require extra hardware.
4. She might use a rule which enforces strong passwords, for example requiring a certain length, or a mix of character types. She might also require users to change their passwords at certain intervals. However, she should be careful – if rules are so strict that users are forced to write down their passwords rather than remember them, this could be making the system less secure.

Network security

1. This is a signal sent between two devices at the start of communication. It lets each device check that the other is genuine, and establishes a private link between them.
2. Genuine websites will have a certificate that is issued by a recognised certification authority, and this is checked and validated during the handshake process.
3. The certification authority issues certificates to websites so they can prove who they are when establishing connections (handshaking). Someone connecting to a website can check with the certification authority that the certificate they are being shown is valid (your web browser does this for you).
4. A MAC address is assigned to each piece of hardware. It is used to route traffic to the correct place across a LAN (a local area network). An IP address is assigned when connecting to the Internet, every web host has an IP address and it is used to route traffic across the Internet.

Encryption

1. Cypher text has been scrambled or changed using a formula only known by people who are supposed to be able to read the message. This formula should be very hard to guess, so if someone just sees the cypher text, it should not make any sense without knowing the formula.
2. Encryption is done with a mathematical formula that does not change from user to user, however, each user will use a different key – which is some sort of code, like a number or string of characters, and the encryption will work differently for each key. This means that we can write the algorithm for encryption once, and everyone can use a different key for security. This enables websites to offer security as standard to all users.
3. Passwords are used to let a service (e.g. a website) check you are who you say you are. The user must remember the password, and they can use it from multiple locations to log in. Encryption is used to make sure that anyone

looking at the computer traffic cannot read your personal information. It happens automatically, the user does not need to know any details such as the encryption key.

4. In symmetric encryption the same key is used for encoding and decoding the data. This means that both parties must know the key before they can communicate. They could share this information offline, but if they are forced to send it through the Internet, then there is a risk that someone else might intercept it which defeats the purpose of the encryption. Asymmetric encryption is safer because each user has a public and a private key. You can send messages to a website using their public key, and only they can read them using their private key. The website can send you messages using your public key, and only you can read them using your private key. There is no need to share a key first, so the risk of interception is eliminated.

Penetration testing

1. Penetration testing is where someone tries to break into the system, but they are only doing it to test, not to try to steal data. It helps improve security because if flaws are found which allow access, then they can be fixed.

2. Black box testing will try to break through any security like a firewall, it is used to emulate an external threat.

3. For internal threats you should use white-box testing, which assumes the testers have access to passwords or other information.

4. She could be hired by a company to test their system, and therefore has permission to attempt to hack the network. If she is successful, she will find areas of weakness that the company can fix to make the system stronger.

10 Databases

10.1 Database design

Introducing databases

1. There are 200 records (one for each car), and 12 fields (one for each fact held on each car)

2. Possible answers include: customer table, supplier table, reservation table

3. Answers include: customer table, supplier table, order table, product table, warehouse table, staff table. There could be many others. The important component is that a table should store data about only one type of entity.

4. Some example fields include: the airline, the starting airport, the destination airport, date, time, the type of aeroplane. Other answers are fine if they are facts about individual flights.

Table design

1. Name: Cost
   Type: real/float

2. The Sales field is a numeric type because it stores numeric data. It is a value we can measure. We might want to use the data for calculations later e.g. total number of albums sold.

3. The Title field is text data because it contains other albums which use text and not just numerical values. For the example of 1989 specifically, it still makes more sense to represent this as text, because it is a title, not a quantity that is being measured.

4. Date of release is one example

Primary key

1. The artist is not unique for an individual record. One artist can have more than one album, and the primary key must be unique.

2. Almost every school will have assigned a code number to students. Whether students see it will depend on your school arrangements. Do students have a pass card? Does it have a code number on it? Is the code number included in any documentation or online system such as the register?

3. Text data type, because the value is not a quantity that we will use in calculations.

4. There are many correct answers. ISBN codes on books and barcodes on shop goods are familiar examples.

Relational databases

1. When a fact is stored in more than one field in a database.

2. Redundancy is unnecessary work. It should be avoided because it is a waste of time and space.

   Inconsistency means the data does not match. It should be avoided because it could introduce errors later when we do not know which source of information is correct.

3. The customer has these details
   Surname: Limbu, First Name: Subid, Country: Nepal, City: Kathmandu

   The product has these details:
   Product Name: M3 Slimline 2 TB hard drive, Supplier: Samsung, Description: USB 3.0 Portable Hard Drive - Black, Cost: 207.00

   We found these details by looking at the foreign keys in the Order table. The Customer Code is CUST0010 and the Product Code is HD003, so we looked at these records in the Customer table and the Product table.

4. A foreign key in a table is where a field represents a primary key from another table. It is used to link the details of records from one table to another. For example, the primary key from the Customer table is used in the Order table, so it is a foreign key. Each order has an associated customer via this key.

Database design

1. Seven fields: matchcode, date, time, teamcode1, teamcode2, score1, and score2

2. There are ten teams in the football league, so there are ten records

3. `teamcode`, this is the primary key from the Team table so it is a foreign key in the Player table

4. *Player table*
   playercode: Text
   firstname: Text
   surname: Text
   email: Text
   teamcode: Text

   Team table
   teamcode: Text,
   teamname: Text,
   Points: Integer

   Match table
   matchcode: Text,
   date: Date,
   time: Time,
   teamcode1: Text,
   teamcode2: Text,
   score1: Integer,
   score2: Integer

10.2 Structured query language (SQL)

Add data with SQL

```
INSERT INTO Team
VALUES("T0004", "Aston Vila", 12)
VALUES("T0005", "Manchester City", 20)
VALUES("T0006", "Dortmund", 0)
```

Edit data with SQL

1. `DELETE FROM Customers`
2. `DELETE FROM FaultLog`
   `WHERE Year = "2016"`
3. `UPDATE Team`
   `SET Points = 0`
4. `UPDATE Team`
   `SET Points = 10`
   `WHERE TeamName = "Anderlecht"`

Select data with SQL

1. Taylor Swift
   One Direction
   Ed Sheeran
   Coldplay
   AC/DC
   Michael Jackson
   Pink Floyd
   Sam Smith
   Katy Perry
   Beyoncé
2. Katy Perry
3. `SELECT Month, Date, Time`
   `FROM Appointments`
4. `SELECT Month, Date, Time`

`FROM Appointments`
`WHERE Month = "April"`

Select data from two tables

1. This will result in a list of matches, with the team name displayed alongside. If you take the example values from page 273, this SQL will return:

   Juventus, 11-19-18, 15:00

   Real Madrid, 11-19-18, 15:00

   Even though there is only one match record, there are two results for the SQL query because there are two team code fields in the Match table. So, the Match specific information (date and time) is returned twice, once for each team that links via the foreign keys.

2. `SELECT Match.score1, Match.score2`
   `FROM Match, Team`
   `WHERE (Team.teamcode = Match.teamcode1`
   `OR Team.teamcode = Match.teamcode2)`
   `AND Team.teamname = "Juventus"`

11 Web pages

11.1 How web pages are made

What is HTML?

1. HTML stands for Hypertext Mark-up Language
2. HTML tags are used to switch features (such as bold text, or web links) on and off. The first tag turns the feature on, the second turns it off.
3. There is no end tag, it should be <h1> Section1: Computer systems.</h1>
4. Four possible answers:
   - It has made it easier to add multimedia such as audio and video.
   - Various sections of a web page are now easier to define with new tags such as header and footer.
   - Support for complex applications that talk to other applications within HTML has been improved.
   - Other features that were previously only available as add-ins (extensions) have been built in.

Designing web pages with cascading style sheets (CSS)

1. CCS are used for specifying style options separately from the content itself. For example, you can specify the background colour for all <h1> tags inside a CSS definition, then the HTML code actually uses the <h1> tags and specifies what content they should contain.
2. Three possible answers:
   - It saves time because the same styles can be used on multiple pages, so they only need to be written once. Plus, if they ever change, they only need to be changed in one place.

- Using a single CSS file across an entire website ensures a consistent experience and makes the site look more professional.
  - Design and content teams can work independently meaning that work can be done in parallel saving time.

3. Multiple pages are usually linked to a single CSS file, so changing the CSS file 'cascades' down through all of the linked pages, like a waterfall.

4. If you do not use a CSS file, then changing the design of a website would mean changing every page on the site to match. If it uses CSS well, then the changes will only need to be done in one place, which is the CSS file itself.

Client-side and server-side scripting

1. A client-side script runs on the user's computer (the client). They can perform tasks like checking input is sensible before submitting it to the server.

   A server-side script runs on the server, in other words the host of the website. For example, if you use a search engine, the script that finds the search results is running on the search engine's servers, not on your computer.

2. Javascript is the most common.

3. The main reason is because the bank would not want code that has access to a user's details (such as bank balance) to be running on a computer out of their control – the user might be able to interfere with the code. Other reasons might include the security of the data from 3rd parties, or the fact that the code might be too intensive (take too much power) to run on a client's computer.

4. As well as e-banking and search engines, server side scripts are used whenever the data to be processed is controlled by the website host rather than the user – particularly when they need to access a database. Other examples include e-commerce, online news, and social media sites.

11.2 Creating web content

Building a basic web page

1. The content that the users see when they visit the site.

2. The head section includes important information about the site, such as the title, styles or scripts, but it is not displayed on the website itself.

3. The title tag determines what shows in the title area of the browser – this is often displayed on the tab at the top of the page. (See the screenshot above the question for an example.)

4. There are no <html> tags
   Corrected version:

```
<!DOCTYPE html>
<html>
<head>
```

```
<title>Page Title</title>
</head>
<body>
<h1>This is a web page</h1>
</body>
</html>
```

Using inline and block-level tags to improve web page layout

1. It will appear in a bold font

2. The `<ol>` tag creates an ordered list – the items are numbered. The `<ul>` tag creates an unordered list – the items simply have bullet points.

3. Inline tags are used to affect a group of words in a line of text, for example making a single word bold or italic. Block-level tags affect an entire section, such as setting the font for an entire paragraph.

4. An attribute is an extra piece of information used to modify a tag, for example in `<h1 style="colour:blue">` a style attribute is used to change the colour.

Selection, images and links

1. The `<div>` tag is used to create a section, then any style changes will affect the entire section marked by the `<div>` and `</div>` tags.

2. This is called the anchor tag, and it is used to create hyperlinks.

3. Some users may be using assistive software such as a screen reader because they cannot see the page. If the alt attribute is used, then the software will be able to provide a text based alternative to the image.

4. This specifies the destination for the link that is being created.

Designing a web page using CSS

1. The selector is h1
   The property is color
   The value is grey

2. The p should not have angled brackets, since it is not a tag, it is the name of the selector; background-color and center should use the US spelling.

   The end brace is missing

   Corrected version:

```
p {background-color:blue; text-align:center}
```

Index